THE BEST OF THE LEGENDARY COMICS FANZINE

Edited by
Roy Thomas
and
Bill Schelly

From *Alter Ego* #1-11
Originally Edited by
Jerry Bails, Ronn Foss,
Roy Thomas, and Mike Friedrich

Acknowledgements

The editors of *Alter Ego* (past and present) wish to thank:

John Benson
Kevin Bermingham
John Broome
Len Brown
John Buscema
Bob Butts
Pauline Copeman
Al Dellinges
Steve Ditko
Mark Evanier
Tom Fagan
John Fahey
Gary Friedrich
Paul Gambaccini
Jeff Gelb
Steve Gerber
Michael T. Gilbert
Dian Girard
Jean Giraud (Moebius)
Ronnie Graham
Grass Green
Sid Greene
Beth Gwin
Mark Hanerfeld
Ron Harris
Randy Haynes
Kenny Heineman
Carmine Infantino
Larry Ivie
Gil Kane
Howard Keltner
Jay Kinney
Ellen Kuhfeld
Richard Kyle
Ed Lahmann
Marshall Lanz
Stan Lee
Randy & Jean-Marc Lofficier
Pat Lupoff
Richard Lupoff
Russ Maheras
Pat Masulli
Drury Moroz
Dale Nash
Fred Norwood
Fred Patten
Bill Pearson
Bruce Pelz
Joe Pilati
Linda Rahm
Kurt Schaffenberger
Julius Schwartz
Marie Severin
L. L. Simpson
Jeff Smith
Bill Spicer
Art Spiegelman
Steve Stiles
John Teegarden
Dann Thomas
Maggie Thompson
Mike Tuohey
Mike Vosburg
Ella Wells
Alan Weiss
Biljo White
Ruthie White
Ted White
Dorothy (Roubicek) Woolfolk
John Wright

And posthumously:

C. C. Beck, Otto Binder, E. Nelson Bridwell, Sol Brodsky, Wendell Crowley, Bill Everett, Sam Grainger, Gardner F. Fox, Ron Haydock, Ted Johnstone, Jim Jones, Jack Kirby, Russ Manning, John McGeehan, Paul Reinman, Sam Rosen, John Ryan, Phil Seuling, Curt Swan, Don Thompson, John Verpoorten, Mort Weisinger, and Wally Wood.

Special thanks to Paul Levitz and Joe Kubert

This book is affectionately dedicated to the three patron saints of *Alter Ego*: Julius Schwartz, Gardner F. Fox, and Otto Binder.

ISBN 0-9645669-2-3

Library of Congress Catalog Card Number 97-61092

Publisher: Hamster Press, P. O. Box 27471, Seattle, Washington, 98125. For additional copies of this book, send $17.95 plus $4.00 postage and handling to the above address. Wholesale prices provided upon request. Cover and book designed by William Schelly and Roy Thomas. Cover production by Nils Osmar.

Photo: Beth Gwin

Introduction by Julius Schwartz

I love reading fan mail. It was one of the things about working as an editor at DC Comics that I enjoyed most.

In order to save time when preparing the letter columns, I graded each letter as it came in. An "A" for a really good letter, then a "B," and so on. Positive letters received a plus sign after the letter, and negative letters got a minus sign. Therefore, an "A – " letter was a well-written negative letter. When it was time to choose letters, I'd take an "A+" and an "A – " and work my way down until the column was filled.

Around 1960, after we had begun revamping the Golden Age characters, I noticed that I was receiving a more literate type of fan letter. And I began to think that it would be nice for these comics people to be able to get in touch with each other.

After all, it's not inaccurate to say that a letter column changed my life. Some thirty years earlier, I first learned of the existence of a fellow by the name of Mort Weisinger through a letter column in *Amazing Stories*.

Amazing Stories, the first true science fiction magazine, was started by Hugo Gernsback. In addition to being a publisher, Gernsback was also an inventor. He predicted television, among other things. Gernsback printed full addresses in his letter column (called "Discussions") and urged fans to get in touch with people in their town to talk science fiction and form clubs.

In order to attend a meeting of a science fiction club called the Scienceers, I walked a mile or so through the Bronx (I didn't have carfare). As I was going into the basement of Mort's house, where the meeting was held, I was met by the club members angrily storming out. Finally Mort and I were left alone.

"What happened?" I asked.

"I'm the treasurer," Mort explained. "When I told them there was no money in the treasury, they left."

"What happened to the money?" I ventured.

"I spent it on science fiction movies ... wine, women and song," he replied, unperturbed.

Because we were the only ones left, I hung around and got to know Mort – which would never have happened if those other twenty members were there, with twenty different people talking. This

Julius Schwartz, for those few readers who don't know, is responsible for what is sometimes called the Second Heroic Age of Comics – by introducing a re-tooled version of The Flash in 1956. This led to revivals of other Golden Age heroes such as Green Lantern, Hawkman, and The Atom. Not only did the Schwartz-edited comics become favorites with the older fans – they spurred the movement to start an ongoing comics fandom by printing full addresses in their letter columns.

"When you nutty fans came around, we nutty professionals went along with you because, deep down inside, we were still fans. To this day, I'm still a science fiction fan."

was a turning point for me. Together (with Allen Glasser), Mort and I started the first science fiction fanzine, *The Time Traveller*, and became lifelong friends and colleagues. We ended up as editors for many years at DC Comics, and I carried on as editor on the Superman family titles after Mort retired.

You can understand, then, why I thought it would be nice if my letter columns could help comics fans of 1960 make contact with one another. Therefore, I decided to print full addresses in the DC letter columns.

I got a call from publisher Jack Liebowitz. He said, "You cannot put full addresses in the magazine." I said, "Why not?" I told him that's how I got started with Mort. He said, "We have a fear that some pornographer may get hold of the magazine and send the kids his literature." After all, we had mainly younger readers, eight to twelve.

I don't know how I eventually got around that... but, with *The Brave and the Bold* #35, full addresses became a fixture of the letter columns in the books I edited. By then I was writing return letters to fans who wrote some of the more intelligent letters. I knew who they were, and when we decided to revive Hawkman, I sent out advance copies to some of them. I knew that Roy Thomas, Ron Haydock, and Jerry Bails would happily fill the letter column in the second revival issue.

"Looks like another one of those days -- four fan letters and 321 requests for fanzine plugs ...."

Cartoon by Roy Thomas from Alter Ego #7 (Oct. 1964)

I remember sitting with Jerry Bails at my desk in 1961. He was on a trip to New York. When he asked if he could visit, I readily agreed – as I did with almost anyone who came into the office in those days. I was very impressed with his credentials as a college professor – and I loved talking to him.

I told Jerry about science fiction fandom. I dug up some fan magazines from a drawer and showed them to him. His eyes popped out. He didn't realize there was a fan movement in science fiction with fan magazines. I told him they were called "fanzines." I realized that sitting before me was a guy who was as nuts about comic books as I was about science fiction.

When you nutty fans came around, we nutty professionals went along with you because, deep down inside, we were still fans. I was always a fan. To this day I'm still a science fiction fan. If I go to twenty conventions a year, at least half of them are science fiction. My biggest thrill was when a convention called Archon in St. Louis invited me to be their *fan* guest of honor.

My main interest in comics fandom, of course, was getting good letters for my columns. I announced that the best letter would receive original artwork. It started when I sent Jerry the artwork for the first issue of *Justice League of America* – for no particular reason. (It may have been another issue – who can remember details like that after so many years?) Years later, Don Thompson told me that the cover of *The Flash* #123 – given to him in my letter competition – put his kids through college.

Not long after Jerry Bails visited me in New York, I received a copy of the first issue of *Alter-Ego,* prepared by Jerry and Roy Thomas. It was much more substantial than the first issue of *The Time Traveller,* which had been a six-page mimeographed thing. Within a couple of years, it became quite impressive.

Three or four years later, Weisinger was looking for a new assistant. He must have been reading my letter columns because he said, "Tell me about this guy Roy Thomas. What do you think of him?" I said, "He writes a very nice letter. I like him a lot. He's a teacher. Why?" He replied, "I'm thinking of hiring him." I said, "Fine." That's when he wrote to Roy, offering him a job at DC. Since many fans became pros in the science fiction field, this sort of thing seemed perfectly natural to me.

In a way, Jerry and Roy were counterparts of myself and Mort. If I played a part in encouraging the formation of comics fandom, and the publication of *Alter-Ego,* it's because I was (and still am) a fan at heart.

An Introduction by Jerry Bails

"The Sound of Celebration"

Hear that sound? It's the sound of celebration and good fellowship. It's been a part of comic fandom since its earliest days. The joys of working together on projects, creating tributes to the medium we love and learning in the process. It was all there in every one of those early issues of *Alter Ego*. Now Roy Thomas and Bill Schelly have managed to bring back the magic once again in this delightful collection.

The news media, when they look at comic fandom at all, see only the collector mania and the high prices some are able to pay for a periodical that was published as a throwaway item. The comics fan is portrayed as an Uncle Scrooge hoarding his rich treasures in some hermetically sealed vault. The general public is never given an accurate picture of the true magic of fandom – the creative energy that has always been a part of our hobby. It is sad to think how many thousands of potential fans were turned away, never knowing that fandom is a celebration of the spirit of creativity. Fans love to publish, write, draw, and share their love of the medium with one another. That's the story Roy and Bill are telling through this book.

This is the third book from Bill Schelly's Hamster Press, and like the others it is dedicated to a return to the values that are at the very heart of comic fandom. Bill's first book was *The Golden Age of Comic Fandom*, which recounted the creative burst of energy that created our hobby in the 1960s. *Golden Age* opened the door and welcomed fans, young and old, to become part of a great creative tradition. It put us in contact with our roots. No one was excluded. Even the youngest fan today tells me how he was made a part of the action, and how the book inspired him to join in the fun.

Then Bill published the beautifully packaged *Fandom's Finest Comics*, a collection of over twenty superb examples of the creativity of early fandom. What a tribute! The roll call of names on the back cover demonstrates just how many great lights there were in the skies in those days and how many of them went on to brilliant careers as professionals. Again, the reader comes away feeling proud to be even a small part of such a wonderful collective effort.

And now, Bill has joined with my old collaborator, Roy Thomas, to pull together the best features that appeared in *Alter Ego* under several fan publishers. I'm waiting anxiously to see the final product myself, because I know not only what great fruit there is to harvest, but that this book will touch the heart of even the most jaded and dis-spirited. They will see that fandom is not just about past glories or collector mania; it's about the possibilities of self-expression, today and tomorrow. Roy and Bill are creators, bringing things alive today, and lighting the way for future talents. That's what comic fandom is really all about.

The articles and features in this book reveal an intrinsic feature of comics that is not present for those who collect coins or stamps. Comics are a story-telling medium, and they pass the spark of imagination from the creators to the audience. Coins and stamps offer nothing like that. Stories are involving and inviting. No matter how excellent the performance, how superb the art, they prompt even the most timid reader/viewer to try it themselves.

A comic is not just an artifact. It is a medium of self-expression that invites the reader to write or draw a story of his or her own. You don't need expensive cameras or equipment to get started, just imagination, a joy in writing, drawing, staging, acting, creating. A simple pencil and paper will get you started. Think back to that first moment when a story first prompted you to create on paper. I can see it in my mind's eye. It must have occurred many hundreds of millions of times. Stories do that, and comics are the

Photo: Dann Thomas

Jerry Bails, Bill Schelly, and Roy Thomas, attending "Fandom Reunion 1997" during the Chicago Comicon

fertile ground in which our storytellers are born.

Comics fans are themselves creators. They are the readers who don't let that first spark of inspiration die. They *fan* it, if you'll excuse the pun. They write, draw, publish, put on shows, and

Above: All-Star #6, *the first issue of the classic All-American comic book that young Jerry Bails ever laid eyes on.*

find new ways to be participants in a wonderful and relatively inexpensive medium.

I was always of the opinion that Roy Thomas would make it big as a professional writer. His talent was obvious to me from Day One. He was sort of my "alter ego," since I had moved on to other dreams. I was delighted when he came back to edit and publish *Alter Ego,* and I felt the same way about his handling of the Justice Society in pro comics. He cared about these projects as a fan, and his love and commitment came through in the final product.

Sure, comics fans cherish and preserve their favorite comics, films and videos, but they want to share their treasures with others, not hide them away. They want to see their treasures reprinted so others will enjoy them. The very thought of sealing an unread comic in a plastic bag is anathema to the spirit of a true fan. Comics are to *read*, to be shared, to become involved with. And no one demonstrates this with greater gusto than my two friends who have put together this book. Their enthusiasm for the medium and fandom is positively infectious. You'll see what I mean when you read this book. It will hook you once again on the delights of this wonderful storytelling medium.

It will not matter if you are 7 or 70, you'll come away committed to the joys of fandom. Fans share; they create; and in return, they receive a priceless lifetime gift of joy. Believe me, I've been at it since I first held a comic in my hands nearly 60 years ago. And in spirit, I am as young now as I was then. I'm proud to say I love comics. And I am extremely proud of my two long-time friends for reminding us what fandom is really all about.

Enjoy.

From The Studio of...

Ronn Foss

Ronn writes: "The 60s was a period of self-discovery, not only for the general population, but also for comics fans, theretofore mostly unknown to each other. *Alter Ego* was the major bridge that brought us together, and my participation was pure pleasure – a labor of love for the comics medium."

Ronn's special introduction to the two issues of *Alter Ego* that he edited and published can be found on page 57.

Believe It or Not ...

One *Final* Introduction

by Roy Thomas

I suppose I could blame Julius Schwartz's early DC comics and Jerry G. Bails' co-founding of comics fandom for my graduating *magna cum laude* instead of *summa cum laude* from college in '61. And I could blame both those gentlemen (with Stan Lee and his burgeoning Marvel line soon added to the mix) for my being a less than dedicated high school teacher from '61-'65.

Blame them?

Rather, I should get down on my knees and *thank* them.

For those comics and fanzines were the salvation of my early-to-mid-twenties. When in *JLA* #16 (Dec. '62) Julie and Gardner Fox named an off-stage character "Jerry Thomas" after JGB and me, I was ecstatic, figuring that was the closest I'd ever get to being in the comics industry.

And of course the combination of writing letters to comics editors and articles for fanzines led to my entering the comics field in '65, where I've been happily ensconced ever since, despite occasional detours into films and television.

Among many other memories of those halcyon days which I mentioned in my preface to Bill Schelly's 1995 tome *The Golden Age of Comic Fandom* and won't repeat here, I very much remember one more in particular:

Namely, standing at the kitchen table on Tuesday evening, November 3, 1964, assembling and stapling copies of *AE* #7 while watching the Presidential election results on the $25 used television set which a fellow teacher and I had purchased specifically to watch the returns. (The TV's innards and Barry Goldwater's challenge to LBJ both gave up the ghost early, but I kept on stapling.)

But mainly, I remember the wonderful correspondences I had and the friends I made:

Ronn Foss, whose art-laden letters were a welcome treat;

Biljo White, whose dedication and talent were always a source of awe;

Richard "Grass" Green, the one fan-artist equally at home with humor or action;

Don and Maggie Thompson, whom I usually thought of as a single two-headed entity, and whose sporadically-published fanzine *Comic Art* was one of the true class acts of the period;

Julius Schwartz and Gardner F. Fox and Otto O. Binder, a trio of wonderful, giving pros whose encouragement to a young and far-off fan continued unabated when I moved to Manhattan – and even after I jumped ship from DC to work for the competition;

And Jerry Bails.

Most of all, Jerry G. Bails, Ph.D.

Ever since the day in November 1960 when he responded to my first gushing letter by sending me semi-complete copies of *All-Star Comics* #4-6 (can you *imagine?*), and even though he bowed out of active fandom after *AE* #4 to pursue his avocations of gathering and disseminating information on comic book creators, he has been both a friend and an inspiration.

No Olympian gathering at lunch in New York with Stan Lee, Jack Kirby, and John Romita – not even sitting at the head table between Milt Caniff and Charles Schulz at the Inkpot Awards Banquet at the 1974 San Diego comicon – ever meant more to me than the Fandom Reunion Luncheon held at the Chicago comicon in July 1997, where Jerry and I met for the first time in nearly two decades, and shared a great good time with Bill Schelly and other fannish longtimers.

And now this book shows, hopefully, what all the fuss was about.

Sure, some of the writing is dated, because we've learned so much more about the practice and history of comics since then. (Hey, it's been over thirty years since the last non-pro issue of *AE*, after all!)

Sure, we mostly used tracings and approximations of comics drawings back then rather than photostats, for reasons that will be explained later;

Sure, the fannish strips herein are drawn by four people who never went on to become super-star artists at Marvel or DC – but Grass Green did later draw for Charlton and various alternative comics (even doing the Bestest League of America for Charlton, with my blessing); Ronn Foss once illustrated a humor feature for Marvel's *Not Brand Echh*; Biljo White and I made a good stab at getting *Son of Vulcan* revived at Charlton; and by good fortune I stumbled into a writing and editing career in comics, even if no one was ever going to ask me to pencil *The Fantastic Four*.

Still, this book – a compilation of *Alter Ego*'s best and most representative moments, plus an informal history of the fanzine from its humble spirit-duplicator beginnings through its photo-offset issues and even its brief flowering as the inspiration for an actual comic book super-hero – fills a gap.

It shows what it was like to be a comics fan, particularly in the first half of the 1960s: what our interests were, what our obsessions were – what our *dreams* were.

Thanks, Bill, for helping another one of those dreams come true!

Cartoon by Sam Grainger from Alter Ego *#9 (August 1965).*

*Art by Biljo White (*à la *Hasen) from* Alter Ego #7

John Buscema contributed to AE #10 (1969) this grand, graceful pencil illustration of Marvel's modern-day Black Knight, which Roy Thomas had co-created in 1967.

Note to the Reader:

Henceforth, throughout this book, new material prepared for this volume will be printed entirely in italics, like this note. In this way, the reader can easily distinguish between material that appeared in the original eleven issues of AE *or was written at that time ... and that which comprises editorial annotations. (As all captions, both new and original, are italicized, the new ones are also bracketed.)*

We have standardized the spellings of "comic book" (no hyphen), "super-hero" (with hyphen), and possibly a few other words, for the sake of consistency. Also standardized is the way we refer to issue numbers, i.e. "AE-7" becomes "AE #7," and comic book titles which were usually printed in all caps have been shown here in upper-and-lower case italics. Letter column formats have also been standardized, with the writer's name and address preceding the letter, and generally without salutation.

All photos and drawings are from the original issues of Alter Ego *unless duly noted.*

The Editors

Cartoon by Roy Thomas from Alter Ego *#8 (March 1965)*

As the "advertisement" on the preceding page indicates, the following article was originally slated to appear in The Bestest from Alter Ego Nos. 1-3 *in 1965. What follows is an abridged version of the first draft of the piece which was written at that time, months before Roy wrote his first professional comics story.*

Since much of the original correspondence between Jerry and Roy has been lost in the intervening decades, this account of the "secret origin" of Alter Ego *is the most complete (and accurate) record of the events leading up to its publication.*

Step into your time machine and set the dial for the year 1960 – when Dwight D. Eisenhower was President of the United States ... when the Silver Age of Comics was a-borning ... and when a saga began that we call ....

THE ALTER EGO STORY

by Roy Thomas

Alter Ego owes its existence to the Justice League of America. It's as simple as that, actually.

Having learned to read on *All-Star Comics* as a child of five, I had long harbored a latent nostalgic feeling for the Justice Society and its ilk. In fact, when the last issue of *All-Star* had been followed by the putrid mess known as *All-Star Western*, I had vowed to one day possess every single issue of my favorite comic – and had, in desperation, taken up reading *The Marvel Family* with a new vengeance.

So when, without fanfare, *The Brave and the Bold* began carrying the adventures of the JLA, I was overjoyed. After the last of the three trial issues was read and digested, I could not contain myself any longer; I wrote a letter for the first time to editor Julius Schwartz, congratulating him on his super-hero comics in general, and the Justice League of America in particular.

I asked if I might know the name and address of the writer of these stories, so I could express my thanks to him in person. In that day before editors of one-shot comic fanzines had cluttered his desk with dozens of requests every day for exclusive 10,000-word autobiographies, Julius Schwartz was kind enough to send me the home address of Gardner F. Fox – who, he added, had also written the first three dozen or so JSA tales. He also suggested that there, rather than at the National offices themselves, was the place to search for the back issues of *All-Star* after which I lusted so vocally.

Needless to say, the mailman was still on our block as I began to type a nice long letter to Gardner Fox, lauding him for his recent JLA-Amazo episode and offering to buy any old *All-Stars* or related comics collecting dust in his attic.

Fox's reply was gracious and understanding. He stated, however, that only a few months before the decision to revive the JSA as the JLA, he had sold his remaining *All-Stars* to one Jerry G. Bails, with whom he had been corresponding off and on for years concerning the JSA, its authors, and its artists. He gave me, however, Jerry's address and suggested that we might enjoy getting in touch with each other.

Accordingly, on November 21, 1960 – just one day before my twentieth birthday – I dashed off a letter to "Mr. Bails":

"The two of us do not know each other, but I discovered recently that we have at least one thing very much in common – we are both great devotees of the old Justice Society of America, which appeared some years ago in *All-Star Comics*."

Gardner F. Fox (from unused cover of AE #10, by Sam Grainger)

307 Greensferry Road
Jackson, Missouri
November 3, 1960

Dear Mr. Fox,

I hope you do not mind my writing to you at your home address, but I obtained it from Mr. Schwartz of National Comics because I wanted to write a letter personally to the man who has given me so many hours of pleasant comic reading over my twenty years (as of the 22nd of this month, that is). I'm not just a person who can't read anything else--as a matter of fact, I have an A- college grade average. It's just that I like the super-hero comics which DC puts out, especially "Justice League of America." I read the old "All-Star Comics" from the age of five years old, before I was in grade school, and I've liked them ever since. From the demise of "All-Star" till the revival of Flash in 1956 I didn't read too many, but now I have a renewed interest in Flash, Green Lantern, et al.

I'm especially glad that the Three Dimwits have been re[illegible] duced in [illegible]

Armed with Gardner Fox's address, courtesy of Julius Schwartz, Thomas wrote his first letter to the DC scripter on November 3, 1960.

From the Fox archives at the University of Oregon Library, Dept. of Special Collections. (Photocopy provided by Michael T. Gilbert.)

I followed this with an offer to buy any *All-Stars* he might be willing to sell, and an expression of a desire to read any he might be willing to loan, informed him that I was a senior at Southeast Missouri State College in Cape Girardeau and a future high school teacher, and then plopped my hopeful missive in the nearest mailbox.

A few days later, on a Saturday morning, I received in the mail two of the most pleasant surprises of my young life: a package containing worn and partially incomplete copies of *All-Star Comics* #4-6, and a letter from one Jerry G. Bails of Detroit, Michigan.

After glancing for a few moments at the comics -- which I had never seen before, as I had been only a few months old when they had come out – I opened the letter. It began:

"Dear Roy,

"I can't begin to tell you how happy I am to find another *All-Star* enthusiast after all these years. I've been a fan since the first Justice Society adventure appeared in *All-Star Comics* #3 (Winter 1941). In 1945, I began my campaign to collect all the back issues of this magazine, and in 1951, when the JSA was dropped, I began my campaign for a revival of this old favorite. Just last year, as you know, my efforts finally paid off. Now, I'm off on a new campaign – to make the Justice League of America more popular than Superman. First, I want to see the *JLA* published monthly; then I want to see it published in a giant edition. I hope you will join me in working for these goals."

He went on to state that he had duplicates of issues #2-8, 10, and 18-24, but that he had just offered them (through Julius Schwartz) to National, whose own files were incomplete. So far Schwartz had neither accepted nor declined his offer, and until he did so, Jerry felt he could hardly offer the comics to me. In the meantime, as he said, all was not lost, as he had sent me some old, worn triplicates of issues 4-6.

In the more personal part of the letter, he observed that we had other things in common besides our JSA/JLA interests. He, too, was a Missourian, having done most of his undergraduate and graduate work at the University of Kansas City. He had moved to Detroit just that preceding July to become Assistant Professor of Natural Science at Wayne State University. He hoped we could get together sometime, perhaps when he returned to Kansas City to visit relatives and friends.

This was the beginning of a long and voluminous correspondence, which in less than five months added up to in excess of 100 pages.

Among other things, I mentioned an idea that I wanted to see reinstated in comics. *Star-Spangled Comics* had, for years, contained a teenage bunch of boys in association with a shield-toting crimebuster called the Guardian (invented by Simon and Kirby, who, I was to discover later, had also created the shield-toting Captain America years earlier). I wanted to see such an idea used in connection with National's weakest super-hero, J'onn J'onzz, or perhaps with a revival of another old favorite, Robotman.

His reply was that, besides liking my idea for a "news legion," he had one of his own, which he had suggested to Gardner Fox already in a letter the previous summer: "I also think that DC should revive the Atom as a character like the old Dollman. Do you remember him?"

Did I? The idea immediately obsessed me that a new Atom should be the next hero to be revived after Hawkman joined the JLA. (Ha.) The next day (December 4), I fired off a letter myself to editor Schwartz, and asked Bails who he thought would be the best artist for such a comic. (His answer: Murphy Anderson, who, of course, did do the inking until he took over Hawkman and left the Mighty Mite to Sid Greene.)

Our first attempt at working together on any common goal came about as a result of a three-page letter I received from my college-professor correspondent on December 13. It began:

"I am 'Jerry' to my friends, 'Mister' to those who don't know me, and 'Doctor' to those who insist on formalities. I hope that you are one of the first group." (So, exit the "Mr. Bails" bit.)

Jerry went on to state that he had sent Julius Schwartz a rather complete description of his suggested version of the Atom, who should have only limited power (as I concurred). His suggestion was the following:

"Al Pratt, a young physics professor, discovers how to replace the normal atoms of his body with heavy metastable isotopes. For an hour at a time, he can compress the atoms of his body and acquire a six-inch stature with strength to smash ordinary matter with some exertion, and to leap several stories high. If trapped in a lead box at the end of his 'hour,' the tiny titan can't absorb the cosmic rays he needs to resume normal size and he shrinks into a subatomic world, return from which is always replete with new danger."

He also mentioned that he had included my idea for a group of boy companions, who might carry the main action, with the Atom helping them – perhaps even unknown to anyone but the boys. "What I really wish," he went on, "is that I had the time to write an occasional Atom script for *Showcase*. Maybe you and I could collaborate in some way and submit a script and cover panel to Julie. How about it?"

This suggestion, plus the fact that Jerry offered to send me his duplicate *All-Stars* to read over the Christmas vacation, cheered me immensely, and I immediately plunged myself into the project.

In fact, even before receipt of this letter, I had already dashed off my own two-page synopsis of an Atom origin which in many details resembled his own idea. In my version, Al Pratt was a college student (as the old one had been), who was given his power to shrink by MOM (Molecular Order Modifier), the invention of a physics professor with whom he was friendly, and who was killed in the first story by spies. I also included a non-talking parrot named Copernicus (Copey for short) who would serve as short-range transportation for the Mighty Mite. I had even created a host of subsidiary characters: a roommate, a girl friend, and a grandmother, who would now seem like a wealthy version of Spider-Man's Aunt May.

At the very end of this December 17 letter to Jerry, I added as an afterthought a paragraph that was to have far-reaching repercussions as far as my own leisure time for several years was concerned:

"Oh, by the way, also during the January lay-off, I begin work on a project long dear to my heart – a *Mad*-type take-off on the JLA called the Bestest League of America, and starring Green Trashcan, Wondrous Woman, Cash, Aquariuman, and S'amm S'mithh, the Martian Manhandler, and featuring Superham, Wombatman, and Aukman. If you wish, I'll let you see it when I finish it in February or March."

I had, you see, long before done a similar parody of the JSA, as lorded over by Mean Lantern, with members Hogman, Dr. Mid-Day, Trash, Blunder Woman, and Mildrat (for Wildcat, since I didn't like Black Canary).

Jerry's next two letters (each, like most of mine, several pages long) outlined in more detail his ideas for the Atom. Things were about at this pass when I received, on January 10, 1961, a discouragingly encouraging note from Jerry:

"I have just received a letter from Gardner. DC will revive the Atom. They have already considered several ideas and art samples. The Atom will definitely have the ability to shrink. They presently intend to make him a college student, but this is not definite yet. Gar will write the stories.

"In view of this news, I suggest we abandon our plan for the Atom. I am sending Gar a list of our final suggestions. I recommend to you that you get to work immediately on your Dr. Fate script."

So that was that. I had already sent my own few suggestions to Julius Schwartz and Gardner Fox, including a sketch of the Atom riding Copernicus which was mildly praised and then ignored. Jerry (with perhaps a little extra help from me) had very likely influenced National to "revive" the Atom – a feat for which he was never given any recognition – and had given them a little scientific information to make the thing more palatable to today's accuracy-hungry comicmongers.

While Jerry and Roy were crafting their proposal for a 6-inch-high revival of The Atom, Julie Schwartz went ahead with his own version.

However, Jerry and I were not the type to sit around stewing in our own Kryptonite juice. His letter quoted above suggested that I commence work on a revival plan for Dr. Fate, which I immediately did. And, for his part, Jerry began to talk of a "JLA newsletter" that he wanted to publish and distribute to such JLA fans as he could contact, both through the letter pages of the comic itself and in other ways.

The road to *Alter Ego* took a giant step forward when, on January 26, I received a letter from Jerry stating that he had just received an invitation to visit and lecture at Adelphi College on Long Island the following month. He and his wife Sondra were planning to make the visit the occasion of a long-awaited holiday, and of course he intended to "drop in" at the DC offices.

He added: "I am going to suggest my plan for a JLA newsletter and see if I can get their support for it. I also hope to see the drawings of the Atom and other projects in the works. If you have any ideas for the newsletter, let me know by return mail."

My one immediate suggestion, a Junior Justice League of America organization as in days of old, in which coded messages told of future JSA tales, turned out to be one which Jerry had already been pondering, so it was incorporated at once.

Also in that letter I included a resumé of the first chapter of the Bestest League story I was doing (in twice-up size) on poster paper. I also included Green Trashcan's oath:

"In little shack or circus tent,
No evil shall escape this gent.
Let those who are of evil bent
Beware my power
– Green Trashcan's scent."

The next day – Jerry's and my letters often crossed in the mails – I suggested something else that was to mushroom into something more personal than I had intended.

Jerry and I had been discussing an idea of mine for a revival of Dr. Fate, one of the mightiest of JSA heroes. In my version he was an archeologist who discovered and donned a strange blue-and-gold costume he found in Egypt, only to find that touching the belt in a certain place tossed him back into time. There, he regained the three missing parts of the costume – teleportational cloak, lingua-translating amulet, and telekinetic helmet -- to become Doctor Fate, a sort of time-traveling Adam Strange.

However, when Rip Hunter arrived on the scene in his own colorless way, I turned my thoughts to other things. And then, suddenly, one day in late January not long before Jerry's upcoming journey, I suddenly dashed off on the typewriter – and later drew an illo for – a revival of another super-powerful JSAer of old, The Spectre.

As I originally planned him, he was scientist Jim Corrigan, who discovered that an invention of his had accidentally picked up dimension-hopping characteristics, so that any object he placed before it vanished and shortly returned in triplicate – the original object and two other, weirder forms.

Naturally, it wasn't long before Corrigan himself became sliced into two other beings, the Spectre and the Shade, embodiments respectively of the good and the evil that are in man.

Jerry responded enthusiastically: "I certainly like your idea for the Spectre. May I suggest the name 'Count Dis' for his evil counterpart. (I chose 'Dis' rather than the Greek, 'Pluto,' because the latter has so many other connotations for comic readers.)"

He also suggested that I use Freudian terms, such as the super-ego and id, rather than the simpler "good" and "evil," and that I make Corrigan a psychiatrist who traveled to India to learn the secret of the mystics. With some revision – Corrigan became a doctor who, in India to see his dying uncle, gained possession of a mysterious gem that caused his personality division – the idea had taken form almost overnight.

After commenting favorably on my Bestest League ideas, he went on to say, "My thoughts for a newsletter are still pretty muddy. I can have the thing hectographed for nothing, but I would prefer to at least have it mimeographed, but that costs money. So does postage, if the number of copies is very great. I don't want to charge for it, because that involves all sorts of complications and DC might not give their approval, and their approval is essential if I am to get the kind of advance info I need for a good start.

"Right now I think I'll send *The JLA Subscriber* (as I might call it) only to adult readers who write in to one of Julie's magazines. This audience would supply many new ideas and help to boost the JLA with the younger set. They would also be interested in gossip about the old JSA stories and other DC Comics, and might want to trade old mags, just as we have.

"The number of JLA fans over 18 shouldn't be so great that I couldn't afford the postage myself, and perhaps different issues of the newsletter could originate from different fans. In other words, any one at any time might get a newsletter off to other fans. However, only subscribers to the *JLA* would receive the code chart when they send me the address label from the brown mailing wrapper. What do you think? I think that each editor might include an editorial. I have one I want to write on the good and bad effects of the Comics Code. And I'm sure you could write many interesting features."

This, of course, was in the days before Jerry or I – or anybody, I suppose – realized just how large a potential readership an amateur publication on comic book heroes really had. It was in the days when both Jerry and I were more enthusiastic about the Justice League than we have had occasion to be since – when we still had dreams of a monthly *JLA* comic, not to mention a giant 25¢ annual following the style of the old *All-Stars*. It was also, need I mention, in the days before Stan Lee had semi-revolutionized the field with his own uninhibited super-do-gooders.

After this, Jerry and I were not in close contact for about two weeks, during which he made his New York trip. Besides seeing "Camelot," the Nichols-and-May show, and sundry other big-city benefits, he did of course manage to give his lectures and visit the National offices, and he returned home full of new fire:

"First of all, let me say that my five-hour visit to the DC offices, my luncheon with Julie and Gar, my private conversations with writers and artists, and my perusal of AA [All-American] classics, gives more than I could relate in a half dozen king-sized letters; and besides, I don't want to steal all my own thunder, because I know now (for sure) that I want to bring out a 'fanzine' devoted to the Great Revival of the costumed heroes.

"I even have what I consider to be a brilliant title and format. It will be called *Alter-ego* and each contributor will sign his article with the name of the hero he wishes to see revived, or created. It seems natural for me to choose the Atom to start, while you, who (I hope) will serve as co-editor, could use either your Dr. Fate or Spectre or both.

"I have enough background info, promise of advance previews, support in Julie's letter columns, and hope for fresh ideas from a guy named Thomas to make this fanzine go, go, go, as Snapper might say." (Even then, you see, Jerry knew what every fanzine contributor needs to keep him going: flattery.)

He also included inside information on the forthcoming Atom, who had been temporarily frozen by DC, which feared, he said, "flooding the market with costumed heroes." A worry, of course, which has since been shown by Stan Lee and his cohorts to be unjustified. Jerry had seen Gil Kane's preliminary sketch of the Atom, which pictured him astride a dog, but he didn't know if the canine was to be a permanent fixture in the strip or not and said that the topic never came up in the conversation.

He concluded: "Now, get to work and supply me with material for the first issue of *Alter-ego*. I would like to run about a dozen pages, including your Bestest League of America in serial form. Hold it to four 8x11 pages per chapter if you can. Send me your shaded pencil drawings and I'll do my best to reproduce them in Ben Day tones. I suggest you use typewriter characters in balloons and legends."

Most of which I immediately did – as a matter of fact, I never did do anything more than the first chapter of the BLA on poster paper at double size after that. I also sent him an intended "cover" that would have gone inside the fanzine and which he decided to use as the cover of *Alter-Ego* #1. (Though still hyphenating the word, we now capitalized both halves, which is something of an improvement, anyway.)

Jerry responded by saying he had written Bill Finger, the original author of Green Lantern and other heroes, for an autobiographical sketch and that he himself was working on a history of the JSA for the first issue of *AE*, "describing a few of the better stories in detail."

A few days later, while I was hard at work redrawing the Bestest League on typing paper as per Jerry's instructions, I received another message from him, this one suggesting that I write up in short story form my revival version of either Dr. Fate or the Spectre, to be published in *AE* for reader reaction. For various reasons, I decided the Spectre was the more interesting of the two, and accordingly started work on an as-yet-unnamed story about the most powerful comic hero of all time.

By early March Jerry had things pretty well whipped into shape. For some weeks he had been sending out feelers to comic readers "by the dozens" across the country, and on March 3 he reported that he was getting a couple of responses a day. These people, he said, would receive our first issue free of charge; from then on, copies would sell for the staggering sum of 20¢ (in coin or stamps) unless the person had an article, letter, or ad in it. He also sent a list of the projected contents of *AE* #1: "Cover: BLA splash (possibly in color); 'The Mystery of the Vanishing Detectives'; Part 1 of a JSA history, with my art; 'A Code That Needs Breaking' – an editorial on the Comics Code; 'The Reincarnation of the Spectre' – (suggested title for your 2-pager); 'A Finger in Every Plot,' the Finger autobiography (No word yet!); 'Swaps and Sales,' 50¢ per quarter-page. (What do you think of this rate?)"

Jerry Bails' thank-you note to Julius Schwartz and Gardner Fox, written immediately after his visit to the DC offices. (From the University of Oregon Library Dept. of Special Collections)

2/12/61

Dear Julie & Gar,

Thank you both very much for a most pleasant day. I was truly overwhelmed by your hospitality. You have been exceedingly generous.

To partially repay you for your kindness, I hope to bring out soon a "fanzine" (Alter-ego) devoted to your past and current creations, and designed to promote the Great Revival of the costumed heros (which I believe has only just started) and to insure that these heros (as a league) will never die again.

May the team of Schwartz and Fox live forever!

Your oldest fan,

J. G. B.

There were also to be a very limited want-ad section; coming events at DC; a letters section; a cryptogram; and "last but not least," he claimed, the Bestest League of America. He planned on a "well-balanced issue, totaling about 20 pages."

A few days later I sent Jerry the tentative splash panel of the BLA story. Jerry, however, thought that the drawings of the six members inside their little circles were too small, and proceeded to substitute for these the heads from a rapid sketch I had sent him earlier. This didn't work out too badly, except that I had not yet succeeded (if I ever did) in giving Wondrous Woman the Brigitte Bardot-type appearance I wanted. In *AE* #1 she came out looking like a young Marjorie Main.

Jerry also made a number of suggestions on the tentative cover I had sent. He wanted all the figures a little larger, and wanted things a bit more confused in general. I concurred with some, though not all, of his suggestions and went to work in earnest.

When he received the first chapter a week later, his reply was very enthusiastic and he immediately prepared the five-color master for the cover. He changed it somewhat, so that Wondrous Woman came out upside down and a "Comics Code" seal replaced the caption I had done. At the same time he changed some of the past perfect tenses in my Spectre story to simple past tenses and announced that it was ready to be included.

On March 28 Jerry announced that, with Sondra's help, the final ditto masters had been prepared on the 21-page *Alter-Ego* #1. The cover, the Spectre-Count Dis drawing, and one he had done for an article on the Wizard were to be in color, while the rest of the fanzine would be in black and white. He wrote:

"As you will see, I have written features on different topics than I originally intended. This I did for several reasons. One, because my story of the JSA was anticipated by another fanzine, *Xero*, devoted to science fiction and the comics."

The rumor persists, I think – I even believe it myself, sometimes – that *Alter-Ego* was inspired by Dick Lupoff's excellent SF fanzine, *Xero*. However, the facts show otherwise. Jerry had already worked out tentative contents of the first issue when he discovered the existence of the other zine, with its fine series on the comics entitled "And All in Color for a Dime." The three parts published so far had dealt with Captain Marvel, National Comics in general, and the Justice Society in particular. I tried to get the back issues, but was only able to start receiving the zine with issue #4, which contained the really outstanding article on the Timely (now Marvel) heroes by Don Thompson.

Jerry was able to obtain, from SF fan Julius Schwartz, the first three issues of *Xero* on loan so that I could read them, but, through an error in judgment on my part which I still regret, they were later lost in the mails.

There still had been no word from Bill Finger, despite many letters sent by Jerry. He hoped to add the autobiography (or whatever) to *AE* #1 as a bonus, if it came in time, but it never did. Jerry also dropped his editorial on the Comics Code Authority. The last thing I saw before I received the finished fanzine was the secret code chart.

"The Alter Ego Story" ends soon after this point, upon mentioning the final item to be added to AE *#1 ("Merciful Minerva," an article on Wonder Woman by Jerry), and appending some initial comments about the genesis of features that appeared* AE *#2. Though left incomplete in terms of Roy's original intent, the piece succeeds in providing a vivid impression of those exciting months just before the fanzine was unleashed on an unsuspecting world.*

Without further ado, we begin the main portion of this book: the best material from each issue of the fanzine, beginning with the innocent early editions, through the progression until its demise, some seventeen years later....

For a brief historical perspective on the entire publishing history of Alter Ego, *turn to page 183.*

About the cover of* Alter-Ego *#1 (March 1961): *Originally drawn as a sort of "cover" for a Bestest League of America comic book, to be run inside the fanzine with the first chapter of the parody strip, Roy's sketch was transferred to a ditto master unit by Jerry Bails. In the process, Bails added the "Forbidden by the Comics Code" seal.*

ALTER-EGO

IT'S A MATTER OF POLICY

This is the first issue of *Alter-Ego*, a new comic fanzine devoted to the revival of the costumed heroes. As you can see, it features portraits of the great heroes and villains of the comic books, stories about their creators, fiction in the best tradition of the comics, and the latest news about coming events in the fantastic world of the good 'n' the bad guys. *Alter-Ego* also has the regular features of any serviceable rag – it has the usual classified section and column for readers' reactions, and the margins may be used for droodles.

Sprinkled through this and all future issues, you will find cryptograms (you know – code messages), which will contain information of interest to comic fandom. To get your copy of the secret code chart, just send yours truly a self-addressed, stamped envelope and address label from the brown mailing wrapper on your subscription copy of *Justice League of America.*

Alter-Ego will be published on an irregular schedule (as most fanzines are), but in all probability, it will hit the mails as a quarterly. Because of the high cost of production and mailing, the print run for each issue will be geared pretty closely to demand. The demand will be gauged by the advance sales of each issue. *No* subscriptions will be sold, but I will reserve a copy of the next issue for any reader in return for:

(1) An article, feature, ad, news, or comments that I accept for publication; or
(2) 24¢ in postage stamps.

Reserve your copy of *Alter-Ego* #2 now! Include a letter telling me what you think of this issue. I will enjoy hearing from you, and I can certainly use the stamps.

J.G. Bails, 14242 Dale, Detroit 23, Michigan

◆ ◆ ◆ ◆

Alter-Ego #1 (Spring, 1961), a comic fanzine edited and published at 14242 Dale, Detroit 23, Michigan. No subscriptions accepted. Single copies of the next issue: 24¢ in postage stamps. Advertising rates: 50¢ per quarter page. Editors: Jerry G. Bails and Roy Thomas. Deadline for material to appear in issue #2: June 1, 1961.

ON THE DRAWING BOARD

by Jerry Bails

This coming summer is going to be one of the most exciting seasons in the history of the comics. DC Comics already has on the drawing board and on the four-color presses some of the most unusual stories that have ever been written; and to top it all off, they plan to revive (on the heels of Hawkman) another great JSA hero. Here are some of the details.

Where there is a shadow, there must be someone – or something – to cast it. Or so Hawkman and Hawkgirl believed until they met the mysterious "Shadow-Thief of Midway City," who could pass through steel and stone, robbing at will. This elusive new villain is featured in the third great Hawkman issue of *The Brave and the Bold* (#36, June-July).

Is it possible for both the Flash and Barry Allen to be present at the same time? We can hear you say, "No, it's impossible – since the Flash and Barry are one and the same person!" But before you jump to conclusions, take a good look at the full-page panel on page 8 of the upcoming Flash adventure, "Secret of the Stolen Blueprint." This story, along with a Flash-Trickster rematch, appears in the June issue of *The Flash* (#121).

[The cover of the first Secret Origins *annual was shown in* AE *#1 as a full-page tracing.]*

Who would make the most formidable enemy for Green Lantern? Naturally, another Green Lantern! And in the July-August issue of *Green Lantern* (#7), the Emerald Crusader faces a renegade GL, Sinestro, who is banished by the Guardians to the universe of Qward. Don't miss the titanic battle of the power rings.

I predict! *Justice League of America* #5, "When Gravity Ran Wild," will top *every* JLA adventure that has appeared so far. In addition to introducing a brand-new villain named Dr. Destiny (who is bound to plague the JLA again and again), this story pits the JLA members against a collection of their most formidable enemies, organized by Dr. Destiny as an Injustice League. As if this isn't enough, the story has Green Arrow placed on trial for betraying the JLA. For those of you who already have your secret code charts in hand, here is a message that will heighten your enjoyment of the story still further.

Gauufoekhuoui Bcbuz, Jenqgdhr Ahinqbiby Dwylalukzavil!

This great JLA story will be in the mails to subscribers about the first week in April, but it won't hit the stands until some two weeks later.

And now for even a further look into the future – *JLA* #6, "Wheel of Misfortune," will pit the all-star heroes against a new kind of villain, who will try to control the hidden luck glands in the body. Oh yes, for those of you who didn't know – our fortunes (good or bad) are determined by a pair of luck glands. When something goes wrong with one or the other of those glands, almost anything can happen – and it does – to the JLA, that is, in the August-September issue, on sale the third week in June.

In the September-October issue of *Green Lantern* (#8), the Emerald Crusader will set a new first – in a book-length novel entitled "Challenge from 5700 A.D.," GL will assume a third, new, and entirely complete identity as a man of the far distant future. Can't you just imagine the complications when this third identity takes over the body of Hal Jordan, without the latter's knowledge? It looks like Carol Ferris is going to get competition for GL's attention in a wholly unexpected way. Incidentally, the cover for this issue will be treated artistically and reproduction-wise in a different fashion. Don't miss it. It will hit the stands the last week of July.

Talking about comic book first – *The Flash* #123 (September) will feature a story, "Flash of Two Worlds," which I never expected to see. It will co-star the new Flash (Barry Allen) and the old Flash (Jay Garrick) together in one book-length novel. How these two Flashes can co-exist on earth today is told in a convincing way by the creator of the original Flash, Gardner F. Fox. The cover of this unusual issue will portray both Flashes in their individual costumes. Both old and new fans will want this issue for their private collections.

Now, about the two new giant anthologies – the first, of course, is the *Batman Annual* that we have been promised. It will feature replays of some of the greatest adventures of Batman and Robin that have appeared over the last two decades. This promises to be a real collector's item.

The second new 25¢ book also holds out promise of being a collector's item, but it holds out an even greater promise – promise of things to come. This book will feature the origin of the Superman-Batman team, as well as the origins of Flash, Green Lantern, J'onn J'onzz, Adam Strange, Green Arrow, Challengers of the Unknown, and last but not least, Wonder Woman. (See the reproduction of the cover on the facing page.) When I say that this anthology holds out promise of things to come, I mean that it may very well lead to a second great issue starring "The Origin of the Justice League of America." Of course, this would not be a replay, since the origin of this team has never been published, but I think it would sell half a million copies. I know many fans would like to see a regular, giant edition of the *JLA* (possibly entitled *All-Star Comics*), and this new annual is a step in the right direction.

And now, for what I believe is possibly the best news of all – the revival of another JSA hero. *JLA* author Gardner Fox and *GL* artist Gil Kane are teaming up with editor Julie Schwartz to create one of the most unusual heroes on the modern scene. I feel especially happy about this one, because I suggested the idea initially in a letter to Gardner Fox dated August 29, 1960. I followed it up with another letter to Julie Schwartz on December 8, but by this time this industrious gentleman had already taken up the idea and developed it along lines very similar to those that I suggested in my second letter. This new hero with a familiar name will be given a try-out in *Showcase* #34, which should appear in early August. So, there is still time to get your secret code charts and decipher the following message, which reveals the name of this hero, and gives the lowdown on his new super-powers.

Aqcnb Bhvsopwzwhm Cwrfrpsuhvv

Dopzivkfpuav Eqgvglafcq

Fxowdlunjaoxaln, Anbcmgcabns

Bawhskwzzhfizm Jadsgdzsnl.

ALTER-EGO SECRET CODE CHART

This code chart is essentially ten codes in one. In an ordinary message all ten codes may be used. The initial letter of each code-word is the key, signifying which one of the ten rows of the code chart is to be used in translating the remaining letters of the code-word into English.

For example, the code-word "Chjr" means "ego." The capital letter "C" designates the third row of the code chart. In that row, "h" corresponds to "e"; "j" corresonds to "g"; and "r" corresponds to "o."

SAMPLE MESSAGE [see Page 18]: Gauufoekhuoui Bcbuz, Jenqgdhr Ahinqbiby Dwylalukzavil!

TRANSLATION: Keep your eyes on GL, for he is not who he pretends to be!

	a	b	c	d	e	f	g	h	i	j	k	l	m	n	o	p	q	r	s	t	u	v	w	x	y	z
A	G	H	I	J	K	L	M	N	O	P	Q	R	S	T	U	V	W	X	Y	Z	A	B	C	D	E	F
B	M	N	O	P	Q	R	S	T	U	V	W	X	Y	Z	A	B	C	D	E	F	G	H	I	J	K	L
C	X	Y	Z	A	B	C	D	E	F	G	H	I	J	K	L	M	N	O	P	Q	R	S	T	U	V	W
D	T	U	V	W	X	Y	Z	A	B	C	D	E	F	G	H	I	J	K	L	M	N	O	P	Q	R	S
E	C	D	E	F	G	H	I	J	K	L	M	N	O	P	Q	R	S	T	U	V	W	X	Y	Z	A	B
F	R	S	T	U	V	W	X	Y	Z	A	B	C	D	E	F	G	H	I	J	K	L	M	N	O	P	Q
G	K	L	M	N	O	P	Q	R	S	T	U	V	W	X	Y	Z	A	B	C	D	E	F	G	H	I	J
H	H	I	J	K	L	M	N	O	P	Q	R	S	T	U	V	W	X	Y	Z	A	B	C	D	E	F	G
I	I	J	K	L	M	N	O	P	Q	R	S	T	U	V	W	X	Y	Z	A	B	C	D	E	F	G	H
J	B	C	D	E	F	G	H	I	J	K	L	M	N	O	P	Q	R	S	T	U	V	W	X	Y	Z	A

[Jerry's secret code chart wasn't included in AE *#1, of course; but we've reprinted it here, because JGB's personal copy may well be the only one still in existence.]*

THE WILES OF THE WIZARD

THE PORTRAIT OF A VILLAIN

by Jerry Bails

[Jerry Bails' Wizard illo re-drawn by Al Dellinges in 1988]

The searchlight on the prison wall is trained on one of the most dangerous villains the Justice Society of America ever faced – the Wizard, alias W.I. Zard (introduced in *All-Star Comics* #34, April-May 1947).

In his youth, Zard was just a stupid, trigger-happy gunman. However, when he was caught and sent to prison, he began to realize that crime is a big business, with all the pitfalls and competition of any other business, and he resolved to study hard, to learn new methods... different angles... to become successful at crime.

When he was released from prison many years later, he traveled to Tibet to study the magic of the mystic lamas. During his apprenticeship, he mastered the complete art of hypnotism – he learned to create illusions so real that he could actually kill a victim by paralyzing his nerve centers. When he had learned enough to teach himself Black Magic, he turned on the master lama who had taught him, and ruthlessly destroyed him.

Returning to the States, Zard started his new crime career as the Wizard, and executed an elaborate scheme to realize his greatest ambition – to join the Justice Society of America. You see, the Wizard thought that the JSA was a great criminal gang; he believed that real honesty is a myth – that the only people who don't steal are those who are afraid of being caught. He therefore thought that the members of the JSA were just posing as champions of justice to fool the police, and that they really intended to commit the most colossal crime in history. Naturally, he wanted *in*.

Only by defeating the Wizard's every ingenious scheme could the JSA convince the mad magician that the joke was on him. When he realized his mammoth mistake, he tried to destroy the JSA with his illusions; however, Dr. Mid-Nite learned the secret of the Wizard's deadly illusions and destroyed them with the inky darkness of one of his famed blackout bombs. Facing defeat, the Wizard broke into hysterical laughter and dove into a vat of acid. Green Lantern remarked at the time, "I guess that's the end of the Wizard," but Flash cautioned, "It would seem so... but don't forget we were dealing with the Wizard, and with him you never can tell – you never can tell – ."

The Wizard, of course, did not die; the vat of acid was just another one of his many illusions. Instead, he hid out for several months, during which time he organized his own "Injustice Society of the World" *(All-Star* #37). This Injustice gang included some of the greatest criminals listed in the files of the JSA: the Brain Wave, the Thinker, the Gambler, Vandal Savage, and Per Degaton. Believe it or not, this gang actually managed to take over the entire United States, and placed the JSA on trial for their lives. In the end, however, the newly reorganized Junior Justice Society of America helped to bring about the humiliating defeat of the Wizard and his gang.

But still, the Wizard wasn't through. He escaped from prison and organized a second Injustice Society – a new band of notorious villains – the Icicle, the Fiddler, the Huntress, the Sportsmaster, and the Harlequin. To determine their leader, these master criminals competed in a gigantic crime contest, which is recorded in the files of the JSA as "The Case of the Patriotic Crimes" *(All-Star* #41). This new gang managed to steal the most cherished objects of the American people: Plymouth Rock, the Liberty Train, Old Ironsides, the Washington Monument, the Freedom Bell, and Gotham Stadium. And by a cruel twist of fate, the members of the JSA were captured and turned into the mindless slaves of the Injustice gang. However, the Harlequin, who delved in crime only to attract the attention of Green Lantern, betrayed the Wizard. She enlisted the aid of the Black Canary, a new heroine, and together they freed the JSA and aided them in the defeat of the Wizard's new gang. For her part in the adventure, the Black Canary was inducted into the JSA, filling the recent vacancy left by Johnny Thunder (not to be confused with the late western hero of the same name who appeared in *All-Star Western*).

The Injustice gang was captured, but the Harlequin escaped, leaving behind a note: "Dear GL, It was fun being partners in this adventure! But fair warning – from now on, watch out for your loving enemy – The Harlequin."

The third defeat was too much for the ego of the Wizard, and he was never heard from again. However, his great dream of an Injustice Gang is being given another tryout in the July issue of the *JLA*.

BESTEST LEAGUE OF AMERICA - Part I

As related in detail in "The Alter Ego Story," in December of 1960 Roy Thomas decided to amuse himself during his senior college year by creating a parody of the Justice League. Influenced by the super-hero spoofs in the earliest Mad *comics ("Superduperman," "Black and Blue Hawks," "Batboy and Rubin"), Roy made no attempt to draw the heroes to closely resemble their DC precursors. When Jerry Bails decided to turn his projected JLA newsletter into a full-fledged fanzine, he invited Roy to redraw the first chapter of "Bestest League" on 8½" x 11" sheets. Jerry traced those five pages onto ditto masters, and "BLA" became the first comic strip published in this brave new fandom. (The full-sized rendition of Part I was printed, for the first time ever, in Bill Schelly's volume* Fandom's Finest Comics*; it is 95% identical to the one that appeared in* Alter-Ego *#1.)*

One of Jerry's editing changes was to move Green Trashcan's oath from the splash page to Page 2. In Roy's version, a caption recapping GT's origin had replaced all but the last line of the oath; Jerry thus coined the term "The Emerald Asphyxiator" for the splash.

Part I served mainly to introduce the six most active BLAers (with Superham and Wombatman absent, as usual). They assembled, then split into three pairs – with each of the males vying to team up with the Glamazon princess – to search for the mysterious entity known only as "It." The BLA would return in AE *#2, and thus became also fandom's first* continued *comics story ....*

THE REINCARNATION OF THE SPECTRE

by Roy Thomas

Dr. James Corrigan sat gazing intensely at the weird blue gem before him on his desk. He was lost in thought, remembering the strange circumstances under which he had received the jewel....

It was only a few months before, when as a young society doctor bored with his practice, he received a cablegram from his uncle – Dr. Peter Corrigan, a physician in India. As he opened the cable, he was unable to keep from comparing his own easy life, treating rich hypochondriacs, with that of his uncle, who had given up wealth and fame to minister to the ills of the poor in an over-populated nation.

The cable contained terrible news. His uncle, his only living relative, was dying in a small village near Bombay. Within the hour, the young doctor was on board a plane to India, hoping against hope that he could find a way to save his uncle's life.

When he arrived at the village, he was greeted by his uncle's devoted servant, Ali, who led him to his uncle's side. His uncle was sinking fast, but he recognized Jim at once. Knowing his time was short, the elderly Dr. Corrigan handed his nephew an ornate, jeweled box containing a blue Spectral Sapphire, and gasped the story of the strange gem with his final words.

"A dying Hindu fakir gave me this a few years ago," he said with difficulty, "in return for my making the last days of his life less painful. He told me that it had great and strange powers for both good and evil. He said it will bring out the best that is in man, and also the worst. I – I feel I *must* give it to you – perhaps you will be the one to unlock its awesome secret."

With these final words, Peter Corrigan died.

From Ali, Jim learned the legend of the Spectral Sapphire: "Legend says that one man, many years ago, found the secret power of the magic stone, but the legend also says it caused great fires and earthquakes, and huge monsters, to appear from out of nowhere, till finally a great hero came, who drove out the monsters and saved the people of the land."

And now once again Jim found himself looking at the sapphire of mystery, before him on the desk. He thought of his uncle's phrase – "the best that is in man, and also the worst." Had his uncle really been compelled to give him the jewel, or had that just been his imagination in a time of approaching death?

Just then a lone ray of sunlight drifted through the venetian blinds into the dimness of Jim's office, striking the gem and causing that weird phenomenon which only the Spectral Sapphire could produce – a black-and-white spectrum, with incredible degrees of darkness and brightness. Although Jim had seen this phenomenon several times in the past, it never failed to amaze him.

But this time it was different! This time the sun's lone ray struck the gem so that the spectrum fell on Jim's face, bathing half of the young doctor's features in great light and the other half in extreme blackness. Jim felt strange almost at once. His first impulse was to rise, but he stayed in his seat as if held there by a super-powerful force.

Slowly an intense drowsiness descended upon him. As he drifted ever nearer to sleep, Jim was dimly aware of two figures appearing near him, one on each side.

On the side where the spectrum blinded him with light was a strangely-clad man – or was it? – with flesh of white, wearing a jade-colored cowl and cloak. Jim felt, even in his drowsiness, an aura of *good* emanating from the figure.

On the dark side of the spectrum was a figure similar in build and appearance, semi-transparent as was the first, but with flesh of a bluish shade, wearing a cloak of dark purple. The feeling of *evil* which came from this second figure was almost as great as the aura of good coming from the first.

Just then, a cloud drifted over the face of the sun outside, interrupting the ray which had caused the black-and-white spectrum. The lights vanishing from his face, Jim instantly snapped back into a wakeful state. In that same instant the two figures vanished.

But where had they gone, if they had really existed at all? Had they been only figments of his imagination? Were these two figures part of the "good and evil" which could come from the Spectral Sapphire? If they once again were to return to the land of the living, would the evil one bring fires and monstrous beasts as legend said he had done in India centuries before? And if so, would the other spectral figure be able to stop him this time? Jim shuddered as he returned the mysterious gem to its jeweled box and stared out the window at the now-setting sun. What did fate have in store for him? Only time would tell!

[1961 pen-and-ink illustration by Roy Thomas, previously unprinted]

COUNT DIS
The
SPECTRE
RT
JB

About the cover of* Alter-Ego *#2 (June 1961): *Jerry asked Roy to draw a dramatic confrontation between the Spectre and Count Dis. Roy's cover showed that, even in that pre-VCR, pre-old-movie-channel era, "King Kong" was one of his favorite films.*

Alter-Ego #2 – Notes & Commentary

When Jerry Bails mailed out copies of AE *#1 in the spring of 1961, his major emotion was probably one of relief. But Roy Thomas clearly remembers his own feelings, a few days later, when his copy of the fanzine arrived from Detroit:*

Elation.

Though Roy had been writing and drawing since childhood, at age twenty he'd never seen anything of his in print except in a book of poetry by Missouri high school students, in a college newspaper, and in a few DC letters pages, commencing with Green Lantern *#1.*

Now, thanks to Jerry's tracing-hand and Sondra's typewriter, Roy reveled in the realization that his work would be seen by 150 or more people all over the U.S. This inspired him in the midst of work he was already doing for AE *#2, an issue for which, oddly, Jerry himself would do no real article.*

For Part Two of the BLA, Roy worked from the outset on 8 ½" by 11" pages, though whether on typing paper or on ditto masters, neither he nor Jerry can recall after more than a third of a century. This volume reprints a few selected panels from that six-page installment.

Roy finished his "Reincarnation of the Spectre," Jerry made some revisions, and the result was duly credited to both of them. In it Count Dis escaped from Jim Corrigan's body and conjured up huge bats and lizards, and a "black viper of tremendous power and length" which wrapped itself around "the world's tallest building." Defeated by the Spectre, Dis vanished into the crowd below. The End...?

(Curiously, in the mid-80s, AE*-reader Steve Gerber – whom Roy had helped enter the comics field – would make plans, with Thomas' permission, to incorporate Count Dis into a Spectre revival of his own – for DC Comics. But somehow Dis never quite made his pro-comics debut.)*

Roy's want ad in AE *#1 for "comics starring Human Torch, Sub-Mariner, and Capt. America together in one story" had soon brought the information that there had been only two such –* All-Winners *#19 and #21 – though for years he and many other fans looked hopefully for a #20. Somehow he acquired a copy* of *A-W #21 and wrote about its All-Winners Squad tale for* AE *#2. However, that copy was missing the final pages of the Namor chapter, leading him to ask in print: "I wonder how the hell Sub-Mariner stopped that tidal wave...?" (Although "tidal" accidentally got mistyped "tital" throughout).*

The fact that Roy would write, and Jerry would publish, an article about a single issue of a 1947 comic – and an incomplete one, at that – shows how eager both were to fill gaps in comic book history, and how dedicated they were to the Justice Society and its various offshoots, past and present.

Because of AE*'s irregular schedule, Jerry still wasn't accepting subscriptions. He instinctively knew that otherwise he'd waste time answering irate letters from people who would send off their money one week, then fire off a letter of complaint when the issue hadn't arrived a week later.*

"On the Drawing Board" spotlighted two secret code messages, one of which revealed the heady news that a vintage illustration of the Justice Society would be reprinted in Showcase *#34, an Atom issue. Advance info in* AE *was still solely about Schwartz's DC comics, except for a final P.S.: "Don't forget to be on the lookout for the appearance of the new Archie heroes: Jaguar and Fly Girl."*

Jerry also devised a simple acrostic which used letters from the civilian ID's of various JLA/JSA members to spell out the name of a certain comics professional. We don't want to let any cats out of the bag, since you'll find "The Alter-Ego Puzzle Tree" on the very next page, but it was a fun touch.

AE *#2 also initiated a letter column: "Conversation – with Jerry Bails." There were missives from Dale Christman, John McGeehan, Harry Thomas, Ted White, Steve Gerber, and Don Thompson. Don's letter was actually a paragraph-long plug for the second issue of his and wife Maggie's fanzine* Comic Art, *which had debuted at roughly the same time as* Alter-Ego *but which covered the entire spectrum of comic art, not just super-heroes. Despite his own orientation, Jerry was willing and eager to see comics readers widen their tastes, and had undoubtedly solicited Don's note.*

At the end of the letter column, Jerry attempted to stir fans to action in several areas. He wanted to hear about their collections, for future articles; he invited readers of The Fly *and* The Jaguar *to send their comments on those comics to* AE*, since Archie mags didn't yet have letter columns; and he asked for information about the names of any artists who worked on the final ten issues of* All-Star Comics. *He also offered for sale (for $35) the portable duplicator with which he had prepared the first two issues of* AE*, because he planned to buy "an expensive electrical model."*

Jerry likewise compiled a two-page index of comic books in which JLA and JSA members had appeared during the 1940s, and wrote a short piece about the new Hawkman and his creators Gardner Fox and Joe Kubert, as well as drawing renditions of six of the Winged Wonder's varying masks from 1940-61.

And, for the first time, someone besides Jerry and Roy had something published in AE*: a two-page recap by fan Douglas Marden of Hawkman's origin in* Flash Comics *#1, 1940. More fans were creeping out of the woodwork, and the horizons of both* Alter-Ego *and comics fandom in general would soon be greatly extended....*

The Editors

ALTER EGO PUZZLE TREE

HINT: His picture appears in nearly every issue of *Mystery in Space* and *Strange Adventures.*

INSTRUCTIONS FOR SOLVING THE PUZZLE

Fill in the blanks in the statements about the current heroes, and transfer the letters from the blanks to the correspondingly numbered squares in the diagram. Then fill in the rows of the diagram with the real names of the heroes listed. Make use of the fact that each numeral, no matter how many times it may appear throughout the puzzle, corresponds to one and only one letter. When the diagram is completed, the vertical axis of the tree will spell out the name of the mystery personality. (The solution is given elsewhere in this issue, but *don't peek!* The puzzle can be solved without *any* knowledge of the long-dead heroes.)

ACROSS:

1. Original Flash
2. Green Arrow
3. Sandman
4. Spectre
5. Aquaman
6. Dr. Fate
7. Original Green Lantern
8. Wonder Woman
9. Present Green Lantern
10. Batman
11. Present Hawkman
12: Hourman
13: Wildcat
14. Martian Manhunter

A. Aquaman's mother came from the sunken island of ____________
2-24-12-2-23-24-20-17

B. Green Lantern often battles the Weaponers of ____________
13-15-22-7-18

C. One of Superman's mortal enemies is ____________
12-25-29 12-14-24-27-11-6

D. GA's Arrowcar is equipped with a ____________
9-5-24-5-26-14-21-24

E. Hawkman is the only super-hero who is ____________
12-2-7-7-8-16-18

F. Batman is sometimes aided by ____________
28-22-24-4-8-6-21

G. The secret identity of the Flash is known by ____________
15-2-12-12-3

THE SOLUTION TO THE PUZZLE (Turn page upside down):

The mystery personality is Julius Schwartz, editor at DC Comics, who is captured on the pages of his own magazines by artist Sidney Greene. See page 2 of the third story in *Mystery in Space* #69 and page 3 of the first story in *Strange Adventures* #130. Now go back and work out the rest of the puzzle yourself.

This 6-page chapter picked up where Part I had left off. In their search for the mysterious "It," each of the three teams captured a criminal set of twins. Roy got in a few good-natured swipes at such 1960s standbys as Green Arrow's trick arrows, Wonder Woman's lasso and tiara, and Aquaman's dependence on his finny friends. Since Roy was an inveterate Hawkman fan, naturally "Aukman" made a cameo appearance.

CONVERSATION

with JERRY BAILS

John McGeehan
405 E. 5th St.
Santa Ana, California

You asked me about the 68-page British annuals. Well, I just got in a few spares of the *Flash, Superman, Tarzan, Batman, Superboy,* and *Superadventure Annuals*, and if you want copies you can have them at $1.25 each. While they sell for 6 schillings (84¢) over in England, for us to get them, we have to pay from 16¢ to 20¢ each for overseas postage fees, international money order fees to send the money, and postage to send the letter to tell them what you want. This raises the cost to about $1.10 each. Then you have the cost of sending them on to someone else here in the States. So, while it may appear at first that I'm making a profit, actually I just break even. I bought the spare copies in the first place mainly to sell to my good correspondents who would like them for their collections. Not too many fans want them, though, as they are just black-and-white reprints of last year's American stories. It took me 7 weeks just to get these annuals from England. The main reasons are: it takes about a month for them to get the international money order, and three weeks to get the 1st class letter. While I send my letter via air mail at 10¢, the companies always answer by first class mail. The above gab was just to let you know, in case you didn't realize, that it is a time-consuming and expensive business to order items from overseas.

[The cover of All-Winners *#21 (1947) was traced as a full-page illustration in* AE *#2.]*

Say, John, do you know where I might find copies of *Flash* or other DC Comics published in French, Spanish, or German?

Don Thompson
Room 36, Prospect Ave.
Cleveland, Ohio

Dick Lupoff has an excellent article on super-heroes and costume-heroes coming up in the second issue of my fanzine, *Comic Art*, and here's some of the other material promised for future issues: Hal Lynch on "Minute Movies" by Ed Wheelan; Buck Coulson on a strip called "Lone Spaceman"; Bill Sarill on TV cartoons; Mike McInerney on "Uncle Scrooge"; and much more. Please let your readers known that they can order *Comic Art* from me for 20¢ a copy or 5 issues for $1.00.

In the opinion of yours truly, *Comic Art* is a high quality zine, which every fan would enjoy reading. I recommend it.

Ted White
107 Christopher St.
New York 14, New York

AE is an intriguing publication; however, it does strike me as slightly "gosh-wow" and perhaps too slanted to the current comic reader.

The mastering of the art is impressive; Roy Thomas seems to have some talent for cartooning, and whoever put both his work and the *Secret Origins* cover on masters did a good job.

I'm afraid I'm not terribly interested in your cryptograms, especially since I don't subscribe to any comics. Once, many years ago, I did. Not only were copies sent haphazardly, but they were invariably sent folded or rolled up, and I prefer to get my copies as mint as possible.

Your complaint is typical of several I've received, particularly from old fans. All I can say is my current subscriptions to DC mags come regularly two weeks in advance of the newsstand sale date, and although they are creased, I don't mind, for I can buy mint copies later. Personally, I like to get copies of my favorite mags in the mail early, so I can be among the first to get a LOC (letter of comment) off to the editor. Now that Julie Schwartz is giving away original art for the best letters, I like to keep in the running, and having a sub helps.

The write-up on the Wizard was interesting and fairly complete, but I wish you'd have included some mention of the artists and writers who worked on those *All-Stars*. For instance, the introduction and conclusion of *AS* #34 were drawn by Irwin Hasen, the artist-creator of the syndicated strip "Dondi."

The author of AS #34 was none other than Gar Fox.

Roy's version of the Spectre was surprisingly fine. It would be wonderful to see DC make use of this idea. The weakness of the original character was that he was all-powerful and in one story he even talked with God. In the stories written by Jerry Siegel [creator of Superman], the Spectre had a habit of reshaping the cosmos to suit his own needs. Indeed, if the Spectre had been allowed to, he could've solved the JSA's problems instantly in every adventure in which he was involved. Roy's version corrects this fatal defect very nicely.

Your Wonder Woman feature was far too uncritical. You glossed over the extremely strong lesbian, fetishistic, and flagellant overtones which dominated the earlier stories, and which still appear to a slight extent today. Wonder Woman's face has grown extremely dykish and unbeautiful; I find Andru's art generally gross and unpalatable. You showed, almost unwittingly, how played out the modern series is, with WW able to do almost anything, including flying, thus forcing the writers to rely more on Wonder Girl and, so help me, Wonder Tot in desperation. Let's face it: the writing today is extremely bad, filled with bald impossibilities and *deus ex machina* solutions.

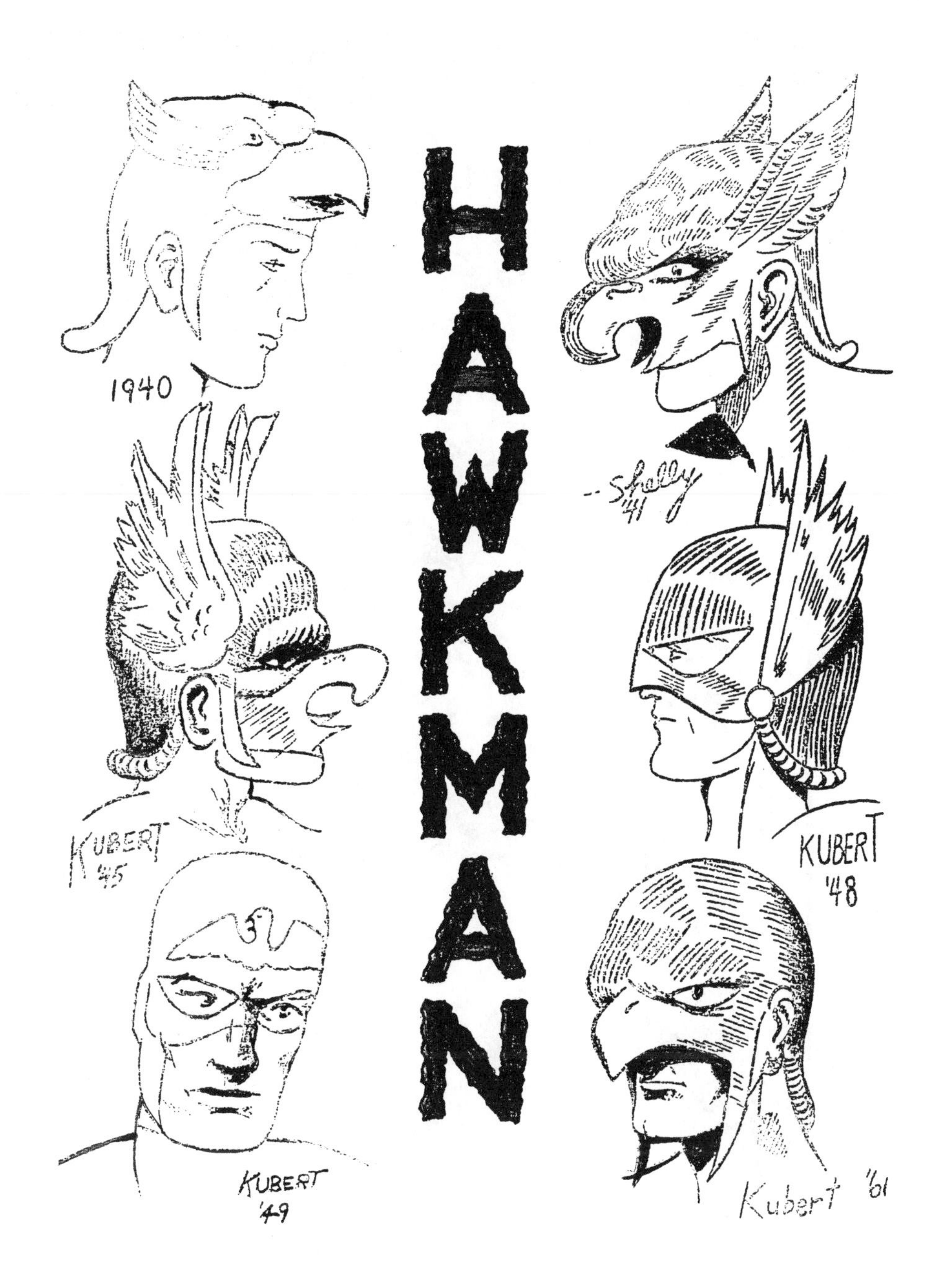

Steve Gerber
7014 Roberts Ct.
University City, Missouri

While *AE* #1 was exceptionally good, I felt that you went too far ahead with "On the Drawing Board"; however, I think it was an interesting feature and I hope to see it in all future issues.

The reason "On the Drawing Board" dipped so far into the future is that it had to cover the several months between *AE* #1 and this ish. In the future, I plan something a little different little different in this connection. I will mail out a supplementary news bulletin in late summer. It will go out to all readers who have ordered *AE* #3. Then sometime in the fall, *AE* #3 will be mailed out with its full quota of features, articles, and news.

Why doesn't DC publish a new semi-annual which could be called *The Best of All-Star Comics* or perhaps *Those Good Old Days*, which would reprint many of the best JSA tales? If they used the second title, it could also contain stories of the original Flash, Green Lantern, etc. I think it would sell many, many copies.

I agree: it would sell many copies, but there are several good reasons why it won't be done quite as you suggest. First, and foremost, many of the old JSA stories, because of the violence they portrayed, could never pass the Comics Code Authority today. Second, the original drawings and plates for those stories have long since been destroyed, and it is nearly impossible to get good, clear reproductions from the color magazines themselves, because of their size and color. However, there is still hope. When I was in New York last February, I happened to see the original drawings of a number of unpublished stories of the original Flash and Green Lantern. As far as I know, these drawings are still in the files at the DC offices, and if I know the publishers, they would happily publish these stories in a special edition if they could be assured that they would sell. What do you say we each send a postcard to encourage the idea!!

By the way, in *JLA* #2 Robert Lindsay wrote that all the copies of *Brave and Bold* #28 received at his shop were sold out in three weeks. If, perchance, you are a correspondent of his, tell him that in less than *one* day nearly 30 copies in one drugstore were sold out!

According to my inside sources, during the first part of this year, the *JLA* was (percentagewise) the highest selling DC mag. If it isn't published 8 times a year soon, then I'll miss my guess.

I hope that until DC revives the Spectre you will continue your series on the Spectre and Count Dis in *AE*. Also, "Merciful Minerva" was an interesting article and I hope to see more like it – perhaps one on Dr. Mid-Nite.

In response to many requests, *AE #3* will feature a spectacular article on the original Green Lantern, his sidekick, his girl friends, his enemies, and, of course, the artists and writers who created them. If you have any material on the original GL that you would like to contribute, please send it along to me and you'll receive a free copy of the Alter-Ego Secret Code Chart.

About the cover of* Alter-Ego *#3 (November 1961): *This time around, Jerry drew the cover, a montage pitting GL, Doiby Dickles, and Streak the Wonder Dog against the Gambler, Vandal Savage, Solomon Grundy, and the Harlequin. Can you spot the homages/swipes from the 1940s art of Irwin Hasen, Martin Naydel, Alex Toth, and Mart Nodell? (Reproduced from the original ditto master courtesy of Mike Touhey, who as a young Detroit fan assisted Jerry in assembling and mailing out* AE.*)*

Alter-Ego #3 – Notes & Commentary

Alter-Ego *#3 (November 1961, with a print run of over 300 copies) came the closest to being a "theme issue" of any early edition of the fanzine. Having covered JSAers Wonder Woman and Hawkman in the first two issues, this time Jerry threw the spotlight on the original Green Lantern. (Few fans would have used the term "Golden Age Green Lantern" in those days.)*

Soliciting fan George Paul to retell his origin, Jerry wrote the first of what was intended to be two articles on the Emerald Gladiator. Despite Jerry's fine composite cover and other illos depicting GL and his supporting cast, Part One dealt solely with the hero's editors, writers, and artists. Part Two was to be titled: "Green Lantern – His Friends and His Foes"; but alas, it never appeared.

Jerry's piece, the longest to appear in AE *up to that time, clearly shows his bent for research, and his talent for sharing it with others. Most fan-writers of this period would have squeezed facts about both creators and characters into one article, no matter how much condensing it took; but Jerry was already casting a far wider net with this piece, which would win an Alley Award for "Best Article/Amateur Division." The germ of his later volumes of* The Who's Who of American Comic Books, *and its current form as an on-line database, can be found in "The Light of the Green Lantern," reprinted in the pages to follow.*

*Jerry asked Roy to cover the then-*new *Green Lantern. That piece illustrates how the "revivals," as they were then called, were viewed by the first generation of quasi-organized fandom.*

Roy writes of stealing away from his job as ticket-taker at a local movie house and stumbling upon the first appearance of the new, improved Green Lantern. Though unnamed in the 1961 article, the "popcorn boy" Roy left in charge was his high school chum Gary Friedrich, who would later take "Joy Holiday" photos for AE *#7-9 and still later write for Charlton and then Marvel in the late 60s and early 70s, including a memorable stint on* Sgt. Fury and His Howling Commandos.

Another denizen of Roy and Gary's hometown of Jackson, Missouri, made a less oblique appearance in AE *#3: Linda Rahm, whom Roy had been dating for several years. With no prompting from him, Linda sat down one day and wrote a "Letter to Ersel" that undoubtedly expressed the sentiments of many a young female with regard to comics and their mostly male fans, in that era and in this. (P.S.: Linda eventually became a college teacher of English literature, though her resumé probably never mentioned she had been* AE*'s first "real" Joy Holiday, appearing in* AE *#5-6 in photos taken by Roy, wearing a red shirt of his turned backward so the buttons wouldn't show.)*

This third issue saw yet another a slight expansion of the roster of contributors. Jerry had first contacted Ron Haydock after both had been "guest critics" in The Brave and the Bold *#34. Ron, who had led a rockabilly group in the late 1950s, was an inveterate fan of old movie serials; his "SERIALously Speaking" became a regular feature in the next four issues of* Alter-Ego. *Since no serial stills could be reprinted in a spirit-duplicator fanzine, his first piece was accompanied by a Bails version of a Simon and Kirby drawing of Captain America – minus mask-wings, shield, and boy partner, since the 1943 serial lacked these items. One of Ron's* AE *articles appears in the* AE *#5 section of this volume.*

AE *#3 also saw the 6-page conclusion of "Bestest League." For this final chapter Roy tossed in the kitchen sink, bringing onstage Wombatman, Superham, Adamn Stranger, The IPOM ("Infinitesimal Particle Of Matter"), and the entire Bestest* Society *of America. We've reprinted a few choice panels.*

The letters section featured lengthy missives from Irving Glassman, Bill Sarrill, Larry Ivie, and Ronnie Graham, as well as shorter ones from Louis B. Cohen and Frederick Norwood.

Jerry was now listed as "Publishing Editor," with Roy as "Contributing Editor." Ron Haydock, Linda Rahm, and George Paul were listed as "Contributors," and Detroit-area locals Donald Foote, Michael Touhey, and Jerry Sorek as "Production Staff." AE *was growing by leaps and bounds, though the offset* AE *#4 would not be published until a year later, with a "Fall 1962" cover date.*

In the meantime Jerry had branched out, moving the "On the Drawing Board" and advertising sections of AE *into a new fanzine called* The Comicollector, *which debuted as "The Companion to* Alter-Ego*" with a cover date of September 1961. Though it was the first comic-book "adzine," to use the vernacular of the day,* CC *#1 also carried Roy's short review of* Fantastic Four *#1, written originally for* AE. *Considering that less than four years later Roy would become Stan Lee's protégé – "Roy the Boy" and "Rascally Roy" – and eventually The Man's first successor as editor-in-chief of Marvel Comics, we thought this first-ever fanzine review of Marvel's flagship title deserved a second look – along with a matching BLA cartoon he drew for* CC *#2.*

By its second issue, The Comicollector *already had a print run of "over 500."*

Now, read and savor a few selections from Alter-Ego *#3... and a couple of anomalies from* The Comicollector....

The Editors

AND THEN THERE WAS LIGHT – THE LIGHT OF THE
GREEN LANTERN

by Jerry Bails

Part I

Today we speak of a revival of the costumed heroes, but what do we actually have? A few long-dead heroes from the glorious forties have been revived and updated for the modern comic book market, and a few "new" heroes have made the scene. If you add to these the old standbys that have been around for two decades, like Superman, Batman, Aquaman, Green Arrow, and Wonder Woman, you have a grand total of just about two dozen. This is nothing – but *nothing!* Why, back in the days just before World War II, more heroes than this were created in a single month. At that time well over a dozen different publishing houses were competing with one another to see which one could turn out the greatest number and variety of heroes. Just for fun I sat down the other evening to see how many of these costumed heroes I could list from memory. When I hit a hundred I stopped; but as a preliminary survey of my files shows, I wasn't even halfway through the costumed heroes that were on the scene by the time America entered the war. And this is not to mention the several hundred nondescript adventure heroes who were too modest to don a costume – *even* in the comics.

The real reason that all these characters were created, of course, was to capitalize on the success of Superman. Even the most adamant Disney fan (*viz.*, my wife) has to admit that it was the Man of Tomorrow (as he was known in those days) who was responsible for the phenomenon we call "comic books," and it was the costumed hero – in particular, the super-hero – who really dominated the comic books during the war years. What happened after the war is a story too painful to relate, but happily that isn't my task. My task is to tell you what I can about one of the most bizarre supermen of them all – the original Green Lantern.

The Master of Light

The Green Lantern of the forties was, of course, the model for the modern-day hero of the same name, and so, as you might expect, he had many of the same powers and paraphernalia that are the trademark of the current hero. He was the possessor of a "power battery," only they called it a magic lamp in those days, and he had a power ring which he had to recharge every twenty-four hours. And, as with his modern counterpart, the original Green Lantern controlled his ring by will power alone. However, according to the original legend, the ring also provided the Emerald Crusader with automatic immunity to all metals, which meant, for one thing, that bullets couldn't harm him – *even* when he didn't bother to use his will power. However, the Green Lantern of old took great delight in using his ring to melt bullets in mid-flight. He performed the trick so often that one tended to forget that he didn't *really* need to waste mental effort in this way.

Although his ring gave him special control over metals, the Master of Light had to exercise restraint in the use of the ring whenever he was in the presence of a great deal of metal – especially flammable metals like magnesium. One stray pencil of light from the power ring could create Dante's Inferno. Ironically, therefore, metals could be used to turn the power ring against the Green Lantern himself. One time, for example, a master criminal got the bright idea of throwing iron filings into the green beam. This caused the beam to backfire into Green Lantern's eyes, temporarily blinding him. Another time, a criminal used a silvered mirror to reflect the beam back at the Green Lantern. This time the effect was even more serious; it knocked the Emerald Crusader right off a cliff. Fortunately, however, our hero recovered his senses and power of flight just in the nick of time, but it gave the villain the customary ten seconds he needed to escape.

The power ring of the *modern* Green Lantern has one fatal flaw: it cannot be used directly against anything yellow. In the case of the *original* power ring, it was anything non-metal; and once in nearly every story, and sometimes twice, the Green Lantern would (quite accidentally) have his head bumped by a wooden object. Sometimes, for a change, the object was made of glass. Despite the frequency with which these accidents occurred, it seems that the underworld never caught on; for, in a return bout with the Emerald Crusader, they would almost always insist on using guns, knives, and blackjacks, as usual.

The most glaring inconsistency in the matter of the original Green Lantern's powers appeared in his ability to walk through walls. Although his head was quite impervious to a wooden club, the Master of Light had no trouble at all in passing through a wooden door. In the early years, he was always using this trick, but in the later years he used it so infrequently that one began to think he had forgotten the "magic words."

GL's power ring also gave him the power of flight, and at the speed of light, no less. And as the years rolled by, our hero

Jerry Bails à la *Paul Reinman '44*

discovered that he could also use the ring to travel in space, time, and from dimension to dimension. The one thing that made these trips a little different was the fact that they were all acts of will and usually left the Emerald Crusader quite exhausted. This was not physical exhaustion so much as it was mental fatigue, but it offered the same beautiful possibility – a helpless Green Lantern. Unfortunately, the writers didn't capitalize on this possibility.

As I mentioned before, Green Lantern had to recharge his power ring every 24 hours. This seems like a simple enough thing to do, but something our hero managed to forget from time to time and this occasionally left him and his sidekick, Doiby Dickles, with nothing but their fists to protect themselves. Fortunately, as with most heroes of the forties, the Emerald Crusader had no aversion to using his fists. In fact, he would often forestall using his ring to wrap up a fight until he and Doiby could get in a few good "rights" and "lefts." In this way, the writers often stretched a five-page plot over thirteen pages.

The Guardians of the First Green Lantern

It is pretty clear that the Emerald Crusader was born with a silver spoon in his mouth. He came from a long line of stars – the DC line – and was destined for stardom almost from the time of his conception. With his first appearance in *All-American Comics* #16 (July 1940), he was made the headline feature of one of DC's six monthly magazines, right up there with Superman, Batman, Flash, Sandman, and the Spectre. A few short months later, he became one of the top stars of DC's new quarterly anthology of heroes, *All-Star Comics*. He first appeared in the second issue, at which time he shared the cover with Flash and the Spectre. When the Justice Society was formed in *All-Star* #3, Green Lantern naturally became a charter member, and when Flash stepped down as the chairman of the group to become an inactive honorary member, the Emerald Crusader was elected over the Spectre and Hawkman (supposedly by the readers) to be the second chairman. Our hero served as chairman, however, for only one meeting (*All-Star* #7), after which time he too became an honorary member with a new magazine all his own. *Green Lantern* #1 was published for Fall 1941, just a little more than a year after the Emerald Crusader's debut in *All-American Comics*.

Except for Superman, Batman, and perhaps Wonder Woman, Green Lantern appeared more regularly on more covers of DC magazines during the 1940s than any other hero. Only rarely, for example, did another character replace GL on the cover of *All-American*, and *this* despite the fact that the magazine featured another famous hero (of considerable radio fame), Hop Harrigan, and three other features that appeared regularly in other DC books: *viz.*, Red, White, and Blue; Dr. Mid-Nite; and the Atom. Of course, none of these subsidiary characters were super-heroes like Green Lantern. In this respect, GL had no real competition on his home ground. This sort of preferential treatment accorded was not the policy for *All-American*'s companion magazine *Flash Comics*, which alternately cover-featured Flash and Hawkman. One can only conclude that Green Lantern's early success was due, in part at least, to the special consideration he received at the hands of his Guardians. It is pretty hard to imagine that Hawkman, the Spectre, or Dr. Fate couldn't have gone just as far if they had been given the same chance.

The number-one Guardian of the Emerald Crusader was the late M.C. Gaines, the man encyclopedias of Americana now call "the Father of the Comic Book." It was Gaines who recognized the potential of the Superman strip, and who attracted many a talented young artist and writer to the comics field. But Gaines' claim to fame predates even Superman. Comic books got their start in 1933 when Gaines began publishing reprints of popular newspaper strips in the comic book format. This in itself would have been enough to earn for him the title "the Father of the Comic Book"; however, a number of my friends argue that Gaines actually won this title for having been the sire of William Gaines, who was later to become the publisher of the EC line of *Mad* comics.

In 1938 M.C. Gaines joined DC Comics. (By the way, the symbol "DC" is derived from the name of the first comic book to contain original material -- *Detective Comics*.) Gaines became the managing editor and publisher of one of two groups of comics under the DC label. (EDITOR'S NOTE: In point of fact, there were as many as seven different publishing corporations under the DC label; however, as far as management and editorial policy were concerned, there were essentialy only two groups. This is only conjecture, but I suspect that the larger number of separate corporations may have been formed to minimize the tax burden.)

It is not possible to fully understand the whys and wherefores of many events in the background of the Green Lantern without a knowledge of this partition that existed in the management of the early DC publications. Gaines managed the so-called All-American group, which published all of the comics in which Flash, Green Lantern, and Wonder Woman appeared, including the 15¢ anthology, *Comic Cavalcade*, which featured this trio of All-American stars from 1943 to 1948. Superman and Batman were not in the All-American stable; they were the mainstays of DC comics proper, which was under a separate management. One of the most important results (from a fan's point of view) of this partition of the DC line was undoubtedly the exclusion of Superman and Batman from *All-Star Comics*, which was an All-American publication.

*Jerry Bails' drawing of Doiby Dickles (*à la *Hasen) originally appeared on the back cover of* AE *#3.*

To this day, the early split in the management of DC is preserved at National in the distribution of editorial responsibility. The modern Green Lantern, Flash, Hawkman, Atom, and Justice League of America are handled by one editor, while Superman is handled by another. I leave it to the reader to see if he can detect in this situation the deeper reasons why Superman and Batman are not featured more prominently in *Justice League*. Of course, the story is even more complicated today, where there are five editors at 575 Lexington Avenue (not counting the editor of the National Romance Group, which also occupies the same offices). But all this is getting me too far afield. I wanted to mention the All-American group at DC because of its editor, Sheldon Mayer, one of the Guardians of the original Green Lantern.

In the early forties, comics were not edited nearly as closely as they are today; however, because such a long string of writers, artists, and assistant editors worked on the Green Lantern over the years, whatever continuity the strip had ought probably to be attributed primarily to the chief editor, who in this case was Sheldon Mayer.

I am told that Sheldon Mayer, as much as any man, deserves credit for recognizing the potential of the Green Lantern strip, and I'll bet he had a big hand in making GL a star of the first magnitude. Be that as it may, this much I know for sure: when Sheldon Mayer turned his editorial cap over to another man in 1948, an era came to an end – Green Lantern was one of the first stars to fall. Oh yes, he did continue to appear as an active member of the JSA until its demise in 1951, but he lost out in *All-American Comics* in late 1948 to Johnny Thunder, the western hero; and after 38 issues, his own book was suddenly transformed into *Rex the Wonder Dog*. Pretty disgusting, isn't it?!

Today Sheldon Mayer is still with DC, although not as an editor. His time is now spent creating for the younger set the humorous comic *Sugar and Spike*. This pair of characters will always remind me of the Cyclone Kids, a couple of hooded youngsters who, along with the Red Tornado (a comical hero – rather, heroine), romped through the pages of the "Scribbly" strip which Sheldon created for *All-American Comics*, and which served as a bit of comic relief to the more serious Green Lantern.

In 1948 Whitney Ellsworth became top editor of all the comics in the DC line, which by this time had been consolidated into one group owned and published by National Comics Publications, Inc. This is not to say that Mr. Ellsworth was directly concerned with the plotting of the Green Lantern stories. It is my understanding that he was not. Nevertheless, he was undoubtedly an important figure in the destiny of the Green Lantern. Ellsworth had been the editor of the Superman books since about 1941. By the time he had taken over the responsibility for Green Lantern and the other features of the "All-American" group, comic sales had dropped off. (This was an industry-wide phenomenon.) It was Ellsworth's job to weed out the deadwood, and to bring forth new features that would keep DC on top. The decisions went against Green Lantern and his JSA buddies in favor of new western features like Johnny Thunder. Only Superman, Batman, Wonder Woman, and a few secondary costumed heroes survived those dark days. It may be only coincidence, but it is strange that the *real* revival of the "All-American" line didn't take place until Whitney Ellsworth left the comics field to become the producer of the Superman TV series. (EDITOR'S NOTE: Mr. Ellsworth is currently producing the Superboy TV series, which should begin to appear on some local stations before very long.)

The Lesser Gods

So far I've been talking only about the higher gods who directed the fate of the Green Lantern. How about the lesser gods – the artists, writers, and editors who actually produced the Green Lantern stories? What do we know of them? Well, let's begin at the beginning and consider the creators.

The Green Lantern was created by the artist-writer team of Martin Nodell and Bill Finger. The credit, however, for the initial, polychromatic flash of insight goes to the artist half of the team – Martin Nodell. Martin was a frustrated young actor, having played a few small parts in stock company productions – all flops. He moved from Chicago to New York when he was 18, hoping to meet a casting director with the good sense to recognize his talent for acting; however, he spent most of his time creating caricatures for theatrical publicity, thus building a fairly good reputation as an artist with art directors and editors. At the age of 25, Martin finally decided that something had to be done. If he couldn't act, he'd do the next best thing -- he'd create a dramatic new hero for the comics. When Gaines and Mayer saw his Green Lantern idea, they immediately introduced him to Bill Finger, one of the young writers on their staff, and before long a collaboration was born.

Bill Finger, who was just a year younger than Nodell, had lived most of his life in New York. He grew up in the atmosphere of his father's tailor shop. His parents wanted him to be a doctor, and although Bill always wanted to be a writer, he tried to fulfill his parents' hopes. However, these hopes were dashed by the Depression, which closed Dad Finger's tailor shop and forced Bill to quit college and to take on all sorts of odd jobs, from waiting on tables to driving a taxi. One night during those lean years, Bill was at a party where he met Bob Kane, the artist-creator of Batman. They got into a discussion on comics, and Bob discovered that Bill had many good ideas. They became fast friends, and even collaborated on early Batman stories. (By the way, Finger still turns out Batman scripts, as well as occasional scripts for TV detective shows.) It was through Bob Kane that Bill met the editors of All-American Comics, and was finally able to dig his fingers into the first juicy writing assignment of his career – Green Lantern.

One of the first problems to face the new team of Nodell and Finger in 1940 was that of picking a name for the alter-ego of their new hero. The first thing that came to mind, Bill recalls, was Aladdin and his magic lamp. A corruption of the name "Aladdin" led them to *Alan Ladd*, a name which had not yet been made famous by Hollywood. They discarded this name, however, as too "obvious," and finally settled on *Alan Scott.*

In the early stories Martin Nodell followed the pattern of other artists and signed his work with a pseudonym, "Mart Dellon." Later he used his real name. This sort of thing may have confused some readers at first; however, there really is no mistaking Nodell's work. Martin seldom did the Green Lantern covers. Most of the time the covers were handled by Irwin Hasen or Paul Reinman, and I seem to detect the work of Sheldon Moldoff (of Hawkman fame) on at least one early cover, and the work of Howard Purcell on others. In any event, Martin Nodell was ultimately replaced by many other artists.

One of the first artists to relieve Nodell in the drawing of the Green Lantern was Irwin Hasen. Hasen's first version of GL will always stick in my memory. Hasen gave the Emerald Crusader a most un-hero-like hair style, a part right down the middle of

Jerry Bails' illustration based on GL by Martin Nodell

his blond locks. Even at this time, I thought the central part was just *too passé*. It went out of style when my father was a young man. So naturally I was quite relieved when GL started combing his hair straight back. It didn't seem to bother me – at the time, that is – that Hasen portrayed Green Lantern with straight hair while other artists gave him naturally wavy hair.

Hasen's work on the Emerald Crusader was broken into two periods: an earlier period which ran from 1941 to about 1943, and a later period which ran from 1947 through 1948. The interruption presumably corresponded with a tour of duty in the armed services for the affable Mr. Hasen.

During his earlier period at DC, Hasen also collaborated with author Bill Finger to create another costumed hero – a kind of Batman without gadgets – the Wildcat. However, probably because he was not superhuman, but only the heavyweight champion of the world in real life, the Wildcat never did become the star that GL was.

When Hasen returned to his work on Green Lantern in 1947, he also handled the introductions and conclusions of the Justice Society adventures. In fact, Hasen's return to DC was signaled by an exciting *All-Star* cover (#33), picturing Solomon Grundy, GL's most formidable enemy, lording over the entire Justice Society. The members were shown imprisoned in one of GL's energy bubbles. Of course, this was just symbolic. Ordinarily, the situation was just the reverse; it was Solomon Grundy who was always being imprisoned by GL's energy bubbles. However, this was a *striking* cover, and will always be one of the cherished items in my collection.

Today Irwin Hasen's work can be seen in the syndicated strip "Dondi," and for those of you who would like to get a quick glimpse of Hasen himself, I recommend to you the movie version of "Dondi." Hasen has a small part in the movie as the police artist who sketches the missing orphan boy.

The next artist of note to handle the Emerald Crusader was Paul Reinman. Older comics fans whose memories date back to 1940 may recall seeing Paul's work on Skyman (*Big Shot Comics*) or on Bently of Scotland Yard (*Pep Comics*). On the other hand, fans whose memories only date back to yesterday may recall seeing Paul's work (along with an occasional self-portrait) in magazines of the American Comics Group and in Atlas magazines.

Reinman began his work on GL in 1943 (apparently as Hasen's replacement) and continued to draw many if not most of the GL stories for several years. Meanwhile, he branched out to handle the drawing assignments on other DC characters such as the Wildcat and Atom. Reinman's Green Lantern was clearly superior to any of those that had come before, and his creation of Solomon Grundy for *All-American Comics* #61 (Oct. 1944) was truly inspired. It seems Mr. Reinman is in his element when he is called upon to illustrate the weird and the bizarre.

In 1945 an event occurred in the publishing world that brought Green Lantern back into *All-Star Comics* as an active member of the JSA. M.C. Gaines pulled the All-American group of comics out from under the DC label, and published the group under the AA label. Now, this separation lasted only about a year or thereabouts, and then the AA group was reintegrated into the DC line, but the separation was long enough to have a radical effect upon the roll call of the Justice Society. Since Starman and Spectre were rightfully the property of DC Comics, and since *All-Star* was among those comics that broke away from DC, Starman and Spectre had to be dropped from the JSA rolls. The vacancies had to be filled, and I suspect that Gaines and Mayer had no trouble deciding that Flash and Green Lantern were the most likely candidates. Gardner Fox, the author of the JSA stories at that time, was instructed to reintroduce Flash and GL into the *All-Star* group. So, in issue #24 (Spring 1945), Green Lantern and Flash made a guest appearance at a Justice Society meeting, and were encouraged by Wonder Woman to become active fighting members again.

Green Lantern's reappearance in *All-Star* allowed many artists to give us their interpretation of the Emerald Crusader. There was the clumsy and comical version of Martin Naydel (the "Martin Dell" who creates the syndicated puzzle "Scramble"). There was the square-jawed version of Jon Chester Kozlak, whose love for fishing invaded the background of almost every other panel. And there was the absolutely superb version of Alexander Toth, whose work, I notice, has begun to reappear in DC Comics. (EDITOR'S NOTE: Jerry DeFuccio of *Mad* has called Al Toth "the Milton Caniff of the comic books," and I heartily agree. Clearly Al was the greatest artist who ever handled the Green Lantern.) Finally, there was a version of the Green Lantern by Carmine Infantino, who (as everyone knows) is the award-winning artist of Adam Strange and the modern Flash.

One of the biggest mistakes that was ever made in the drawing of the Green Lantern was made in *All-Star Comics* #26 when Stanley Asch, who signed his art "Stan Josephs," gave GL Starman's gravity rod. But I guess that it is understandable that Stan was a little confused, for in addition to Green Lantern and Starman, he also drew Johnny Thunder (the comic hero of the JSA), Dr. Mid-Nite, Mr. Terrific, and for a time, Dr. Fate, from a period which extended from 1940 to 1947.

Outside of *All-Star*, the Emerald Crusader was handled by many of the same artists, *and* by still another one who happens to be at DC today – Howard Purcell. Purcell will probably be remembered for his art on the Gay Ghost, Sargon the Sorcerer, and Johnny Peril stories, although his career at DC dates back further than any of these characters. A sample of his current work can be seen regularly in *Tales of the Unexpected* and *My Greatest Adventure.* At times he will sign his work with his initials.

As I mentioned earlier, there were a number of writers and assistant editors who were responsible for the Green Lantern stories during the forties. In the beginning, when comics were 68 pages long and were being produced at a tremendous clip (the rate for Green Lantern in 1943 was 32 stories per year), the editors did little more than approve the stories after they were written. Gradually, however, they began to take a more active part in the plotting of the stories, foreshadowing the day when they would become a dominant force in the creation of the characters, story ideas, and plots.

One of Sheldon Mayer's first assistant editors was Ted Udall, who also scripted some of the early Mr. Terrific stories. When Udall was drafted for World War II, he was replaced by Dorothy Roubicek. (EDITOR'S NOTE: Dorothy is now married to Bill Woolfolk, editor of *Space World.* Incidentally, both of the Woolfolks used to write for the comics.) When Dorothy left DC, she was succeeded by Julius Schwartz, the man most responsible for the current revival of the Green Lantern. Julie Schwartz joined DC in Feburary 1944. Later that year Ted Udall returned to the fold as Julie's co-editor. This partnership lasted until 1946, when Udall left DC. His place in the partnership was taken up by Robert Kanigher, currently the editor of *Wonder Woman.*

As for the writers of the Green Lantern strip, there was a long string of them after Bill Finger – first, Alfred Bester, then Henry Kuttner, and finally Lee Goldsmith, Robert Kanigher, and John Broome. The first two of these writers to follow Bill Finger went on to become *top* names in the science-fiction field. Alfred Bester's *The Demolished Man* won an award as the best science fiction novel of the year, not too many years ago, and the late Henry Kuttner must be regarded as one of the five greats in science fiction. ((Thanks, Julie.)) The last three writers on the list, who were all contemporaries, are all still with DC. Lee Goldsmith currently writes many of DC's romance stories. Bob Kanigher, as I mentioned before, is now an editor. In addition to *Wonder Woman,* he handles all of National's war books. And John Broome, of course, is the author of the highly successful current *Flash* and *Green Lantern* strips, which incidentally started the present trend, however modest, back to the super-heroes.

PART TWO:

"GREEN LANTERN – HIS FRIENDS AND HIS FOES" will appear in a future issue of *Alter-Ego.*

by Roy Thomas

[based on Gil Kane artwork]

The movie business was a little slow in the small Midwestern town of Jackson, Missouri, on that spring evening in 1959. But then that wasn't really too unusual; business was *generally* pretty poor week-nights at the Palace Theatre (or "Theater," as those of you who have never been in Show Business may spell it). It was the kind of night on which everybody who is coming to see the show is already in his seat by the time the movie starts; therefore, if you are official ticket-taker and have already seen the current feature several times, things generally go from dull to duller to dullest after 7:30.

At any rate, on this particular evening I decided that I was in need of a little diversion, preferably of a literary nature. So, entrusting the privilege and responsibility of "watching the door" to the popcorn boy, I meandered up the street a few yards to the nearest drugstore, where I proceeded to rummage about through assorted paperbacks, magazines, and comic books, searching for something – *anything* – that would make the evening pass more quickly.

Abruptly, after mentally weighing and then physically discarded myriad racy pocket-books and movie magazines, I spied a familiar name staring me in my bespectacled face. "GREEN LANTERN," shrieked the title logo in big white letters surrounded by green-colored flames. Could it be?

Grabbing it hurriedly lest it vanish, I surveyed the cover at closer range. It boasted an excellently-drawn picture of a brown-haired man wearing a tight-fitting green-and-black costume and an emerald mask, hovering high above a large city as an over-sized ring on one outstretched hand blasted verdant rays at a plunging rocket. WOW! I thought.

This character didn't look very much like the red-and-green-costumed hero I remembered from some years before, and there was now no evidence of a cape, royal purple or other; but he *was* wearing a magic ring (even though it had been switched from *left* hand to *right*), and it *did* still shoot out those crazy beams that did all those amazing things! Deciding that this was close enough to the old Green Lantern for the comic to be worthy of my sticky dime, I deposited the coin in the hand of a disinterested druggist (who was obviously unaware of my Great Discovery) and hot-footed it back to the Palace, where I found the popcorn boy still unmoved from his grease-covered stool.

I had plenty of time that night to read – and to re-read -- my new magazine. And, along with a fair number of other people both young and old, I have read a goodly number of comics about him *since* that night 2½ years ago. *Eleven* more, to be exact, making an even dozen issues about the Emerald Gladiator of the so-called Sizzling Sixties! And, during this time, I have formed a few conclusions which may or may not be worthy of the reader's attention, but which I shall now proceed to state anyway.

Taking first things first as all good little reviewers should, we come to GL's second origin. If there is one way in which Green Lantern *II* is unlike Green Lantern I, this is it. Our hero's present-day alter-ego, test pilot Hal Jordan, had nothing whatsoever to do with the *making* of the second version of the almighty Power Ring. It was bestowed on him (along with his form-fitting underwear) by a dying alien who had crashed on earth in his space ship. Not only that, but even the *alien* was just a custodian of the ring, which is evidently the invention and sole property of a group of little blue men with receding hairlines who call themselves the Guardians of the Universe and who dwell on the planet Oa in the "central galaxy of the universe," wherever that is.

Worse still for our hero, his is only one of *many* Power Rings given to *many* Green Lanterns scattered at strategic points throughout the universe (with the way GL's are popping up lately, there must be one about every thirty feet of space). These other verdant valiants come in all shapes and sizes – some humanoid in appearance, and others definitely *not*. At times, they seem to treat one of earth's greatest champions of justice not unlike a kid brother who is a little naive and not necessarily on the bright side.

(One wonders how they must have treated his predecessor, Abin Sur, who could not have been too long on brains himself; he had a Power Ring which could have transported him virtually anywhere, but he ran around till the day he died in an old-fashioned space ship.)

Actually, however, this diverse number of Green Lanterns is one of the more intriguing and interesting facets of this relatively new super-doer. After many, many years of Superman's uniqueness as the most powerful human being in the whole gosh-dern universe, it is sort of refreshing to read about one who is merely an emissary of a kind of interplanetary United Nations (though a more effective one).

These Guardians who add so much to the attractiveness of GL-II (will there ever be a GL-70?) are, however, not wholly original with this comic. A similar group with an identical name (though not with identical appearances) existed in the early 50s and was featured in two of the many *Strange Adventures* stories which starred a super-mutant named Captain Comet (of whom more in a near-future issue). These earlier Guardians, however, had not given the captain his futuristic powers; they had merely waited until a menace had sprung up and then had called on the greatest hero from that general area of space to combat it. The *first* Guardians were less like the United Nations than like booking agents.

It isn't surprising, by the way, that the Guardians have appeared in both Captain Comet and Green Lantern stories. They both had the same author in later years: one John Broome, who wrote the tales about the marvel mutant under the pseudonym of Edgar Ray Merritt.

But, as Mort Sahl might say, *onward*.

One of the things I miss most in the new Green Lantern book is Doiby Dickles. True, the chubby little cab-driver was a lame-brain type who sometimes got a little *too* ridiculous even for a small child with a Sense of Wonder, but still....

Starting with issue #2 of the regular *GL* comic, an attempt was made to replace him with a thin young Eskimo mechanic named Pieface, but this has fallen at least a little flat as far as this quarter is concerned, because Pieface (whose face looks not at all like a pie) is usually rather humorless and uninteresting, except on rare occasions such as the second story in #7. He might be improved somewhat if he were fattened up and used for comedy *á la* Doiby, but maybe the Code does not wish to offend overweight comic book buyers. (More likely, wily J. Schwartz, the editor, figures that he, like the Three Dimwits of the old Flash stories, would lay a bomb-- and he may well be right. If so, I hold that the majority of comic-buyers are wrong, wrong, *wrong*.)

The department in which the new GL is *particularly* deficient, however, is that of *villainy*. The original Green Lantern had a host of foes, all different and many great. There was the Frankenstein-like Solomon Grundy, the suave Gambler, the evil Sportsmaster, the ingeniously stupid Fool, the love-started lady-villain Harlequin, and the chilly Icicle (now renovated rather mildly as Captain Cold – even the name sounds less icy – in *The Flash*), to name just the more prominent ones!

Unfortunately, there has been little effort to bring back any of these arch-criminals, nor to create worthy successors in their tradition. The second *Showcase* issue featuring Green Lantern introduced (and terminated, apparently) an anti-matter crook called the Invisible Destroyer (an unwieldly handle, at best), and *Green Lantern* #1 featured the comparatively anemic Puppet Master. But after that there was virtually nothing for a year, unless you count the Qwardians, a sort of evil counterpart of the Guardians. But the Weaponers of Qward seem to form a rather socialistic whole with no outstanding individuals to compare to the Guardians' lantern-boys.

Recently, there has been introduced *one* fairly good villain – Sinestro, who was once one of the Green Lanterns but who decided that crime paid better. So far, however, he has not been proven right, as twice the Emerald Gladiator of earth has defeated him "forever." This last time the Guardians sent him on an eighteen-billion-year journey through space via an indestructible capsule. If that doesn't take care of him, *nothing* will. And, probably, nothing *will*; at least, I *hope* not.

(I suppose this is another digression, but this Sinestro sequence of late has created within my cynical mind doubts as to the infallibility – or just plain common sense – of the Guardians. They don't seem to have much talent for choosing their heroes to go about doing good: first a redskin who was too stupid to use his own Power Ring to fly through space, then an earthman so careless that a grease monkey figures out his secret identity in twelve pages, and now this! Yes, sir, it just makes a body wonder.)

However, even after allowing for all these various faults and some others (such as proximity to omnipotence) which space does not allow me to go into, Green Lantern still comes off a pretty good character, as super-doers go. True, he is in many ways about as stereotyped as the average, being an almost perfect physical specimen and pure as the driven snow; but at times (especially when pursuing his better-than-average-for-a-comic-book romance with boss Carol Ferris), he seems a fairly believable human being. Why, in one issue he was even shown *perspiring*. (No, not *sweating* – that'd never get past the Code Authority.)

I suppose one's opinion of the new version of GL depends largely upon your frame of reference, as Don Thompson would say. Compared to Achilles in *The Iliad* and the very human Winston Smith in *1984*, I don't imagine Green Lantern comes off too splendidly. But if you compare him with others of his supercharged ilk – Superman, the Human Torch, and like that – he begins to glow, I think, with new light.

All in all, I believe Julius Schwartz and his crew (Kane, Giella, and Broome) are doing a creditable job, and have in their GL perhaps the best character National has on the market at this time. As a fan of the *old* Lantern... I can only say: *he never had it so good!*

The following letter was discovered by Linda Rahm when she was rummaging through some of Roy Thomas' old comics. Can you help her locate "Ersel"?

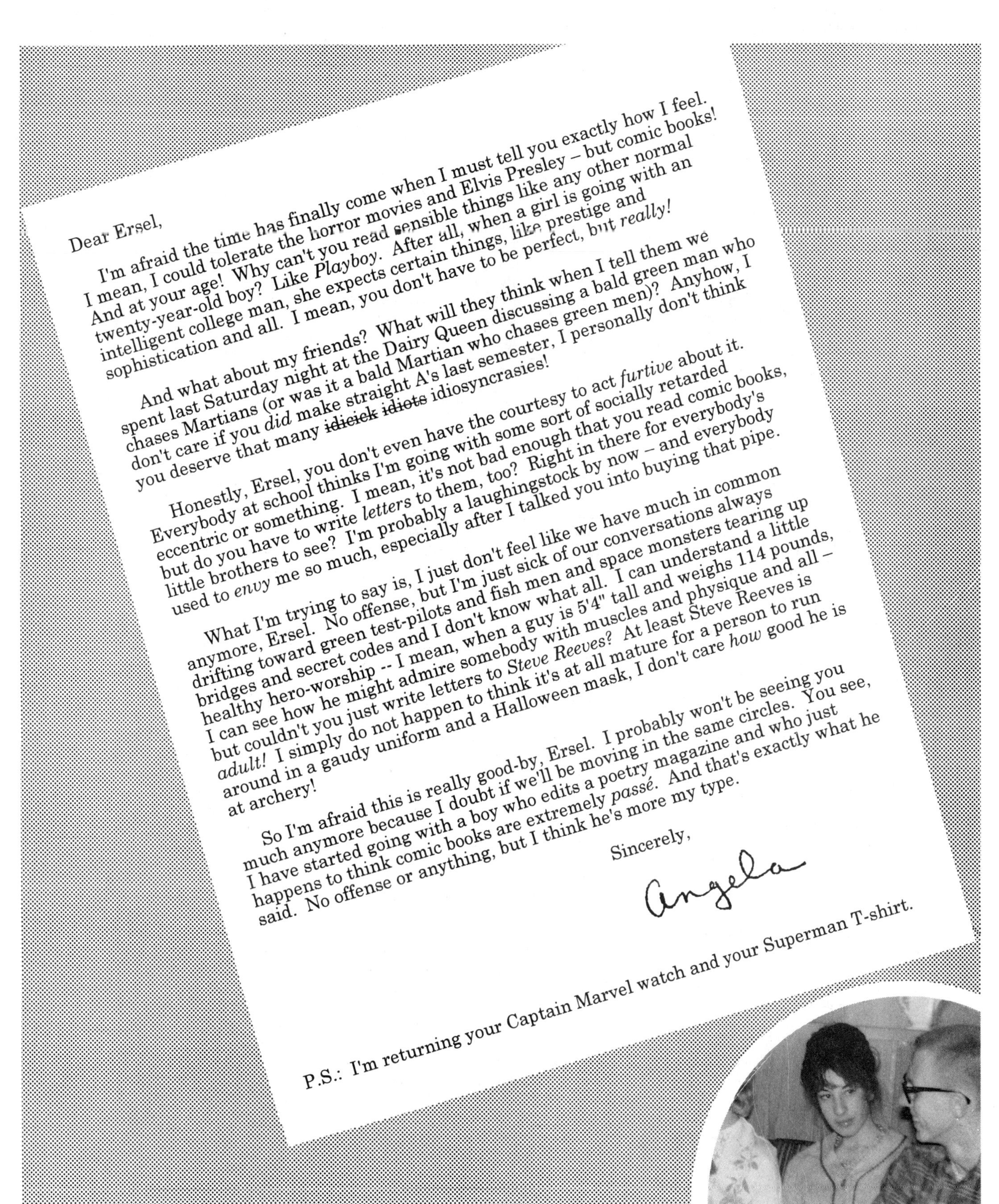

Dear Ersel,

I'm afraid the time has finally come when I must tell you exactly how I feel. I mean, I could tolerate the horror movies and Elvis Presley – but comic books! And at your age! Why can't you read sensible things like any other normal twenty-year-old boy? Like *Playboy*. After all, when a girl is going with an intelligent college man, she expects certain things, like prestige and sophistication and all. I mean, you don't have to be perfect, but *really!*

And what about my friends? What will they think when I tell them we spent last Saturday night at the Dairy Queen discussing a bald green man who chases Martians (or was it a bald Martian who chases green men)? Anyhow, I don't care if you *did* make straight A's last semester, I personally don't think you deserve that many ~~idicick idiots~~ idiosyncrasies!

Honestly, Ersel, you don't even have the courtesy to act *furtive* about it. Everybody at school thinks I'm going with some sort of socially retarded eccentric or something. I mean, it's not bad enough that you read comic books, but do you have to write *letters* to them, too? Right in there for everybody's little brothers to see? I'm probably a laughingstock by now – and everybody used to *envy* me so much, especially after I talked you into buying that pipe.

What I'm trying to say is, I just don't feel like we have much in common anymore, Ersel. No offense, but I'm just sick of our conversations always drifting toward green test-pilots and fish men and space monsters tearing up bridges and secret codes and I don't know what all. I can understand a little healthy hero-worship -- I mean, when a guy is 5'4" tall and weighs 114 pounds, I can see how he might admire somebody with muscles and physique and all – but couldn't you just write letters to *Steve Reeves*? At least Steve Reeves is *adult!* I simply do not happen to think it's at all mature for a person to run around in a gaudy uniform and a Halloween mask, I don't care *how* good he is at archery!

So I'm afraid this is really good-by, Ersel. I probably won't be seeing you much anymore because I doubt if we'll be moving in the same circles. You see, I have started going with a boy who edits a poetry magazine and who just happens to think comic books are extremely *passé*. And that's exactly what he said. No offense or anything, but I think he's more my type.

Sincerely,

Angela

P.S.: I'm returning your Captain Marvel watch and your Superman T-shirt.

[Photo of Linda Rahm with Roy Thomas by Ruth White, not from **AE.***]*

BESTEST LEAGUE OF AMERICA - Part III

Roy's lampoon of the striking cover of Justice League of America *#3 was designed as a possible cover for* AE *#3. When Jerry's own Green Lantern pastiche illustration was used as the cover instead, Roy's drawing (along with his parody of a full-page Hawkman/*Brave and Bold *house ad) preceded the final six-page chapter of "BLA."*

One of writer/artist Harvey Kurtzman's recurring motifs in the early Mad *comics had been to have the hero overthrown by a traitorous sidekick (see "Black and Blue Hawks," "The Lone Stranger Rides Again," "Woman Wonder," "Mickey Rodent"). So Roy decided that the mysterious "It" should turn out to be none other than Wombatman, for reasons explained in the panels at right:*

Yes, what about *Superham? Well, just like the real McCoy often did in early issues of* JLA*, Superham shows up for a single panel – just long enough to haul all the captured crooks off to jail and get all the credit!*

If Wombatman and Superham be here, can parodies of Adam Strange and the Atom be far behind? Obviously not, as shown in these two panels:

Years earlier, Roy had drawn a takeoff on the already-defunct Justice Society, so, to wind things up, he now decided the BLA should be swamped by JSA parodies leaping out of limbo. Fleeing the BLA, Wombatman throws wide a door marked "Danger – Do Not Open!" – and unleashes a plethora of costumed types, in a moment unconsciously predictive of the super-hero explosion that, in fall of 1961 after the debut of Fantastic Four *#1, was poised to begin....*

And so it ended, with Wombatman reinstated in the BLA (because he owed them $200,000 in back dues and they wanted to build a swimming pool). For the remainder of AE's mid-60s life, Roy would utilize the Bestest League in one-panel cartoons and house ads, but there would be only one more actual BLA story – in AE #6 – and that one would reflect the changed realities of a bipolar comic book world, in which DC and Marvel were battling for supremacy in the universe of super-hero comics....

Here are some more one-sided

CONVERSATIONS

... if you like that sort of thing (and we hope you do).

Larry Ivie
31 West 76 St.
New York 23, NY

The story behind my Atom drawing on the cover of *Xero 5* extends back several years to the time of National's revival of The Flash. An enthusiastic youngster in my early days of art school, I immediately phoned National to see if they had plans for revival of any of the other old characters. (I had an intense desire to do Hawkman.) They said they would see how well sales went on The New Flash first, and gave me the standard "We'll keep you in mind."

When the Green Lantern hit the stands, my enthusiasm was revived, and I ran immediately to the National offices, and was graciously consented an interview with Julius Schwartz. Two people who had seen my art school work had suggested Schwartz to me – Jack Kirby, a former National artist, and Sheldon Mayer, a former editor. And so I arrived with an armload of samples.

I had actually done comic book work by this time – at least a small bit of it – with an artist by the name of Al Williamson, and I knew that the samples, as far as comic book drawing went, were above average. I had a page that was completed for reproduction, a page that was penciled only, and a page that was half penciled and half inked. Mr. Schwartz looked at these and said they were fine, except for the use of cross-hatch, which did not fit in with National's way of doing things, and the use of shading sheets, which "confuse the color artists." It resembled too much the work of the late EC comics group, which had "failed to reach an audience because it was too complicated for the age level of the comic book buyers." In general, he commented that he liked the drawing, but wouldn't really be able to tell what I could do unless I brought in a complete story, from first page to last. He said there were occasional openings for new artists, and would keep my name on file, just in case.

So I began work on a complete story of Hawkman. I wrote a script which was not only consistent with the earlier version, but brought the character logically up to date. I feel that this script still has more audience appeal than any National has used to date. I then lettered and drew the second page. Then I panicked. It didn't match the National "house-type" in any respect. The lettering was too precise, the panel borders too thick, and the balance of black and white was completely different – more like the old Hawkman by Moldoff. I showed the pages to a dozen artists, along with the first issue of the new *Green Lantern.* I asked kids which of the pages they preferred. Every one favored mine over the printed *Green Lantern,* but still my confidence faltered. A few months later I began anew. I redrew the second page with National-width borders, standardized the figures as much as possible, kept the backgrounds to a minimum, and even imitated the faltering hand lettering in *Green Lantern.* All told, I did four pages of the story – the first two and the last two, as close as possible to what I sensed to be the National way.

I took these to Julius Schwartz. He said they might have seriously considered the work, when they had decided to revive the Hawkman the week or so before; but the script was now already written, and Joe Kubert had been reassigned to the artwork. The sad part was that the new Hawkman was only the old National cliché of an extra-powered hero from another planet; and the artwork, for Kubert, showed only mediocre enthusiasm. But, again, Schwartz was not discouraging, and promised to keep me in mind should another character revival become imminent, and even asked me if I would be able to write my own scripts. I showed him a page of Sandman, but he was not familiar with this old JSA member. The Sandman would have been my second choice.

I then mentioned my interview to Ted White, a long-time National fan, full-time science fiction fan, and part-time professional writer. Ted was immediately enthused with the idea that National would accept new writers, and immediately set to thinking out a substantial plot situation (which he felt had been lacking in recent National efforts) for another character revival, which he wanted me to illustrate. We then hashed over possible characters and possible new origin ideas. We knew if things were left in National's hands, Starman would be a super-being from another star; Sandman would be a being from a planet made of sand, who could, on earth, transform himself into a minute grain and travel on the air currents; the Atom would explode like a bomb, or turn into an atom, etc. This we didn't want. We chose the Atom, and, as in the original version, made him slightly smaller in size than ordinary men. This created a timely and interesting occupation for him – astronaut – where his lack of weight would be to advantage.

The cover of *Xero 5* was the first of three pages that were started on this idea. Unknown to us, National has already started an Atom revival, so our efforts would have been better spent on another character. I haven't as yet seen any artwork on it; but two-to-one his powers are incredibly alien.

[Cover to Xero *5 featuring Larry Ivie's visualization of a revived Atom. Illustration did not appear in AE.]*

I doubt if I will have much time to attempt another possible fiasco for National. I definitely feel I could have given them a character of good circulation, and had a long talk with Schwartz as to what I felt were the drawbacks in the current line, based on my own feelings as a reader during the old era.

The major drawback I sense in National *today*, as an *adult* bystander, is imitation. National was ahead once, with the accidental acceptance of Superman. From there on, it has been imitation. The editors have been "borrowing" Superman (the being from another planet concept) to this day; the writers have been "borrowing" pictures. Other companies have imitated also, of course. But National has always been renowned for this, I think, because of a greater awareness among the competition. It was during the days that every other National panel was traced from Alex Raymond, Hal Foster, or Milton Caniff, and every being was of supernatural origin, that Quality Publications came up with Blackhawk, the Spirit, and Plastic Man, and the superb original artwork of Reed Crandall, Lou Fine, and Will Eisner. There was seldom a swipe in the early Fawcett Group, which, in 1942, brought forth a feature that has never been surpassed in artistry by the super-hero comics – Raboy's Capt. Marvel Jr.

A lot of National's panels would be different today without the all-too-handy products of EC publications. And today's Green Lantern would be a lot different if Dan Barry had never started the daily Flash Gordon.

When National hits upon artists willing to rival – not *trace*, but *rival* – the Raboy of 1942, they can prepare themselves for a revival of the "Sense of Wonder" on the part of the buying public. When a writer and an artist lack the inspiration of originality, their product will forever lack the full range of its selling potential.

You may quote any of all of this, as I've already expanded on these views quite extensively for Schwartz himself. I doubt if they will see fruit, however, as even Raboy was an Inspired Young Man for only one year.

Then his work fell into the same rut as that of National today, and finally into the depths exhibited by his current Flash Gordon Sunday page. Comic books seem to do that to people. Only a few – Reed Crandall, Frank Frazetta – were able to maintain and improve their ideals as time passed. Mostly, the enthusiasm wanes as the years pass. After all, it takes twice the amount of work to turn an adequate product into a superior one. Sometimes three or four times the amount. And most of the National staff has been at the grind for an awful long time. I can see their point.

Ronnie Graham
Box 923
Berkeley 1, CA

Alter-Ego arrived yesterday. In *Alter-Ego*, "The Bestest League of America" is the best article. Artwork not great, but it is good for amateur publications of this kind. Also enjoyed greatly story of the Spectre, Bernard Bailey's old creation. Is he (BB) still around? Last I remember of him was a one-shot *Cisco Kid* comic book published around 1944; he illustrated the cover and some of the insides.

It was published by a small, unknown to me, comic-publishing house. The Wonder Woman history was also very interesting to me. I hope *Alter-Ego* continues to be published for many moon to come.

B. Bailey is now on the staff of *Cracked*.

I have about 150 original drawings, mostly by comic book artists of the super-doer variety. They are in Lafayette, Indiana, where I am originally from. I collected them from 1948 through 1953. I have originals of (this isn't a complete list, as I'm relying solely on my memory for them): Airwave by Lee Harris, late 1940s issues of *Detective Comics*; Batman, a 1945 daily McClure syndicated strip by Bob Kane; Kerry Drake by Alfred Andriola; Green Arrow and Speedy by George Papp; Capt. Compass by George Papp (late 1940s *Star-Spangled Comics*); Tomahawk

[adapted by Bails]

by Fred Ray (signs his name "Fray"); Black Diamond by Wm. Overgard from the Lev Gleason publication, *Black Diamond Comics* (Overgard is presently illustrating the Steve Roper syndicated strip); Big Ben Bolt by John Cullen Murphy (this is a huge water-color painting, not a mere pen and ink strip; I got it a few months after Ben Bolt began in the papers); Pee Wee, one of *Daredevil*'s Little Wise Guys, by Al Borth; Pvt. Pete by Henry Boltinoff, from early DC publications (this strip was revived after the Korean War but Pete's features had changed by this time).

Powerhouse Pepper by Basil Wolverton, a long-standing favorite of mine, also the best of the comic strip artists in my opinion (Wolverton got me started in collecting originals by answering a postcard I sent him quite accidentally in 1948 asking him if he were the same Wolverton who drew Lena the Hyena in the 1946 Li'l Abner contest); Lin Thorne, the Flying Fool, by Paul Reinman from late 1940s *Airboy Comics*; Sniffer by Carl Hubbell from *Daredevil Comics* (Hubbell is also from Indiana – Indianapolis, to be exact; he originated a syndicated daily strip called "Merry Chase" which appeared in the *Indianapolis News* around the 1950s; this strip was later drawn by Paul Reinman, who sent me several originals from the strip); also some pages by Fred Guardineer, who created Zatara in *Action Comics* #1; the Katzenjammer Kids and Elmer by Doc Winner; Curly Kayoe by Sam Leff; Priscilla's Pop by Al Vemeer; Muggs & Skeeter by Wally McGinner; Bud Fisher's personal card, sent by his secretary (he was on vacation at the time).

An item about Ogden Whitney you may find of interest; in the Mar/44 (#44) issue of *Big Shot Comics,* Whitney signed his strip Skyman "Cpl. Ogden Whitney"; by issue #53, Feb/45, Skyman was being drawn by Chollie Stern (possibly a pen name); then in issue #67, July/46, we find the following notice placed at the beginning of the Skyman strip, which Whitney again illustrates:

"Welcome Home, Ex-Sgt. Whitney! Hello, Fans. *Big Shot Comics* is happy to announce the return of Ogden Whitney to its fine art staff. After drawing Skyman for four years, Ogden enlisted in the U.S. Army. Now, back from the Pacific War Zone with a chest full of campaign ribbons and an honorable discharge, Ogden has settled down to the task of offering our readers the finest quality of comic strip entertainment. We are sure all of you will join us in saying, 'Welcome Home, Ogden Whitney!'"

The *Big Shot Comics* group are to be admired for establishing this personal relationship of artists and writers with the readers, for those discriminating enough to be interested in such things. They also gave Boody Rogers a welcome home from the army, as Captain Boody Rogers, when he returned to his original and successful *Sparky Watts* strip. This strip was drawn by Tom DeAngelo while Rogers was in the army. An interesting item about Mark Bailey, who drew The Face (later changed to The Adventures of Tony Trent) for *Big Shot Comics.* In the strip of issue #73, Jan/47 (which contained two Tony Trent strips, by the way), Tony Trent faints in the last two panels of this strip after glancing at newspaper headlines. The headlines: "Marion Ryan to Wed Mark Bailey."

Great Scott! It's ten after five in the morning, Jerry Boy. Must close. Keep up the good work. Get rid of the silly codes that you have to translate.

Frederic Norwood
3 Ames St.
Cambridge 39, Massachusetts

I just made a tremendous find, hundreds of early comics from the forties, including a copy of *All-Winners* #21 with no pages missing. My copy of *AE* is at school, but if I remember correctly, it was the ending of the Sub-Mariner incident that was missing from Roy's copy. In the center four pages, a mermaid tells Prince Namor that a queer man is undersea, along with dozens of divers from a submarine. Sub-Mariner swims into them, but is stunned by Future Man, whose mental bolts cannot kill underwater. Then Namor is tied to a torpedo which will be used to start a tidal wave and drown Asia. He regains consciousness and orders his finny friends (shades of Aquaman) to gnaw through his bonds. Then he manages to pull the fuse cap off the torpedo and swims back to the divers, whom he takes on single-handed, knocking out half a dozen of them. Future Man gives up and moves on to Africa.

COMING SOON TO *ALTER-EGO*:

* * "Shades of Neptune" – New information on the early Wonder Woman.

* * "The JLA Branches Out" – An hilarious new parody by Roy Thomas.

* * Bill Everett's Amazing-Man of 1939, by Ed Lahmann.

* * SPECIAL: In the next issue, *Alter-Ego* will conduct what is destined to become the biggest annual event in comics fandom. I can't say any more about it now, but I'm sure you won't want to miss out on this great historical event!

FOUR OF A KIND

From *The Comicollector* #1 (September 1961)

It was bound to happen! The Human Torch is back, flaming his way across the heavens, scorching everything in his fiery path.

But wait – something has been added. For this Human Torch is a blond-haired *teenager* whose major interest in life, when he's not setting fire to USAF jets, is tinkering with hot-rods! And he's not *alone*, for with him are three other, new super-heroes: his sister, the Invisible Girl, who fades in and out of sight with alarming irregularity; the group's leader, Mr. Fantastic, who possesses the ability to stretch to an amazing variety of sizes and shapes; and, to top it all off, The Thing, endowed with tremendous physical strength which he (it?) generally uses for good, but looking like a monstrous cross between a walking boulder and a Gila monster!

Yes, these are *The Fantastic Four*, heroes of a new comic put out bi-monthly by Canam Publishers Sales Corporation. Produced by Stan Lee*, and Jack Kirby (of the old-time Simon and Kirby team, which originated Captain America, the Guardian, Stuntman, Challengers of the Unknown, and many others), this comic stands somewhere between the *Challengers* and the new *Justice League of America*.

Despite its faults – and this first issue has some glaring ones – *The Fantastic Four* holds promise of becoming one of the better comics now on the stands, in this reviewer's opinion. Especially gratifying is the re-revival of the Torch, undoubtedly one of the most interesting super-hero concepts of all time. The Four's leader, Mr. Fantastic, is also a welcome character, as appearances by Elongated Man in *The Flash* have so far been too spotty to be satisfying.

The *really* outstanding feature of this comic, however – which somehow seems more like a mag of the 40's than of the 60's – is the hero known as The Thing! Not since The Heap ran rampant in the old *Airboy Comics* a decade or more ago has there been such a frightening champion of justice. Perhaps the readers of *this* comic era – who do not appear to like some of the old ideas – will not take kindly to such an unlikely hero; but I sincerely hope that they do, for something is needed in a period of all-too-handsome supermen to remind us that goodness of heart and an attractive physical appearance are not necessarily synonymous.

Unfortunately, this first issue also leaves a lot to be desired. Invisible Girl's power, apparently unsupplemented by the ability to walk through walls, etc., is such that her role is a minor one; the three humans wear drab clothing that would never really stand the rigors of a monster-filled adventure such as this first one; Mr. Fantastic's stretching power (like that of Elongated Man) is still too limited for him to be considered the true successor of Plastic Man or a great one in his own right; and, worst of all, the drawing of this third version of the Human Torch is almost pathetic in some panels, *crying* for a return to something like the old Burgos version.

It is too early yet to judge fully the Fantastic Four, but I, for one, cast my vote in favor of them. With a little added imagination in both stories and artwork – plus perhaps the addition of a fifth character, such as the Sub-Mariner or someone like the old Purple Claw – I think this comic would be worthy of a large circulation. One interesting aspect of this comic – are you listening, Don Thompson? – is that The Thing is a rather rebellious creature who is often at the point of fighting to the death with the leader, Mr. Fantastic, and is, to say the least, extremely contemptuous of his leadership. This feature alone, especially if and when the Torch begins to get in on this running feud, would make it well worth any super-hero fan's dime.

However, *Alter-Ego* would like to hear from others who have read the first issue, or who purchase the second issue, which will hit the stands the first week of October. We'd like to hear what other comics fans think of *The Fantastic Four*, its good and bad points. Who knows – this reviewer may have been the only person who bought a copy!

– Roy Thomas

---

*EDITOR'S NOTE: Mr. Lee was formerly an editor of the Timely group of comics, which featured the original Human Torch.

About the cover of* Alter-Ego *#4 (October 1962): *Out of the dozens of fans who submitted drawings of Alley Oop for the cover, Jerry selected that of Ronn Foss and Richard "Grass" Green (who was adding an "e" at the end of his name at this time, because he thought it looked better) as the contest winners, adding luster to their debut in the pages of* AE. *The black-and-white cover was printed with an unusual overlay of* gold *ink, to simulate the gold paint that Foss applied to his ten hand-crafted Alley Award statuettes sent to the award winners.*

Alter-Ego #4 – Notes & Commentary

In the editorial for AE *#4 entitled "A Parting Shot," Jerry Bails wrote, "As most of you know by now, this issue is my last as publisher and editor of* Alter-Ego."

The reason for this momentous decision, made just a little over a year after inaugurating the fanzine? "I am engaged in collecting data on artists and writers, and all costumed-hero comics published before 1948," he explained. "With a big assist from Howard Keltner, I hope to publish a big index to DC titles before too long." Bails was also busy photographing the covers of all comic magazines through the end of the 1940s. He was simply more interested in indexing and researching the early days of comics than he was in publishing a magazine. (He would continue The Comic Reader, *with the help of Mike Tuohey and others, until spring 1964.)*

Alter-Ego *would be continued by a group of fans in California who called themselves "Triad." This group, consisting of Ronn Foss, his wife Myra, and Richard "Grass" Green (whose nickname is a shortened version of "Grasshoppa"), volunteered to take up the reins of both* AE *and its companion* The Comicollector. *(As you will see in the next chapter, Triad's "best laid plans" almost immediately collapsed, leaving them in the hands of Ronn alone.)*

Why didn't Roy Thomas assume the full editorship at this juncture? He had been listed as "editor" (along with Bails) of the first two issues, and "Contributing Editor" of #3. Yet, despite the fact that Roy never sought editorial credit, it seems strange that he did not receive this status in #4. Could there have been a rift between Bails and Thomas? If so, neither Jerry nor Roy has any memory of one. Though occupied (none too happily) with a full-time teaching job, and therefore unlikely to have accepted the position, Thomas cannot recall being offered the helm of the fanzine. This will probably remain shrouded in mystery, though of course Thomas would eventually edit more issues of AE *than either Bails or Foss, and become the only person to contribute something to every issue.*

The cover and early pages of AE *#4 were devoted to the somewhat tardy announcement of the winners of the first Alley Award poll. The announcement of the winners and report on the results by Academy Secretary Roy Thomas (reprinted in full herein) offer a fascinating glimpse back to a time when DC Comics had few serious competitors. Despite grumblings from fans who were growing increasingly dissatisfied with the* Justice League of America *comic book, Julius Schwartz continued to ride high in the overall estimation of fandom.*

*A number of other firsts surfaced with this issue: the first photo-offset edition (allowing a print run of 1000 copies); the first costumed-hero fanzine to feature pro contributions created especially for its pages (the Jack Kirby sketch of the Thing, inked by Bails, and the letter from Paul Reinman); and, interestingly, the first (as far as we know) fanzine photograph of a comic book cover (*Jackpot *#1), which was among the initial group of one hundred covers photographed by Bails. Soon Jerry would be transferring hundreds of comic book covers to microfilm.*

The number of contributors this time around grew to include some of the most active, best-known fans in 1960s comics fandom. Ed Lahmann of Indianapolis offered "Maximo, the Superman before SUPERMAN'S Time"; Ronn Foss provided not only a cover, but illustrations for another segment of Ron Haydock's "SERIALously Speaking" column, this time relating "The Exploits of Batman and Robin"; L. L. Simpson contributed a "Hall of Infamy" column focusing on The Claw and Iron Jaw; and Howard Keltner weighed in with "MLJ Leads the Way," written a year before he teamed up with Buddy Saunders and Larry Herndon to form the Texas Trio and launch a popular fanzine called Star-Studded Comics. *"MLJ Leads The Way" is reprinted here in full, including the illustrations by Jerry Bails, not only because it placed second in the 1962 Alley Award poll for "Best Article," but because it exemplifies the kind of personalized, informal research pieces that were fandom's first attempts to chronicle the unknown facts about the history of comic books. Keltner was so infatuated with MLJ's Mr. Justice that he created his own "knock-off" called Dr. Weird, who achieved considerable popularity in fandom. (Dr. Weird has gotten a "new lease on death" in the 1990s, in the pages of Gary Carlson and Edward DeGeorge's* Big Bang Comics.)

Oddly, this issue did not feature a letter column. This may have been because of the high cost of professional printing.

Jerry Bails' editorial concluded, "Let me take this opportunity to thank all of my friends in fandom for their encouragement, contributions, and kind comments." With this 34-page edition, the first part of the Alter-Ego *saga came to a close. Bails had done himself proud, offering quite a challenge to his successors. Could they match this sterling all-offset issue?*

The Editors

THE ALLEY AWARDS FOR 1961

Division One:
Best Regularly Published Comic Book
JUSTICE LEAGUE OF AMERICA

Division Two:
Best Adventure Hero(ine) Having Own Comic Book
GREEN LANTERN

Division Three:
Best Adventure Hero(ine) Not Having Own Comic Book
HAWKMAN

Division Four:
Best Supporting Character
ELONGATED MAN

Division Five:
Best Cover
THE FLASH #123
"Flash of Two Worlds"

Division Six:
Best Single Issue of a Comic Book
THE FLASH #123
"Flash of Two Worlds"

Division Seven:
Best Artist (Pencil or Ink)
CARMINE INFANTINO

Division Eight:
Best Story
THE FLASH #123
"Flash of Two Worlds"

Division Nine:
Best Adventure-Hero Group
JUSTICE LEAGUE OF AMERICA

Division Ten:
Hero or Heroine Most Worthy of Revival
THE SPECTRE

Special Division:
Worst Comic Book Currently Published
WONDER WOMAN

Academy of Comic Book Arts And Sciences

Ronn Foss
Wendell Davis
Donald Foote
Douglas Marden
Jerry Bails
Don Thompson
Ed Lahmann
Bob Barron
Richard Durell
Len Brown
Dale Christman
Ron Haydock
Howard Keltner
Dick Lupoff
Roy Thomas
Raymond Miller
Frank Neussel
Bill White
Irving Glassman
Fred Norwood

A REPORT FROM ROY THOMAS,

SECRETARY OF THE ACADEMY OF COMIC BOOK ARTS AND SCIENCES

Because of a number of various factors, it becomes necessary (or at least advisable) to say a few words on the recently-published first annual poll of the Academy of Comic Book Arts and Sciences, hereinafter referred to as the Alley Awards. These awards are named for the venerable A. Oop, who, being a caveman, is doubtless one of the earliest possible adventure-heroes (by our definition of the term). These first awards are meant to cover a time-period of one year, from January to December, 1961. Since comic books are generally published two or three months before the date for which they are marked, this means that, by and large, all the comics and features eligible for this (the 1961 Alley Awards Poll) were probably on the stands by at least October of last year. Admittedly, then, the announcement of the results of this poll comes a bit late, but this was unavoidable due to the time of the conception of the plan and the amount of preparation involved.

First of all, as many of you know, ballots were sent to the twenty members of the nominating committee. When these were returned, a second ballot was drawn up, featuring the top five nominees in the various categories (except in the Special Division of "Worst Comic-Book" and Division Eight where there was a tie). Then this second ballot was sent out to over 750 active fans. Problems of time necessitated the omission of provision for write-in votes in most cases, but Division Ten and the Special Division even allowed for that.

Despite a number of features and imperfections which should be taken care of by the next voting, we really thought that we had made all instructions as crystal-clear as possible. However, it now appears that in this case we deceived ourselves greatly, because almost every kind of misconception which could possibly happen under such an arrangement occurred on at least one returned ballot, and often on considerably more than one. A number of zealous voters, for example, simply could not bring themselves to decide between two nominees and drew all sorts of elaborate arrows on their ballots to indicate a "tie." These hardy souls, I am afraid, were rewarded for their artistic efforts by having their votes in these particular categories voided.

Also, several helpful well-wishers informed me (often! with! large! and! forceful! exclamation! points!) that the Atom was ineligible in Division Three as he now has his own comic. This mistake is a bit more understandable than that made by the hapless Hamlets mentioned above, but it is still an error. The awards ballot clearly stated that only comics published for the year 1961 were to be considered in this poll, and the first issue of *The Atom* falls well outside that time.

Now to a few general comments about the results of the poll:

In Division One, *Justice League of America* was an easy winner, with *The Flash* and *Green Lantern* as runners-up in that order. A few voters wrote in that *The Fantastic Four* should have been nominated, but one reason that it was not is undoubtedly the fact that only one issue of it was actually eligible for consideration in this poll. We'll have to wait till the next time to see how popular Stan Lee's brainchild is. I seriously doubt if many people would actually have voted for *The Fantastic Four* as best comic book merely on the basis of the first issue.

In Division Two, Green Lantern nosed out the Flash by a few votes to win "Best Hero Having Own Comic Book" award. This was a nip-and-tuck battle all the way, with Superman running a poor third.

Hawkman was a walk-away (nay, a run-away) in Division Three, despite the slightly incongruous fact that it was the Atom who now has won his own comic, with Hawkman still waiting in the wings (an accidental pun, so help me). Believe it or not, Adam Strange ran second here, about ten votes ahead of the Atom, who only beat the Human Torch by eight votes. This seems to me to agree basically with Jerry Bails' view that, as the decision to start regular publication of *The Atom* was made on the basis of sales of the first trial issue only, it was as much the publication of the picture of the first JSA meeting from *All-Star* #3 as the Atom himself that won the day – and the comic book. Be that as it may, I'm extremely happy to see Atom now in his own well-deserved magazine and in the Justice League, albeit I would much have preferred to see Hawkman join first. As soon as the new Hawkman debuted in *Brave and Bold* #34, the JLA became incomplete for me, and will remain such until the Winged Wonder is a permanent member.

Returning to the poll, Elongated Man defeated two runners-up, Robin and Hawkgirl, by approximately a dozen votes each. Any chance he'll get his own well-deserved mag in the near future? How about it, Julie Schwartz, my favorite editor? I'm afraid that I still think that he and the Three Dimwits would make a great team, especially if the latter occasionally did some hectic babysitting with an "Elongated Baby." Ralph Dibny *is* married, you know.

The Flash #123, cover-featuring the full-length "Flash of Two Worlds," which served to team the old and new Scarlet Speedsters in a yarn of considerable human interest, proved to be the "West Side Story" of the Alley Awards, winning everything for which it was nominated. The cover won Division Five, probably less for its real artistic merit, however, than because it spotlighted the old Flash. However, this is not to say that the cover was undeserving of the award. The covers of *Brave and Bold* #34 (the first Hawkman issue) and #36 ("Shadow-Thief of Midway City," also with Hawkman) were runners-up and between them amassed more votes than did the winner, showing that the fans still appreciate a good Kubert cover.

The Flash #123 also won Division Six for the best single issue of a comic-book, with *Superman* #149 (featuring the "Death of Superman" story) its only real competitor.

Carmine Infantino, pencil-artist of *The Flash* and other strips, won the Division Seven award for best artwork. This, of course, is quite consistent with the winning of the best-cover award by *The Flash* #123. Infantino's been doing some great work recently. Joe Kubert's work, which to me has long had a kind of semi-impressionist air, won him runner-up position, though he was far and away the first choice of the nominating committee. Murphy Anderson, Gil Kane, and Jack Kirby finished in that order.

"Flash of Two Worlds" also copped the "best story" award in Division Eight, with slightly over 50% of the votes, with "Secret of the Sinister Sorcerers" from *JLA* #2 and "Challenge from 5700 A.D." (the first GL-future yarn) way behind. This seems to indicate that the two-Flashes tales should have enough popularity to insure their continued and welcome appearances.

In Division Nine came the largest victory margin, however, with the Justice League winning 70% of the votes cast. Second was the Fantastic Four, which may well prove a stronger contender next time. In fact,

[illo by Foss]

several new groups will probably challenge the JLA next year. They are The Metal Men, The Legion of Super-Heroes (*Adventure Comics*), and perhaps a group of heroes from the Archie Comics family. If imitation is the sincerest form of flattery, then Julie Schwartz must have had to change hat sizes several times recently.

In Division Ten, the Spectre nosed out Doctor Fate by exactly one vote, with the redoubtable Captain Marvel only a few votes behind these two. Strongest write-in showings were made by Dr. Mid-Nite (an excellent revival version of which will appear in comic form in an upcoming issue of *Alter-Ego*) and Black Canary (who was patterned strongly after the recently-returned Black Cat).

In the "Worst Comic" division, *Wonder Woman* had no competition, amassing almost 20% of the total votes -- a considerable feat, since all of these were write-ins! The selection is probably much deserved; the stories are abominably weak and trite, what with Wonder Girl and Wonder Tot. Why, now they're even referring to Hippolyta, a regular feature in the comic since the first Wonder Woman story, as "Wonder Queen," a farcical title if ever there was one.

Other receiving five votes or more in this "Special Division" were *The Hulk, The Jaguar, Magic Agent* (now deceased), *Tomahawk, Superman, Blackhawk,* and *Action*. None of these approached *Wonder Woman*'s total, however.

These, then, are the results of the 1961 Annual Awards Poll of the Academy of Comic Book Arts and Sciences. There will undoubtedly be some changes made in the next polling; in particular, the inclusion of a "Best Villain" division seems an inexcusable omission this go-round, and perhaps there should be a distinction between shorter stories and full-length ones in the interests of fairness. Also, if more writers will sign their stories, we will surely have a "Best Writer" division. All I can say in parting is: if your favorite didn't win this time, be sure to vote in the next annual poll conducted by *Alter-Ego*.

Sincerely,

Roy

Roy Thomas, Secretary

[The Thing by Jack Kirby, with inks by Jerry Bails]

From the Studio of PAUL REINMAN

In answer to your letter, I am only too glad to give you a few thoughts about my times with the comics. I remember distinctly the first day I was confronted with this business of illustrating for comic books. I did not start with inking or penciling only for some other artist. I got right into the middle of things and was given a script just on the strength of my samples, which were mostly dry brush illustration for pulp magazines and some fashion drawings for ad agencies.

I remember when the artists were just a page, or sometimes only a few boxes, ahead of the writer. We would come in in the morning and the editor, who mostly doubled as the writer, would say: "Sit down, I'll write a rough outline of the plot in a few minutes." While the artist was working on the first page, the editor broke down the rest of the story and typed it for the artist. The dialogue was not written before the artist had finished his inkings. When the artist looked at the breakdown of his story and a box showed a lot of action, he would let his drawing take up most of the space of this box; if it was a close-up or very little action, he would leave more space for dialogue. Well, that's the way it was in the beginning of the comics.

I remember one artist, a gifted painter and lithographer, who lived in Greenwich Village. He was one of the few artists who wrote his own stories and the dialogue. After getting his assignment he would simply disappear; came the deadline for his story and our editor became frantic. After a hasty search through all the nearby bars and dives, our artist was finally located dead drunk. After sobering him up the artist would promise to do his story in no time at all, if only the editor would lock him up in the studio of our publisher. And, sure enough, after working through night and day, he finished his assignment with perfection and usually within a short time. Only once was he late. While he was putting the finishing touches on his work, he placed his drawings near an open window, and a sudden gust of wind blew the pages out into the street a few floors below. By the time we got to the street – editor, artists, letterers, and office help – a few trucks and cars had run over the drawings and completely ruined them. I'm sure that passers-by must have thought that we were nuts, trying to save a few scraps of paper from the gutters. But again, our production genius and editor had the answer to this emergency. We were about 6 or 8 artists working at the studio of our publisher. Each artist got one page to do over, and by nightfall the job was finished.

Here's another funny story. Our editor received a batch of drawings from an artist who decidedly was not too experienced. These drawings were left at the office for quite some time, and this artist never came around to pick them up again. Finally, one day our editor threw them in the wastepaper basket. But a jokester retrieved them from the basket, straightened them out, and put them back on the shelves. By this time the editor was mad, and to make sure they would disappear, he tore them up. But again we salvaged them and pasted 'em together carefully, and back on the shelves they went. Now we kept a constant watch on our editor, and when he saw the drawings again he couldn't believe his eyes. By this time we could not keep from bursting out laughing while he tore them into tiny bits of confetti.

I'm sure if I had the time I could sit down and write a book about this business. Maybe some day I will. Jerry, I hope this little missile will suffice for the moment, but please don't hesitate to ask me again, sometime.

Sincerely,

Paul Reinman

Paul Reinman

Art adapted by Jerry Bails

In 1938, with the world on the brink of war, Superman made his appearance in the first issue of *Action Comics* (June 1938), and a new fad was born. The Batman followed in the May 1939 issue of *Detective Comics* (#27), and the costumed hero was on his way. By 1940 there were at least a dozen companies in competition with each other in the publication of comic books devoted to the costumed hero. By the time America entered the war, over 200 costumed heroes had seen the light of day. Most of these heroes battled crime and subversion throughout the war years, but with the coming of peace in 1945, there came a thinning of the ranks, as other fads began to dominate the comic books: humor, western, romance, horror, fantasy, science fiction, and war stories, just to name the more prominent ones. Today, after more than a decade in near-oblivion, the costumed hero is again becoming the kingpin of the comic books. This fad, like the original movement, began at DC, but it has now spread to no less than four other publishing houses: Atlas, Gold Key, Harvey, and Stadium. *And this is just the beginning!*

The last mentioned, Stadium Publishing Company, is an outgrowth of MLJ Magazines, one of the first and most successful of DC's competitors. In late 1939 and early 1940 MLJ issued a new comic book every month for four consecutive months. One of them, *Pep Comics*, is still being published today. Another, *Top-Notch Comics,* changed its title to *Top-Notch Laugh Comics* with issue #28, later dropped the word "*Top-Notch*" and is today being published as *Laugh Comics.* The other two, *Zip Comics* and *Blue Ribbon Comics,* lasted 47 and 22 issues, respectively. It was MLJ's intention to publish these books on a monthly schedule, but it was the spring of 1941 before this ambition was achieved. During the first year each of the titles skipped a month here and there. Indeed, when *Zip Comics* #1 appeared for February 1940, *Blue Ribbon* #4 was scheduled to go on sale; but it was June before the latter finally made it, and then with an almost entirely new lineup of characters. Thus, when the periodicals finally assumed an uninterrupted monthly schedule in early 1941, the oldest title had the lowest number.

Like most publishers of that day, MLJ had its own stable of writers and artists, though a few of the illustrators gained recognition elsewhere. Probably the best known among its artists were Irving Novick, Charles Biro, Mort Meskin, Jack Binder, Irwin Hasen, E.L. Wexler, Al Camy, Paul Reinman, Jack Cole, Bob Wood, and Sam Cooper. The names of Harry Shorten (later chief editor) and Joe Blair appeared more often as writers. I strongly suspect that Joe Blair was a fictitious name, used by more than one writer. The variety of strips attributed to this name seem to have been too widespread to be the product of one man. Besides, the name sounds phony! But, to return to the artists, whose work, after all, is more easily identifiable, I cannot but feel that only two of them, Camy and Novick, did their best work for MLJ. Camy left MLJ and came up with some pretty good stuff for Standard and one or two other publishers. His drawings of The Black Hood, The Wizard, and Black Jack are among the best MLJ published. Probably the very best, though, was Novick's The Shield in 1940 and 1941. But then in the middle 40s Novick did an about-face and turned out his worst work. Paul Reinman's drawings of Inferno were good, but the rest of his stuff was mediocre. Sam Cooper was another artist of opposite extremes; his illustrations of Mr. Justice were alternately terrific and sloppy. He was at his peak during 1941, which, in my opinion, was the year for the super-heroes. Mort Meskin is a name perhaps more familiar to fans of today. He regularly turns up in the DC magazines, ranking right up there with the best of the ink-splashers. His *style*, however, has not changed too much from the days when he was doing Ty-gor, Son of the Tiger, Doc Strong, and a few others. About the only difference is a vast improvement in the important item of background. Meskin's best work for MLJ was on The Scarlet Avenger, a pretty good character, incidentally. Many other artists were featured in the pages of the MLJ publications, too many to elaborate on here, but a few deserve a mention in passing. The better ones were Lin Streeter, Frank Volp, E.M. Ashe, Ed Smalle, Bob Montana, Harry Sahle, and Carl Hubbell.

Like most of the other publishers, MLJ had its group of major characters, *i.e.*, the ones given prominence over the others, and then it also had its minor ones; and, also like other publishers, some of the minor or supporting characters were better than some of the stars. It should be pointed out here that I am restricting this observation to the costumed characters, and that the opinions expressed are of necessity my own. I think at this point a breakdown of all MLJ's major costumed heroes would be more appropriate and less confusing than skipping back and forth. So here they are individually, in the order of their origin, from the earliest to the latest.

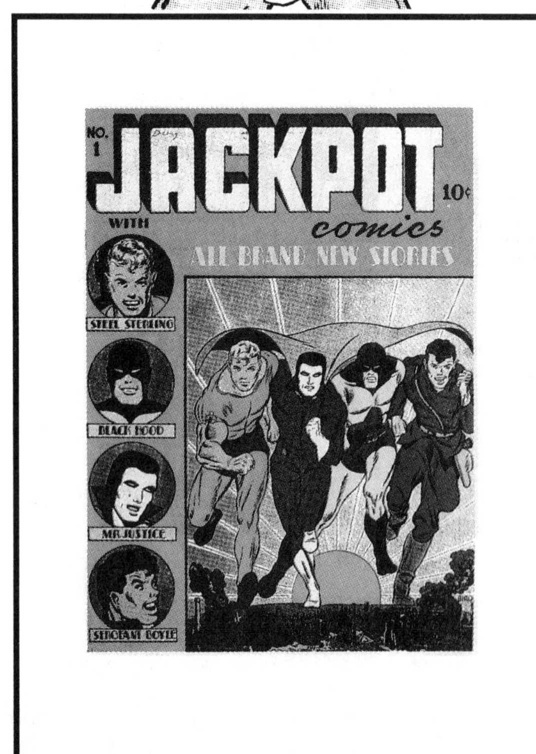

1. THE WIZARD. The Man with the Super-Brain was MLJ's first costumed character, making his debut in *Top-Notch Comics* #1, dated December 1939. (Actually, *Blue Ribbon Comics* first appeared one month earlier, but contained no super-hero until issue #9.) The Wizard must be classified as a super-hero despite the fact that he did not assume his more familiar costume until issue #7. He first appeared in magician-like evening garb, complete with tuxedo, high hat, cape, and mask. However, this outfit was not too appealing, and no doubt the change was made in order to boost the strip's popularity. The addition of Roy, the Super Boy, in *Top-Notch* #11 also added to the strip's popularity. In the earlier issues The Wizard tangled with international spies with an occasional assist from The Shield. Later he and Roy confined their activities for the most part to breaking up domestic crime rings.

2. THE SHIELD. The first of MLJ's real super-heroes was The Shield, G-Man Extraordinary. He was the star of *Pep Comics* from its very first issue (January 1940) until the Archie-type characters finally crowded him out many years later. He, along with The Black Hood, lasted longer than any of MLJ's costumed characters. Blessed with a striking red, white, and blue costume and one of the best illustrators in the business in Irving Novick, The Shield was destined for stardom from the very outset. Indeed, *Pep Comics* was one of America's best-selling comic magazines for a long time. But when the decline came, it came fast, and The Shield was ruined when in a special story in *Pep* #30 his super-powers were taken from him. He was never the same after that. Let it be said to MLJ's credit, however, that it did give The Shield a good initial build-up. Realizing the tremendous popularity of this hero, they quickly proceeded to feature him, along with the new

SHIELD

and rejuvenated Wizard, in a quarterly magazine; thus in the summer of 1940 was born *Shield-Wizard.* Though the comic also featured The Wizard, everyone knew that The Shield was the real star, the prime reason the magazine sold copies. When MLJ revamped *Top-Notch Comics* in mid-1942, The Wizard was dropped; but later, when the "funny" characters took over *Pep Comics*, The Shield remained, vastly degenerated though he was. (EDITOR'S NOTE: A new version of The Shield debuted in 1959, but lasted through only two issues. He now appears only occasionally with The Fly.)

3. STEEL STERLING. Never one of my particular favorites, Steel Sterling was nevertheless one of MLJ's more popular characters. Born in *Zip Comics* #1 (February 1940), he appeared on the cover of every one of that magazine's 47 issues, maintaining a position of prominence until the very end, despite the addition of two other outstanding characters in later issues. (EDITOR'S NOTE: It is rumored that Steel Sterling was forced into an early grave by DC as a Superman-imitator. Can anyone confirm this rumor?) His red and blue costume was simplicity personified, yet somehow appealing. Steel was never blessed with the best of artwork at any time during his career. His original artist, Charles Biro, did some reasonably good work during 1941, but later he began to concentrate his efforts more on *Daredevil*, for another publisher. In late 1942 Biro left MLJ for good, and for the next few years he really turned out some fine Daredevil stories. After Biro's departure, Irving Novick took over the art end of the Steel Sterling strip, but by this time Irv had passed his peak and only for a few issues did he come up with any really good work on the Man of Steel. Yet, despite this apparent handicap of generally mediocre artwork, Steel Sterling prospered, and I suspect that his popularity stemmed mainly from good characterization and better-than-average story plots. Whatever the reason, when the new quarterly magazine *Jackpot Comics* was introduced in the spring of 1941, Steel Sterling was the headline feature, ranking first in the magazine, ahead of even The Black Hood. He maintained that position for as long as the magazine lasted. He outlasted all the other costumed heroes in *Zip Comics*, being the only one left when that magazine folded in 1945.

4. THE BLACK HOOD. Already riding high with the new Wizard, *Top-Notch Comics* became a real leader with the addition of The Man of Mystery in issue #9 (October 1940). (EDITOR'S NOTE: About one year after his appearance in comics, The Black Hood was featured in a pulp magazine entitled *Black Hood Detective Magazine.* This was a rather unique achievement for a hero born of the comic books.) When this terrific new character was introduced, the result was very little short of sensational. MLJ was now approaching its very highest caliber of production. The Black Hood was the crowning masterpiece. His popularity was instantaneous and overwhelming, yet even so it was no accident. Several things attested to the success of this new hero: superb artwork on the part of Al Camy, story-plots far above the standard of the day, and the advent in the very first story of one of the most cunning and diabolical villains in comic book annals, the Skull. Seven times the Dark Knight of Justice came to grips with this insidious fiend, and each story was a corker. But let it be said to MLJ's credit that they did not overdo a good thing, and in *Top-Notch* #19, the Skull received his deserved reward – death in the electric chair. The Black Hood's stories usually bordered a bit on the macabre side, and he battled more of the "weird" type antagonists than any of the other MLJ heroes, except Mr. Justice. Like Steel Sterling, the Man of Darkness was given billing in the new quarterly *Jackpot Comics*, ranking right up behind Sterling in every issue. (EDITOR'S NOTE: Today, The Black Hood, in essentially his original form, has been revived for occasional guest appearances with The Fly.)

5. MR. JUSTICE. No doubt elated by the success of The Black Hood, MLJ decided to go one step farther along this line, and when they introduced Mr. Justice in the February 1941 issue of *Blue Ribbon Comics* (#9), they really went off the deep end. For in the Royal Wraith they now had the ultimate in the weird and fantastic, and they played it to the hilt. Mr. Justice was a spirit, representing, of course, the good element in the world as opposed to every embodiment of evil. In every issue of *Blue Ribbon Comics* and also *Jackpot Comics* he waged a continual war against vampires, werewolves, evil spirits, and demons of all kinds, even to the point of descending to the very depths of Hades at times to do battle with Satan himself. Mr. Justice never attained the intense popularity of The Black Hood, Steel Sterling, and The Shield, but he did have a devoted following during his brief career. (He happened to be my favorite character when I was a young boy.) Naturally, his stories could never pass the Comics Code Authority today, but twenty years ago he was something different and unique. His artist, Sam Cooper, had a flair for the supernatural, and when he took his time he was one of the best MLJ had. I don't know if it was became of the war or poor circulation and low sales, but *Blue Ribbon Comics* folded after the 22nd issue, dated March 1942, leaving Mr. Justice to quarterly appearances in *Jackpot Comics*, where he soon faded into insignificance, both story-wise and in art.

6. THE HANGMAN. By now it had become very evident that what the young comic fan wanted was costumed characters and more of the same, so the editors at MLJ were busy creating one top-flight star after another, yet always coming up with something new and different each time. *Pep Comics* had been including a minor costumed character with somewhat super powers called The Comet. But The Comet was never particularly popular and it was decided to drop him in favor of a new and better mystery man. Yet it was sheer genius on someone's part to inject a very human element into the whole scheme, and as a result something that had never happened before transpired in the July 1941 issue (#17). The Comet was allowed to be killed, and his place was taken by his brother, who vowed a personal vengeance upon all criminals and lawbreakers. And so was born The Hangman, MLJ's newest and one of its best creations form the popularity standpoint. This origin story was written by Cliff Campbell, while many of his later stories were written by Bill Woolfolk. It undoubtedly was the characterization and better-than-average stories that put The Hangman over, because the artwork was, in my opinion, atrocious, the worst of any of MLJ's costumed heroes. (EDITOR'S NOTE: The Hangman strips were handled by several artists: first, George Storm, and later Lucey and King.) Be that as it may, The Hangman proved a great success, and in winter of that same year, 1941, MLJ brought out a quarterly magazine called *Special Comics*, which featured this new character exclusively, and also included special stories of the Boy Buddies, who were none other than Roy, the Super Boy, and Dusty, the Boy Detective, youthful companions of The Wizard and The Shield, respectively. With the second issue, the title of the magazine was changed to *The Hangman Comics*, and it lasted about six or seven issues. Though The Hangman was never one of my particular favorites, I did like his blue and green costume, and I recognize the fact that he was a major factor in the success of the MLJ Magazines, as long as this success lasted. It is worthy of note, however, that he was dropped from the pages of *Pep Comics* long before The Shield.

7. CAPTAIN FLAG. Not too much can be said of this particular character, due to the fact that his stay was so short (only seven months). He was, however, prominently featured while he was around, and I really believe that he was just coming into his own when he was snuffed out of existence. Captain Flag was born in the September 1941 issue of *Blue Ribbon Comics* (#16), and, like The Black Hood, encountered a major foe in his very first adventure, namely, The Black Hand. Four of his seven episodes were struggles with this most worthy antagonist, whom he

finally vanquished for keeps in his very last story (issue #22). Though not a particularly super hero, Captain Flag had a superior origin, very reasonably conceived and worked out, and his costume was a striking combination of red, white, blue, and purple. At first he was accompanied by his American eagle, Yank, who played a major role in the origin story, but who did not appear in the later stories.

8. BLACK JACK. The year 1941 had been a good one, indeed, with all the new stars doing so well. Each of MLJ's four monthly magazines now contained two costumed characters, with the exception of *Zip Comics*, where Steel Sterling was holding out alone. This situation was soon remedied, when in November (issue #20) Black Jack joined the ranks. It was advertised elsewhere that with the addition of Black Jack to a magazine which already contained Steel Sterling, the result was that *Zip Comics* had now become the best comic book in the world! Of course, this was hardly true, but for about a year or so Black Jack did add measurably to the caliber of *Zip Comics*. His stories were above par, and the artwork was by top-notcher Al Camy, who also did The Black Hood. Black Jack's foes were unique in that, like himself, they represented some prominent card or aspect of playing cards, and each was a wily and extremely interesting opponent. Some of the best and most worthy were The Black Seven, Poker Face, The Joker, and The King of Diamonds. The Black Seven and Poker Face each required more than one issue in which to be vanquished. It seems that Black Jack was created fairly close to the beginning of the end, as far as the success of the MLJ costumed characters is concerned, and when in a few months the gradual change-over to the "comic" type character began, he was first subjected to very bad artwork by the likes of "Red" Holmdale and Sam Cooper, and then he was dropped completely.

9. THE WEB. The last of MLJ's attempts at really good costumed heroes, The Web was one of the best for a while. But by the time of his initial appearance (*Zip Comics* #27, July 1942), one magazine (*Blue Ribbon Comics*) had already folded, and evidence of worse things to come could be noted by the careful observer. In fact, it had been previously advertised that The Web was to begin in the July issue of *Top-Notch Comics*. But at the last minute something happened: *Top-Notch Comics* became *Top-Notch Laugh Comics*, featuring Pokey Oakey, The Applejacks, Señor Banana, and such like, and The Web made his debut in *Zip Comics* instead. Nevertheless, as has been previously stated, for a few issues The Web was a very good character with good stories and excellent artwork. (I am sorry to say that I don't know the name of the artist.) However, as has also been pointed out earlier, the caliber of Irving Novick's art had declined to the point that it was difficult to recognize at all. So then when he took over The Web, that was all. I think that probably the most outstanding thing about The Web was his green and yellow costume. Pattered after Daredevil, I admit, but it was still one of the most colorful of any of MLJ's heroes.

There you have them, a star-studded lineup of nine of the most important costumed adventurers of the early and middle 40s, a time when anything could happen, and usually did. These were the leading features of one of the major publishers of the time, and their influence on the comics world as a whole was most certainly felt. Of course there were minor supporting characters, some of which, given the opportunity, could have been equally effective. The best of these were The Firefly, Inferno, The Fox, The Scarlet Avenger, Mr. Satan, Bob Phantom, The Comet, and The Fireball. It is extremely doubtful that any of these old favorites, either major or minor in stature, will ever be restored to their former glory, since MLJ's successors seem content with the promotion of their new heroes, The Fly and The Jaguar. But who can say for certain? Maybe this article will touch off a movement to restore the best of the old MLJ group.

About the cover of* Alter Ego *#5 (March 1963): *The second Foss cover for* AE *featured the Eclipse, Ronn's best-known character from the 1960s. The Eclipse origin represented a noticeable advance in his artistic development, as he brought to bear his excellent design sense, his improving ability to work with pen-and-ink, and a mature approach to characterization that set him apart from most amateurs.*

Editor Foss in his studio in Suisun, California, putting the final touches on the splash page for The Eclipse origin. On the wall in front of him is the cover of Xero 5 *featuring a proposed Atom revival by Larry Ivie.*

Introduction to Alter Ego #5 & #6

by Ronn Foss

I had been a collector of comic books since childhood in the 1940s. A decade later I was busily writing and drawing my own comics with high school buddy Grass Green. We created hundreds, maybe more than a thousand, characters – coincidentally including Supergirl (1953) and Batwoman (1954) – drawn on 3" by 5" cardstock. Many, of course, were "inspired" by established pro characters, like dozens of variations of our favorite hero of the era, Simon and Kirby's Fighting American.

After my discharge from the US Air Force in 1961, and receiving my first issue of Alter-Ego *(#2), I contributed strips and illustrations to early comic fanzines like Don Dohler's* Wild, *Ron Haydock's* Skybird, *Steve Gerber's* Headline, *and Parley Holman's* Spotlite.

Jerry and Roy's Alter-Ego *became the most widely circulated zine, due in part to their "insider" contact with Julius Schwartz. Grass and I did the cover for #4, featuring a drawing of the Alley Award statuette that I'd designed. (I crafted dozens of Alley trophies over the next three years, winning two of them myself in the 1963 poll for "Best Fan Artist" and "Best Illustrated Strip" for The Eclipse.)*

When I wrote Jerry that I planned to do my own fanzine, he suggested I take over AE *and* The Comicollector *from him instead. I agreed that it would be easier to continue well-established titles, rather than starting from scratch, especially in view of all the other zines being initiated at that time (which spread the knowledgeable writers much thinner).*

He had always printed AE *on standard 8 ½" by 11" paper, so I decided to try something closer to comic book size, with wrap-around binding. In the end, I had to settle for 8 ½" by 14" folded on #5. Financial considerations forced me to collate and staple all 1,000 copies myself, because I'd spent the budget on the first full four-color cover.*

Another change, albeit minor, was the omission henceforth of the hyphen in the magazine's title. This was simply a matter of editorial preference.

The lay-out of Alter Ego *was of paramount importance to me. I added more and varied artwork, and photos (there were ten screened images in #5 alone), often in an effort to put a face on the potentially "faceless" contributors. I was naturally eager to continue publishing work by Roy Thomas, Jerry Bails, Ed Lahmann, and others who had earned* AE *its unparalleled reputation for excellence, and was pleased to introduce the art of Biljo White into its pages.*

By this time, letters arrived from fans in Europe, South Africa and Australia, making AE *international. On a firmer footing, the sixth issue was published 10" by 14" size, for the folded comic book size of 7" by 10." In that issue, more letters from industry professionals appear in* AE*'s pages (including the only one from Stan Lee), as well as artwork by Russ Manning, Steve Ditko, and Curt Swan.*

Meanwhile, I was traveling around the country, meeting other collectors. My wanderings took me to get-togethers with Biljo White in Missouri, Glen Johnson in New Mexico, and the Texas Trio in the Lone Star state. The biggest "fan meet" for me was the Alley Tally Party at Jerry Bails' house in 1964, which was attended by nineteen enthusiasts. I came costumed as my second-favorite serial hero (after Flash Gordon) – Rocketman.

Much as I enjoyed the Alter Ego *experience, all the time-consuming work that goes into publishing kept me from the drawing board. Since my true ambition was to create original comics, I offered the reins of* Alter Ego *to Biljo White and Roy Thomas. Fortunately they accepted – and continued* AE *in grand manner.*

R.F.

[illo by Mike Vosburg]

Initially, the plan had been for three fans known as "Triad" to carry on the publication of Alter-Ego *and* The Comicollector. *It is doubtful that Ronn Foss would have agreed to edit and publish both fanzines if his young wife Myra and long-time friend Grass Green hadn't offered their help. Unfortunately, Ronn's marriage would end in the summer of 1962, and Green's contributions consisted of lots of artwork, but little assistance in the more mundane aspects of publishing. Putting out* The Comicollector *involved typing page after page of number-laden advertisements, and maintaining subscription files that included hundreds of addresses. This sort of thing would never be Grass' forte. Thus, Foss was left to plan* Alter Ego *#5 on his own, while issuing* The Comicollector *on a bi-monthly schedule, beginning with #7 in September 1962.*

In the pages of CC *#8, Foss introduced Joy Holiday as a sort of female mascot for fandom. Her name, suggested by the Christmas season when she received her name (in a contest where she might have been called Fannie Fandom – a runner-up suggestion), became synonymous with the "spirit of comicdom" – and her red and green costume was filled by three women.*

The first to don the makeshift costume and pose for photographs was Linda Rahm. A tiny snapshot of her appeared in Alter Ego *#5; fans would have to wait for the following issue to see a somewhat larger, and considerably more enticing, picture as a header for the letter column. In the future, Ronn's sister Beverly Ann would pose as Joy (though never in the pages of* AE*), and Roy's friend Pauline Copeman would become the most photographed of the three, appearing in #7-9. Each of these attractive young women endowed Joy Holiday with charms beyond the scope of any line drawing, though Ronn (whose ability to draw the female form was undeniable) did his best in the pages of* The Comicollector *and* Dateline: Comicdom. *Fandom, being predominantly male (as it is today), found something else to enjoy in the pages of America's leading comics fanzines.*

Through the fall of 1962, Foss worked to cast Alter Ego *into the format he envisioned. He designed a beautiful new logo for the magazine, at last finding a way to marry the title lettering with the mask image. This logo design was retained for the remainder of non-professional issues of* AE.

Foss would establish the amateur comic strip (apart from parody, such as the BLA) as a staple of Alter Ego, *devoting ten of #5's thirty-six pages to The Eclipse. "Dru Moroz and I met as most collectors do; via the mail," he wrote in 1963. "Within just a few letters, I noticed that he wrote with a 'flair' and exuberance of one who really enjoys writing." Before long, they were collaborating on the origin of the "Master of the Midnight Hours." Foss hoped the exposure this comic strip would receive would help him find work at DC or Marvel. (It didn't happen that way, though the reasons are many. Ultimately, Ronn chose to pursue art endeavors outside of mainstream comics, where more variety was available, and one need not move to New York City.) Nevertheless, The Eclipse was quite popular in fan circles (winning an Alley Award), and opened the door for strip-oriented fan magazines like* Star-Studded Comics *and* Fantasy Illustrated.

Can you imagine a time when fans weren't sure which Golden Age comics were worth collecting? In this era before indexes and price guides, in a time when there was no comprehensive source for information about the comics field of the 1940s, Alter Ego *leapt into the breech. In retrospect, Ed Lahmann's "So – You Want To Collect Comics?" may make us smile ... or raise some eyebrows, when one realizes the cost and difficulty involved in amassing the "starter set" that Ed blithely prescribes in this piece. (Although, strangely, Quality Comics was accidentally overlooked.) It's included here just for fun ... and to provide a look back to a much different time.*

Ron Haydock's "SERIALously Speaking" column, highlighting the exciting movie serials of a bygone era, made an appearance in each of Ronn's AE issues, focusing on the dynamic Rocketman in two parts.

Foss introduced two teenaged artists to the pages of Alter Ego: *Alan Weiss, a 14-year-old Las Vegas fan, and Mike Vosburg, who was already making a mark with his fanzine* Masquerader. *Both went on to enjoy successful careers in pro comics. 'Voz' was already fast friends with Ronn, and they have remained close to the present day.*

A pair of fannish articles were presented in Alter Ego *#5. "The Mystery of Fandom" by Stan Woolston, the first reprint in* AE *(taken from the pages of Ron Haydock and Larry Byrd's fanzine* Escape *#1), attempted to analyze the appeal of fan activity, from fanzine publishing to collecting. In "The Future of Fandom – Unlimited!" by "Dr. Jerry Bails, Ph.D.,"* AE*'s founder suggested numerous subjects for articles on costumed heroes.*

Also in this issue was an article by the pseudonymous "F. T. Frost" (with art by Biljo White) entitled "The JLA – Overcrowded?" Rounding out the issue was a full-page Bestest League of America pin-up by Roy Thomas, and a list of recommended fanzines that included fifteen *titles. Comics fandom was growing by leaps and bounds!*

The Editors

SO – YOU WANT TO COLLECT COMICS?

By Ed Lahmann

Occasionally, within my regular comic correspondence of trades and sales, I get a letter from a young fan (or perhaps I should say new collecting enthusiast) who wants to know what kind of comics to start with to form a good, solid collection.

Well, many rabid fans collect everything they can, while others concentrate only on certain titles, runs of comics, first editions, and/or special issues, and so forth.

I myself concentrate on first issues and origin stories, as well as any and all Flash Gordon material. I understand Jerry Bails is one of the few who has the complete run of *All-Star Comics*. Ray Miller is interested in comics of the World War Two era, and Biljo White is a solid fan of Batman and Flash Gordon, while our editor delves into the works of Joe Kubert and Simon and Kirby.

My intention here is to put together a basic list to give the new collector some idea of what comprises a well-rounded collection. The books in this list are not necessarily the rarest of the rare, but are nonetheless surely collector's items. I've tried to pick by title the particular issue number in which time it was at its peak.

Since the National line is perhaps the most popular, we'll start with them, and certainly the biggest name from DC is Superman, so we'll take him first. He was at his peak in the latter part of 1939, so here's what to look for:

Superman #2 – This was the best issue.
Action #15 through 20 – Any one of these.

So now you have two books in your collection and are on your way. Now let's go to The Batman and the rest of the National line...

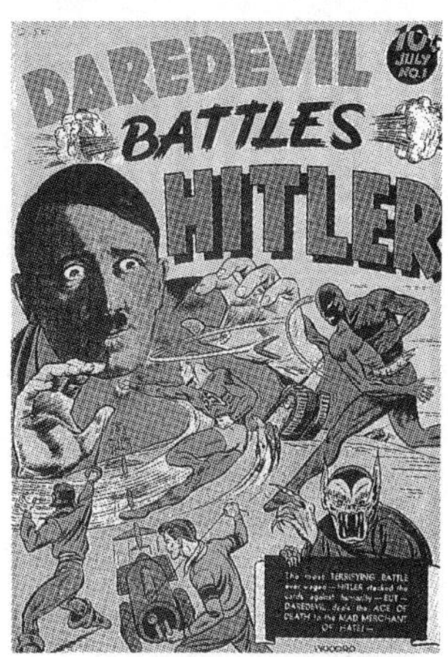

Batman #4 – Easier to get than the earlier ones, and has some fine art by Bob Kane; some of his best.
Detective #33 through 37 – May be hard to find but good examples of Batman before the time of Robin.

For both Batman and Superman let's pick up a copy of *World's Fair 1940*. It'll be hard to find but that's half the interest in collecting. That makes five books and we're beginning to take a little shape.

Adventure #61 through 69 – The transition period in this title line. Any one of these will do.
More Fun #78 through 82 – Easier to find than the old goodies and has more costumed heroes. Just one now.

Now let's go to that favorite among collectors, that gem of a comic, *All-Star*. Pick out a couple of these from the following:

All-Star #10 through 20 – Just two now; we have to make room for...
Star-Spangled #15 through 20 – Let's start here for some of that Simon and Kirby material. One to a customer, please.

Boy Commandos #1 and 2 – If at all possible try to find both of these classics – S&K at their very best.
All-American #5 through 10 – One of these. We'll get Green Lantern in his own mag.
Flash #1 through 10 – Two of these would be nice; good luck.
Green Lantern #1 through 7 – All good; get as many as you can.
Sensation – Any one of these first ten issues would suffice. (Ahem!)

Now, to pick up any loose ends in the National line-up, get a copy of the *Big All-American* – and if you don't have any luck, one of the first five issues of *Comic Cavalcade* will do.

This brings us to the Fawcett group... you know, Capt. Marvel and his gang. While we're about it, we may as well start with the Big Red Cheese himself. It'll be nigh impossible to find his origin story (*Whiz* #1), so we'll just have to do the best we can.

Whiz #5 through 10 – These will be tough to find. #15 through 20 is your next best bet; just one.
Master #1 through 6 – Here's your toughest test. This was a large, outsize comic; if you can even find somebody who's got one, consider yourself lucky. Just one.
Nickel #1 through 6 – Another oddball; just one now.

Another tough one is the *Special Edition Comics* with Capt. Marvel; this is the first full-length book of the Captain. Other Fawcetts to try for are:

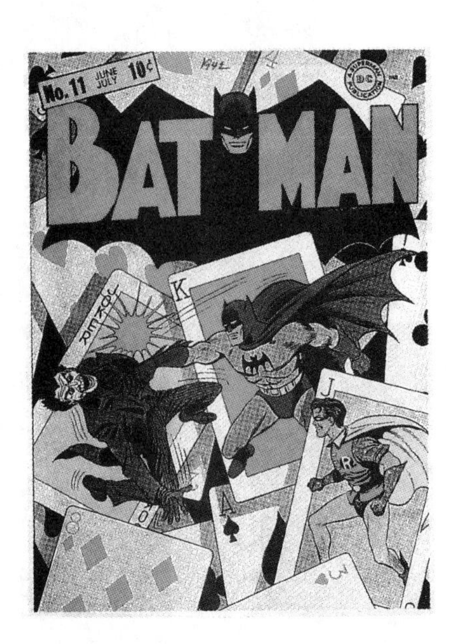

Captain Midnight, Don Winslow, Wow, Slam-Bang, America's Greatest, and *Capt. Marvel Jr.* Try for one issue of each of these titles.

Now is a timely time to get Timely; or, shall we collect a few Timely comics?

Capt. America #1 through 10 – More Simon and Kirby. Be careful, though; these two gave up ol' Cap after issue #10. Only one of these is needed, but you'll probably want more after seeing it.
Human Torch #1 through 6 – Just one; they're too hot to handle.
Marvel Comics #1 through 20 – Try to get at least 4 or 5 of these, and if possible get issues 7 through 10.
All-Winners #2 through 6 – One of these will be doing good.
Sub-Mariner #1 through 3 – Any one; just one.

Onward to another publishing company now; we don't want to corner the market in any one area. Let's see – who do we take next.... How about Fox? As you know, Fox put out *The Blue Beetle.* I didn't know foxes cavorted with the insect world except for fleas. There wasn't a comic called *The Blue Flea,* was there? I wouldn't be surprised.... Back to business:

Mystery Men #10 through 15 – No trouble here and you only need one of them.
Fantastic #5 through 10 – Just one.
Wonderworld #15 through 20 – The Flame stars here and he's similar to the Torch. One will do nicely.
Blue Beetle #1 through 7 – Get a couple if you can; this wasn't a bad character and they're not too hard to find.

That's enough of the Fox line to have in any collection unless you decided to collect Foxes. Now, let's move over to the Centaur outfit. This will be an easy one to cover for me, as in my eyes they only had just one good magazine – but it was a dan-dan-dandy!!

Amazing-Man #1 through 10 – A lot of the big writers and artists got their start with this comic. Real good Bill Everett art, one of the pioneers. Get all you can.

MLJ had a lot of good comics. The basic ones needed for a well-rounded collection:

Black Hood #9 through 15 – Get two of these since it was MLJ's best character.
Hangman #5 through 8 – These had the Bob Fuje art and it's a must in any collection. Try for 2 or 3.
Top-Notch #1 through 5 – The original Wizard. Get one; that's all.
Pep #5 through 9 – The Comet's in here, get one.
Zip #1 through 10 – One's enough.
Blue Ribbon #10 through 15 – The imitation Spectre, Mr. Justice – and it's a crime to have more than one.
Jackpot – A challenge here. Try for the first issue, a fine Black Hood story.
Shield-Wizard – Another task is at hand. Again I say try for the first issue, but settle for any of the first five.

Now, we'll go over to Novelty Press and pick up a few tidbits. Novelty published *Target* and *Blue Bolt* in volumes; 12 issues to a volume. We'll try to get as many of the first volume as possible:

Target Vol. 1 #1 through 12 – Get many.
Blue Bolt Vol 1 #1 through 12 – Ditto.

I've always got an ace up my sleeve and this is it: Ace Publications.

Super-Mystery #1 through 10 – Just one here.
Lightning #1 through 10 – Settle for one but try for two of these.
Four Favorites #3 through 7 – Just one now; leave some for the others. You're not the only one reading this, are you? I sure hope not... bet Ronn does, too!
Banner #1 – Here's another toughie. There was just one issue of this; or so it seems. If you get more than just the first issue, contact Raymond Miller; he's been looking for a long time.
Our Flag #1 through 6 – Just one of these.

I've played my ace and now it's time for staking the house: Fiction House, that is. I'm not a gambler and you can make book on that.

Planet #5 through 10 – Very valuable and not easy to come by, so just go for one of these.
Jungle #10 through 100 – All good, not much difference. Easy to come by from #50 on. Get a handful; say 5 or 6.

Jumbo #10 through 15 – Only one of these; we'll get Sheena in her own book. Nice!
Sheena #1 through 5 – If you're lucky enough, you might just get one of these. If you can find more, get 'em.
Fight #7 through 15 – Shouldn't be too difficult to get one.
Wing #7 through 15 – Same as above.
Rangers #15 through 25 – Try for this one; Firehair, and she's hot-headed.

Now we take leave of Fiction House and head for Family Comics. Now, that's a paradox: leaving the house to see the family. Oh well, anything can happen in the comics. Let's start with the Blue Beetle's cousin, The –

Green Hornet #10 through 15 – Don't get stung on this one; they're not hard to come by and shouldn't cost too much. Get two.
Pocket Comics – Another oddball; get one if you can find it.
Champ #2 through 6 – Early and may be hard to locate; try one.
Speed #1 through 5 – Get one of these, and try for the small pocket-sized *Speed.*
Black Cat #1 through 10 – She's back now but try to pick up one of the old ones – she was a doll.
Stuntman #1 through 5 – More Simon and Kirby, though not as good as Boy Commandos. Settle for one; that's sufficient.

We're really getting a collection together now, but here comes the hard part... the odds and ends – the fill-ins; all that is needed to round out the effort and make the collection one worthy of any collector to have. These books will be hard to find, much less get, but it can be done. For the most part, these are the transplanted newspaper strips needed to supplement a true comic collection:

King #1 through 20 – Any 3 of these; rough.
Ace #70 through 90 – Not too hard; try for 5.
Tip Top #30 through 50 – Pretty tough; get 3.
Famous Funnies #89 through 95 – Rare, but around; try 2.
Popular #55 through 75 – You should be able to get six of these.
The Funnies #55 through 60 – Just one here.
Crackajack #28 through 35 – You'll have work getting this one.
Buck Rogers #4, 5, or 6 – Just one.
Mandrake Feature Book #46 – Not too hard.
Prince Valiant Feature Book #26 – Impossible, but try anyway.

The same applies to the next two as with Prince Valiant...

Flash Gordon 4-Color Comic #10
Tarzan Single Series #20

Also recommended by me are these, all Single Series –

Joe Jinks #12
Looy Dot Dope #13
Jim Hardy #27

To cap it off we'll stop with the one that got it all started:

Okay Comics #1, featuring one of the three original comic-strip creations: The Capt. and the Kids, by Rudolph Dirks.

And there it is, you would-be collectors: an idea of what to put together for a well-rounded collection of comic art. And to gain knowledge of what's behind this collection, I suggest you go to your public library and study Steve Becker's book entitled *Comic Art in America.* This book will show you what an institution the comics really are; pure Americana.

I hope you find this guide helpful, and I wish you the best of luck in collecting. May you enjoy them as I have.

Photo and excerpts from "Portrait of a Collector" in Alter Ego *#6.*

ED LAHMANN

"I was born in Indianapolis and, except for an interlude of three years in the Army, have lived here all my life. My interest in comics goes back to the early thirties. I had a cousin who subscribed to *Famous Funnies* at the time, and I can remember at any early age asking dad to buy me 'the books like funny papers.' I was eight years old when he finally got me my first comic book; it was the third issue of *Superman.*

"I wrote a letter to DC which appeared in *Brave and Bold* #36, and because of it I have met through the mails and in person some of the finest people I've ever known.

"At thirty-two I figure my best years are still ahead, but the ones gone have already given me more than my share; I consider myself fortunate to have been part of the passing parade."

– Ed Lahmann

One fateful evening, serologist Dr. Craig Pierce stumbles across a desperate robbery-in-progress in the hospital laboratory where he works.

The criminals have murdered his colleague, and Pierce refuses to divulge the combination to the safe, which contains the radium they seek.

With police sirens in the background, the frustrated thugs flee – but not before setting an explosion to kill the only witness to their misdeeds ....

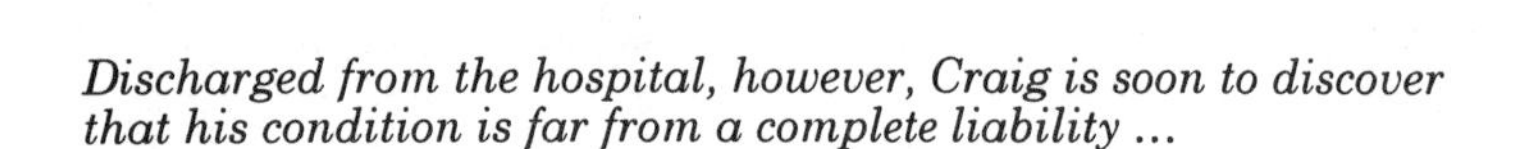

Discharged from the hospital, however, Craig is soon to discover that his condition is far from a complete liability ...

"The molecules of my body," he writes, "seem to be under almost complete control of my will, and by an 'expansion' of my solid-passing capabilities, I can will my molecules to disperse and remain so wide apart that I am, in effect, invisible! But, my powers are valid only under the influence of darkness – light, in fact, cancels them out completely!"

Pierce decides to use his special abilities to become a crime fighter. He restores his daylight vision by devising special infra-red glasses, and designs a special costume to shield his identity.

Using his weapon which emits a pure opaque blackness, the Eclipse quickly subdues the criminals, and delivers them to the authorities ... thus announcing the emergence of a new defender of Crescent City – not that everything *would go smoothly for Craig Pierce ...*

This comic strip is reprinted in full in Fandom's Finest Comics *(Hamster Press, 1997). See advertisement on pages 190-1.*

Portrait of a COLLECTOR

In his second issue of *Komix Illustrated*, Biljo White introduced a series entitled "Profile on Collectors" which became an instant success and has been nominated for the 1962 Alley Awards. This feature, a brief but concise biography of comic collectors with accompanying illustration of the individuals, has given us all a better knowledge and appreciation of the correspondents we deal with. Knowing Biljo, he'd never to a profile on himself – so I'd like to "borrow" his concept for this issue; and who would be better than Capt. Biljo himself. Perhaps, with his permission, *AE* could continue with this series each issue... I myself would like to see one on the "Femmes in Fandom."

Biljo is 33 years old, has been married 9½ years, has one daughter, Sunday Elizabeth, 2½ years old. He lives with his family in a ranch-type house in the country just outside Columbia, Missouri. He was born and educated in the country. After high school, he continued to draw and write stories. Bill has been drawing "strips" since he was a little fella. The first ones were very crude but clever, and one could see that he had a lot of talent. He has collected various comics since 1939, but went into collecting "full-time" in 1955. His favorite collection is Batman and Robin. His favorite artist is Bob Kane. I don't think any one artist influences his style – he claims his style is his own, as do most artists.

Biljo served with the U.S. Army for 2 years. Most of this time was spent in Germany. During these 2 years he had a cartoon strip called "The New Bunch" in the Division newspaper.

Back in the states, he married and settled down. He was working for the Columbia Fire Department at the time, and in his spare time he continued to draw and write stories. Here he created a strip about the guys around the fire house.

Later, he decided to go into the art field, and was employed with a department store chain in Portland, Oregon. When our daughter, Julio Jo, was stricken with Meningitis and died, we were far from home and very unhappy and lonesome for friends. We moved back to Columbia. He was re-appointed to the Columbia Fire Department. Since then, he has been collecting comics, magazines, etc., drawing and writing – anything to keep busy since Julio Jo's death. We now have another daughter who is little Biljo. Maybe she will grow up to be a cartoonist, too.

Among the many hobbies of Biljo, he has up-to-date scrapbooks on sporting events. I believe boxing is his favorite sport, then football. He watches all main events on TV when possible. He also has scrapbooks on all available space information, especially the astronauts.

He enjoys the fanzines. He enjoyed doing *Komix Illustrated* while it lasted, but with so many things "in the fire," something had to go. Maybe this will only be temporary. He tries to keep his correspondence up to date and spends hours answering his many letters. Besides all his hobbies, etc., he manages to be a fine father to his daughter and a good husband. He loves to spend time with his family and likes to putter around the few acres of woods near here. He's a great one in the kitchen, too – his pizza is better than mine and his tuna salad is great. He is very modest and will probably brain me for bragging on him.

Sincerely,

Ruthie White
Mrs. Biljo

[Logo/lettering by Foss]

by RON HAYDOCK

A DISTANT THUNDER OF ROCKET MEN!

He shot through the stratosphere like a guided missile, this steel-helmeted man of tomorrow, garbed in a brown leather flying jacket, trailing showers of sparks and clouds of atomic smoke. His burnished helmet masked his features, but the eyes of the world were fastened on him, blinking with the knowledge that here was an antagonist of evil the likes of which had never before been witnessed.

Republic Pictures titled him "King of the Rocket Men," the hero of a 1949 serial that was destined to be the forerunner of a series of epics featuring this crimefighting and cosmic-flying cinema champion, known to the world only as Rocket Man.

The imaginative rocket suit itself, donned by this spectacular serial hero, was destined to become a popular topic for cliffhanger discussions.

Tristram Coffin was the first of the three actors to sport the bullet-like helmet, leather-jacket-with-rocket-pack-on-the-back costume, starring as Jeff King, a member of Science Associates, introduced to the flying rig by its inventor, Prof. Millard (James Craven).

"King of the Rocket Men" concerns himself with a mad scientist named Vulcan (I. Stanford Jolley), who is after the secrets of certain world-shaking inventions being created by the men at Science Associates. One of these is the Decimator, a powerful apparatus capable of disintegrating anything, or anybody, within a radius of 200 miles. It is Jeff King's pledge to counter Vulcan's every plot.

But though King as Rocket Man shoots throughout the length and breadth of the 12 chapters, with a ready fist at the sight of another Vulcan attempt at the inventions, the insidious scientist successfully manages to steal away the Decimator and install it at his private island off the coast of New York.

Vulcan sends an ultimatum to the mayor of New York City, threatening complete annihilation unless a billion-dollar ransom is paid. The mayor shakes his head woefully, and Rocket Man, in a smashing climax, blasts through the atmosphere and into Vulcan's island hideout. A free-swinging battle with Vulcan and his thugs ensues. However, unknown to them is the fact that American bombers have been dispatched to blow the entire island off the face of the Earth. Even as Rocket Man and his foes toss chairs at each other, the planes with their devastating cargo are nearing their destination.

Rocket Man catches an earful of the bombers' drones, and realizes his plight. Quickly adjusting the over-simplified dials on his rocket suit to ON and UP and Like a Bat Out of Hell, he zooms out of the hideout and rockets to safety.

Fortunately, the same cannot be said for Vulcan and his gang. Completely at a loss for words when the bombs fall, Vulcan sees his plans for world domination go up in a burst of cinema glory, along with himself and his nefarious aides.

New York City has been saved, and Vulcan's reign of terror has showered its last, thanks to the courage and daring of Rocket Man – and the American bombers.

In 1951, Republic re-released this episodic film in a feature-length version, under the title "Lost Planet Airmen." During this same year, the famed serial studio also released the second of their Rocket Man chapterplays, "Radar Men from the Moon," with George Wallace starring as Commando Cody, Sky Marshal of the Universe.

"Commando Cody," according to the Ronald Davidson script, "is an able young scientist who is making rapid strides in the development of a flying suit and a rocketship, the last of which will propel him to the moon."

We see here that Republic created a new serial "character," built around the much-acclaimed rocket suit originally worn by Jeff King.

"Moon Rocket," chapter 1 of "Radar Men," discloses that our national defenses are being sabotaged by mysterious blasts. A government official jets to Cody with this alarming bit of news, and Cody rockets out to get to the bottom of this troublesome business. He immediately swoops over two thugs who are preparing to blast a troop train with their atomic gun. The Sky Marshal drops down behind them, wheels one of the do-badders around, and deals him a crushing blow. Cody reaches out again, and spins the other, utterly dumbstruck at the sight of the henchman's features.

"It can't be!" Cody is heard to exclaim. "But it is – The Lone Ranger!"

The second villain is portrayed by none other than Clayton Moore, stalwart companion of the life-saving Tonto. And Cody realizes that for some unfathomable reason the Early West's fearless champion of justice has turned crooked.

"There's only one thing to do with a good guy who goes bad," Cody thinks.

He immediately slugs Moore in the belly.

Through devious means, both thugs escape Cody, but leaving their atomic gun in their treacherous tracks. Cody rockets back to the lab with the weapon, and analyzes the element used therein. By clever scientific deduction, the Sky Marshal concludes that this unknown ingredient can only be found on the moon – of all places.

Cody blasts through space in his sleek rocketship, and drops to the moon to discover a huge, walled-in city governed by Retik (Big Bad Roy Barcroft), the Ruler of the Moon, who is conducting an all-out campaign to conquer our world. From here on in, Cody faces mortal destruction at every turn in his quest to abdicate Retik from the Luna throne and save our planet: he is blasted by a ray pistol, and disappears in a chapter-ending puff of smoke; he is tossed bodily from a cliff; a Moon Man forces him backwards into an electronics switch panel where he is (evidently but not actually, as you may have guessed) electrocuted; and in yet another episode, Retik zips a nuclear ray gun at our helmeted hero, disabling his air supply, leaving him to suffocate in the rarefied atmosphere of our nearest planetary neighbor.

Fantastic weapons, pretentious action, and foolish carryings-on were the keynotes of "Radar Men," so very much unlike the fine piece of serial footage that was "King," the original.

Serialously Speaking

was created and is written by Ron Haydock, editor of the pro mag *Fantastic Monsters*. *FanMo*, as it is called, is the top quality monster mag in the field. It features not only superior writing and photos, color, a full-size fold-out, and assorted items, but also covers comic heroes! *FanMo* #3 (out now) has a spread on the Blackhawk and Flash Gordon serials; #4 will feature Superman, written by Kirk Alyn, who played him in the screen version; #5 will have Spy-Smasher. If *FanMo* isn't on your local newsstands, write: Jackie Blaisdell, c/o FanMo, Topanga, Calif. Current copies are 50¢; back issues $1.00. (#2 featured Capt. Marvel.)

In *AE* #6 Part 2 of Rocket Man – versus Zombies of the Stratosphere! Until then, read Ron's review of the super-hero serial in *Comicollector* #10: "The Black Commando"!

There were no photos of Ron available as this issue went to press, but you can let him know what you think of his efforts by writing him at: 2771 San Marino, Los Angeles 6, Calif.

READERS WRITE

EDITOR'S NOTE: All the following letters except the one from Carmine Infantino were sent to Jerry Bails, who forwarded them to me.

Carmine Infantino

Thank you for your kind interest in me and my work. I find your magazine a delight and a memory awakener. As for my work and how I approach a story, I will try to explain as best I can.

I begin first by reading the script through so I can get a "feel" of the characters and situations. Once I have established who and what I am to illustrate, I then collect my reference – an important area, since our modern readers are ready to reproach you for the slightest error and it gives the story a credibility not had any other way. I then draw very roughly the entire page – in this method I try to get a "flow" to the action. Once I am satisfied with the action I then go back and make tight finished pencil drawings which are then given to either Mr. Anderson or Mr. Giella and they proceed to make them look good. When inking myself I use a combination pen and brush – I think the above gentlemen use the same method.

My idols of yesteryear were and still are Hal Foster and Milton Caniff; in my opinion they are the giants.

I do hope this note has answered some of your questions. Again, thank you for your kind interest and much success with your fine publication.

Sincerely,
Carmine Infantino

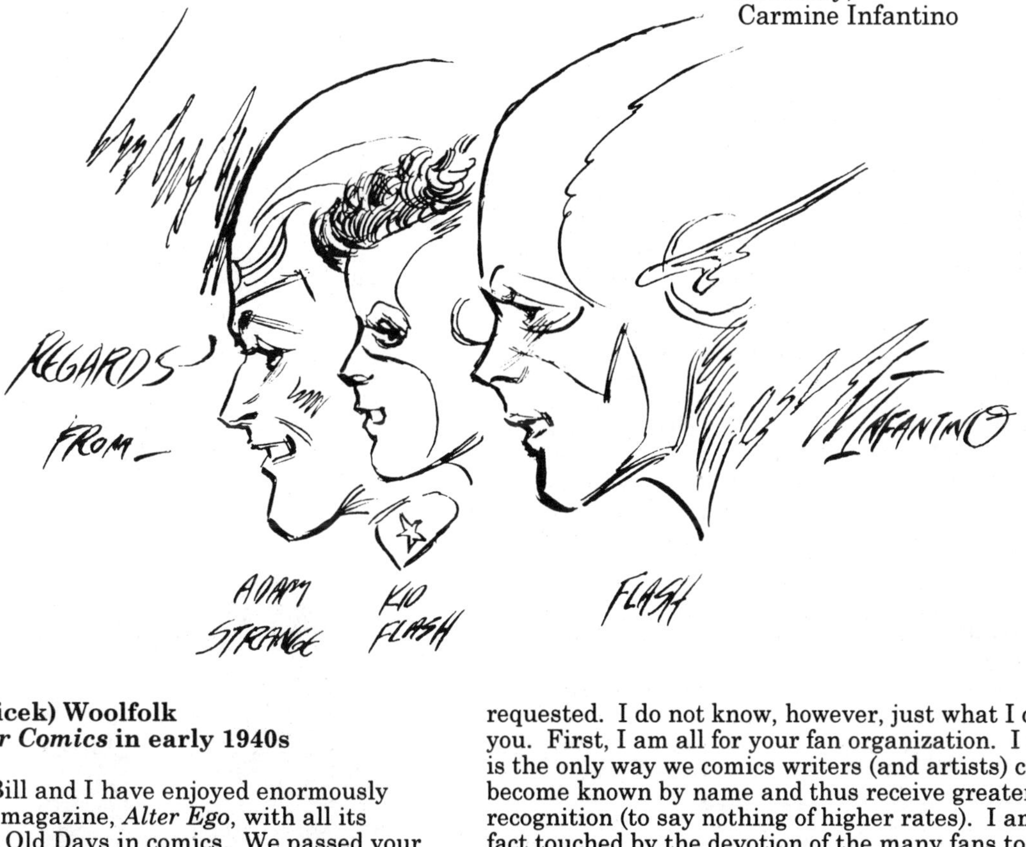

REGARDS FROM— INFANTINO

ADAM STRANGE
KID FLASH
FLASH

Dorothy (Roubicek) Woolfolk
Editor: *All-Star Comics* in early 1940s

My husband Bill and I have enjoyed enormously reading your fan magazine, *Alter Ego*, with all its news of the Good Old Days in comics. We passed your last issue along to Wendell Crowley – he used to edit *Captain Marvel*, remember? – and he was most enthusiastic about it, too. He's married to Dagny Weste, who used to work up at Fawcett Publications as a secretary in the editorial department when he was editor, and they have three children. Their oldest was born on Capt. Marvel's birthday, Feb. 29th. No, they didn't name it Shazam. Lots of luck in the switch-over of editorial jurisdiction.

John Broome

It was very gratifying to learn that I had been one of the recipients of the 1961 Awards in comics, and I am only too glad to let you hear from me as you requested. I do not know, however, just what I can tell you. First, I am all for your fan organization. I feel it is the only way we comics writers (and artists) can become known by name and thus receive greater recognition (to say nothing of higher rates). I am in fact touched by the devotion of the many fans to comics and in particular by your sturdy attitude over the past few years. Personally I have labored hard over almost everything I have ever written in comics, and naturally, it is pleasing to know that some of the things were liked. For this, many thanks.

When you speak of a larger, more stable, and older following to come, I certainly hope you turn out to be an expert prognosticator. If you do turn out to be right, you will be able to lay claim to being a seer and clairvoyant of no mean talent yourself.

Again thanks for the encouragement that your letter and the awards mean to us hard-pressed comics writers. Some day we may attain a certain legitimacy and if we do we will know who was responsible for our change of station.

Gardner F. Fox

I am tickled a lovely shade of purple-pink by the receipt in the mails of the Alley Award for **1961**! Many, many thanks to you and to the voters who awarded it to me. I'll try to live up to it.

I repaired my Alley with epoxy glue (I am a military miniature collector and convert many of the lead soldiers into different postures for painting, hence the epoxy glue) and am about to repair the Alley for Julie Schwartz.

It may interest you to know – or perhaps you already know – that the Jerry Thomas in the *JLA* "Cavern of Deadly Spheres" story was a borrowing of your first name and Roy's last – as a fan of the JLA. Since there are so many fans with artistic and creative talents around, we sort of unofficially dedicated this issue to you and them.

Again, many thanks. My Alley has an honored spot on my – on *one* of my bookcases, that is – in such a position that I can see it as I type.

I will miss your fine touch on *Alter Ego*, but as you can guess, I wish Ronn Foss all the best with his future issues.

It was indeed unfortunate that many of the award trophies became broken in the course of mailing. This year, I hope to have something more durable in the form of Alley Oop statuettes. It has been suggested that all interested readers donate 1¢; this is impractical, since it would cost a 5¢ stamp to get it to me – however, I certainly won't refuse any contributions to this worthy cause. While I'm at it, I'd like to express my gratitude on behalf of all comic fandom for the recognition shown our efforts in the notice of the Alley Awards which appeared in *JLA* #18 and *Flash* #135.

Paul Gambaccini
8 Elizabeth Dr.
Westport, Connecticut

Your last *AE* is the best of all; however, *AE* doesn't seem like *AE* without the BLA. So you see, *AE* #4 left something to be desired. Also, there was no letter column, unfortunately... this took some of the life out of the issue. What there was was good. Roy Thomas' conduction of the ACBAS [Academy of Comic Book Arts and Sciences] results was dignified, not spectacular as some enthusiastic reporters might have written. Keltner's MLJ article was very good; whoever reproduced the illos and photo of *Jackpot* #5 did a fine job. This type of article is very valuable for new collectors as I am, and I hope to see more on other companies when Ronn Foss takes over *AE*. L.L. Simpson's "Hall of Infamy" was the best article in the issue... entertaining, informative, and humorous – a rare combination for zine writing. Grateful for four great issues.

There'll be a letter col from now on, Paul; and next issue, Roy's BLA meets the Frantic 4. Also another fine L.L. Simpson "Hall of Infamy."

Bruce Pelz
738 S. Mariposa, Apt. 107
Los Angeles 5, California

The 7th issue (of *Comicollector*) showed up last week, completely flabbergasting me with the unexpected size and activity of comic fandom. I hadn't realized the provincialism of SF fandom in thinking comic fandom was one of its offshoots, along with such things as monster fandom. In a number of ways, comic fandom *is* an offshoot of SF fandom – the borrowed phraseology, for one thing.... but for the most part it appears to be a fandom to itself. There are, of course, the double-fandom fans such as Lupoff, Don Thompson, Robert Jennings, and the ones who are fans of one fandom and shadow-fans of the other (myself for one).

I didn't have much chance to take pictures of the JSA at the con, as the Dr. Fate mask made me leave my glasses in my room, but I did take four of our local entries, and will take several more when the LA Science-Fantasy Society holds its Halloween party this coming weekend. I can promise pix of Wonder Woman, Green Lantern, Dr. Fate, Flash ... *AE* is welcome to the publication rights.

In *AE* #6, read Bruce's write-up on the Chicago SF con, with photos of the aforementioned JSA-ers. Till then, below are Dick & Pat Lupoff ... as you-know-who!

Richard Kyle
152 East 23rd St.
Long Beach 6, California

AE #4 is a completely marvelous job. If Ronn Foss can come up with any kind of an approximation of it, I'll be well satisfied. The amateurishness that creeps into amateur magazines is virtually absent here. This is unquestionably one of the best looking amateur magazines that I have ever seen, and it is far more pleasing in appearance than **90** per cent of the professional magazines on the stands. You have every reason to be proud, Jerry.

Foss & Green's cover is excellent; the color and Ben Day are very effectively handled.

[Dick and Pat Lupoff at the 1960 World SF Convention in Pittsburgh.]

Harry Thomas' heading for the contents page is clever and amusing, and the layout and type would be hard to improve upon. I agree completely about the Alley Awards for '61, but then the competition was pretty limited. The '62 awards are the ones I'll be most interested in. However, the idea has gotten off to an excellent start and this shakedown cruise is probably just the thing that's needed. As Roy Thomas remarks, the imperfections of this Alley Award presentation should all be taken care of next time. Howard Keltner's article was quite good, and so were the illustrations accompanying it. Isn't there an error about Maximo? It was my impression he didn't come along until the early 40's. Unless they were reprints, which I doubt, the editions I read as a kid came along well after Superman.

> You're right, Dick – my copy of *Maximo*, which is the same (origin story) that Ed reviewed, is dated 1940; and it's not a reprint. Thanks for the correction.

John Wright
Editor: *The Komix*
P.O. Box 1277
Port Elizabeth, South Africa

Regardless of a remark I read in a zine some while back about "Gosh, Wow!!" comments, this cover truly deserves such praise. Like a great many, I am but one admirer of the art of Ronn Foss. I honestly doubt that any of today's professional magazines could have dreamed up, or presented such a cover. The Alley Awards and Roy Thomas' report were interesting and gratifying. Howard Keltner's "MLJ Leads the Way" was something I have long yearned to read, and thus I am deeply grateful to Howard for writing it, and to you for presenting it. "Hall of Infamy" – here again characters whom I thrilled to and who have lived in my memory for a lot of years. If I could find one complaint, it was this: *It ended on page 34!*

> John, the cover idea was Jerry's; Green and I merely executed it! (And I hope you won't take that literally.)

Joe Pilati
Editor: *Enclave*
111 S. Highland Ave.
Pearl River, New York

AE #4 arrived about 2 hours ago. Now, having gone through it 3 times, all I can say is Goshwow. Yes, Goshwow. There's enough Sense of Wonder here to envelope Mort Weisinger. The offset is magnificent, the material is *worth* being published by this process – which is saying quite a lot for *any* fanzine material. If this is your last "major" fanzine you've certainly had the good sense to quit while you're ahead ... in fact, you're on top – I doubt whether there will ever be a better comics fanzine than *AE* #4.

Jerry G. Bails, Ph.D.

L. L. Simpson
1106 W. 4th
Tyler, Texas

Once again, you have outdone yourself, setting a really high, high (get me, Ed Sullivan) mark for *Alter Ego*'s new editor to match. Poor lad, I wish him luck – he'll need some to outgo you. I'm kidding; I know him ... he'll do fine.

Jerry Bails (Former Editor)
17645 Gaylord
Detroit 40, Michigan

I join with hundreds of other fans across several continents in extending you my best wishes. I know that I have left *Alter Ego* in the best possible hands. I am looking forward to your first issue with great expectations. I am sure that fandom is in for a great treat.

> And I'm sure all fandom joins me in expressing appreciation for 4 great issues of *AE*, and our warmest regards for your continued support through the irreplaceable *Comic Reader*.

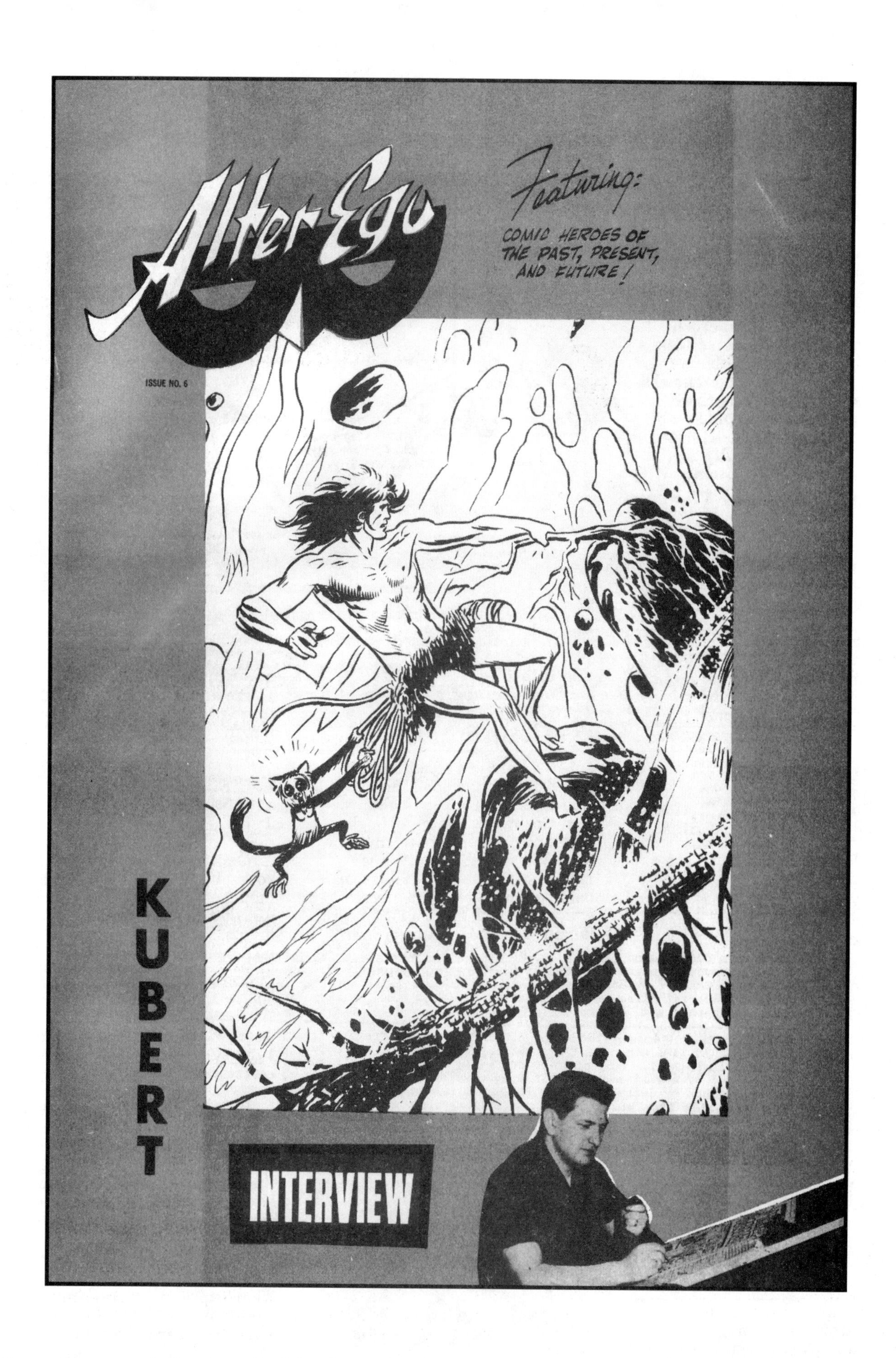

About the cover of **Alter Ego** ***#6 (March 1964):*** *The magazine's first professional cover was derived from a photostat of the cover of* Tor *#3 (1954). The original of this Kubert cover, long thought lost, was offered for sale at the 1997 Chicago Comicon for $5,500.*

Biljo White (left), receiving his 1962 Alley Award for "Profiles on Collectors" in his fanzine Komix Illustrated, *from retiring editor Foss. Along with the trophy were to go the publishing reins of* Alter Ego *itself, to be co-edited by Roy Thomas. Photo from* AE *#6, taken by Ruth White.*

Alter Ego #6 – Notes & Commentary

Although promised by June 1963, Alter Ego *#6 didn't appear until a full year after #5. Its green-and-white Kubert cover can be seen in photographs taken at the Alley Tally Party on March 21, 1964. The wait had been lengthy, but few could have been disappointed.*

In the editorial entitled "Growing Wonder," Foss wrote, "One must consider that the professional editor/publisher earns his livelihood in the field, doing work not unlike we amateurs – who must not only attempt to present some comparable effort, but also have the time to work for a living in some other, usually completely unrelated, field of endeavor.

"The foregoing is one of many reasons I found it impossible to continue AE *and* CC. *My dire hope is that my successor, Biljo White, artist that he is, finds some way of minimizing the time consumption of the painstaking trivialities required of a faned [fan editor]. I will by all means remain active in comicdom – perhaps more so than ever – in the capacity of fan artist and writer."*

Ronn's interview with Joe Kubert, the first interview to appear in the pages of Alter Ego, *provided a blueprint of sorts for this type of feature; many a fan editor afterwards would ask the same questions that Foss posed of Kubert, until they became clichés. From a historical perspective, however, it's important to realize that the basic technical information of drawing for comic books hadn't been available until this piece (and others like it) appeared. (The Kubert interview was conducted through the mail.)*

"Warlock," a succinctly imaginative piece of fiction by Vermont fan Tom Fagan, and Roy Thomas' "The Schwartzian Epic," a parody of literary criticism whose premise was that the only example of 20th Century literature surviving in 5263 A.D. was a dog-eared copy of Justice League of America, *scored well with the readers – as did "The Bestest League of America Meets Da Frantic Four" by Thomas and Grass Green. (The latter parody group had previously appeared in* Comicollector *#8.)*

The BLA/FF strip required a unique collaborative process, as Roy and Grass each drew their respective parody characters. (The script itself was solely by Thomas.) It had been drawn to fit the proportions of AE *#5; when the page-size changed with #6, the extra space at the top of each page was filled with letters of comment on the previous issue. This made use of the available space but couldn't help but draw the reader's eye upward from the comic strip below. For this book, the alternate solution (merely leaving the extra space an aesthetically-pleasing white) has been adopted.*

Of course, devoting the extra space to "Readers Write" allowed for the inclusion of 21 letters – a record number. We have selected some of the most interesting missives, including a few from pros accompanied by excellent artwork. Steve Ditko, Curt Swan, and Russ Manning provided nicely finished drawings, not mere sketches. Even the pros seemed to put their best foot forward in Alter Ego.

In the excerpts from "The Alley Awards for 1962" presented, it's significant to note that Fantastic Four *had won "Best Comic-Book of the Year" – and* Alter Ego *topped the "Fanzine" category.*

Also in Alter Ego *#6: an installment of Ron Haydock's "SERIALously Speaking" column (the second devoted to Rocket Man), "The Super IBM Machine" by Irving Glassman (who died at the age of thirty-two before the article saw print) with art by Ken "Kente" Tesar, and L. L. Simpson's "Hall of Infamy" column spotlighting the villainy of Two-Face and Catwoman.*

Again, "Recommended Reading" in AE *#6 is an eye-opener. Now there were* thirty-five *fanzines offered, twenty more than in* AE *#5. With members of the Los Angeles Science Fantasy Society appearing in JSA costumes at the 1962 Worldcon in Chicago (featured in photos in* AE *#6), fans began to think in terms of putting on a convention of their own.*

The Editors

> "I was quite impressed by your zine (*AE* #5) – both in its quality and the amount of work/energy put into it. Incidentally, Ronn – only someone who has had work reproduced in a mag (or any other form of printed matter) can know the thrill of seeing his efforts in published form. It's a thrill you never lose, no matter how long you're in the business. It's still true with me, and I've been in 'it' going on 25 years."
>
> – Joe Kubert

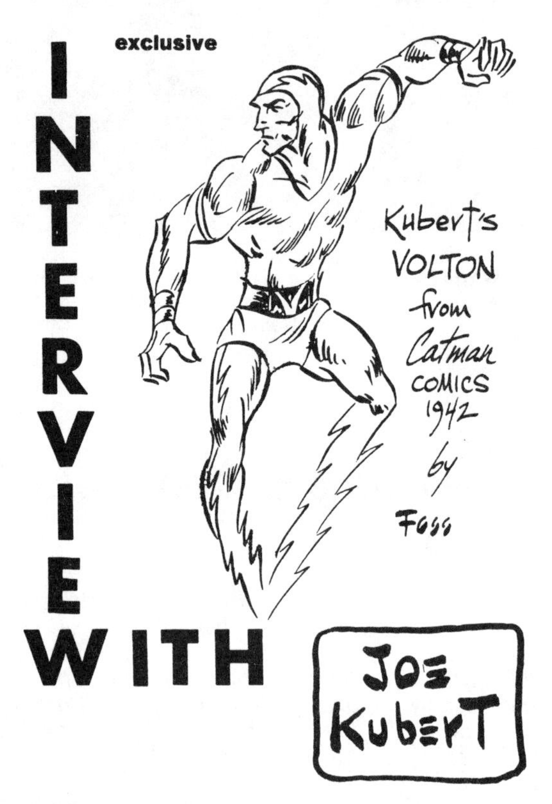

RONN: What is the pay per page? How much more if you also write the script?

JOE: I can't tell you page rates – specifically, but they vary from $25 to $60 per page for artwork only. Story will vary from $8 to $12 per page. The "lows" are pretty much set; the "highs" can vary – depending on the demand for the particular work (art, writing, lettering, coloring, what-have-you). When I started out, my rates were $6 per page.

RONN: Did someone other than you letter Hawkman?

JOE: The latest Hawkman strips I did (circa 1963) were lettered by Gaspar Saladino. However, when I did the strip "way back when" – I did the lettering, and with a very shaky hand, I might add!

RONN: How much are letterers paid?

JOE: Rates are $2 to $5 per page.

RONN: Do you know if all DC artists work "twice-up" (double-size)?

JOE: As far as I know, yes. I think, generally, it's found that one-half reduction tightens, cleans, and clarifies original artwork. After a while you find that you work "for reproduction" – that is, the artist will know what the printed work will look like (which is most important) – rather than gauging full effect from the original drawing alone.

RONN: Who was your personal favorite of all the characters you ever drew?

JOE: Tor was and is my favorite.

RONN: Do you use a crow-quill pen?

JOE: I use a pen similar to it, but very flexible.

RONN: Do you dilute your India (waterproof) ink?

JOE: I "water down" my ink with tap water.

RONN: Do artists ever get original art back? Would you like any of it returned?

JOE: Artists may get their work back, upon request – frankly, I've never had any desire for it. The point here being that once the publisher pays for work, it becomes his property. If the publisher feels he will have no further use for those originals, he disposes of them as he sees fit. At this time, the artist (writer, letterer, etc.) may request the originals.

RONN: According to Archer St. John (Tor #1), you started drawing in 1941. Do you remember what character it was?

JOE: I did a strip called Volton, around 1941, when I was in my second year of high school or thereabouts. Prior to Volton, I worked for Mr. Harry A. Chesler; this was in the early 40's. I worked in his offices one-and-a-half hours a day after school, and he gave me $5 a week for my expenses. This, I believe, was one of my greatest "breaks" I ever had. He had a staff of men, among whom were Charley Sultan, Rube Moreira, Raphael Asterita, and George Tuska. I was allowed the run of the place – to look over the artists' shoulders and watch them work – and to ask their criticisms of my own work. These guys were just wonderful – their patience and their helping hands did much to engender a desire in a very young boy to be a successful cartoonist – just as they were!

RONN: Doesn't D.C. allow the use of zip-a-tone? You used it so advantageously in Tor.

JOE: Yes, they allow it – or anything else the artist wants to use – so long as the effect is a good one.

RONN: What kind of paint is used to white-out a mistake?

JOE: Some white paint has a plastic base, so that ink will not dilute it. One is called "Sno-Pac."

RONN: How long does a brush last you? A pen tip, before it either spreads beyond usefulness or becomes caked up with ink?

JOE: A brush will last through 30-40 pages; pen, only 2-3.

RONN: Do you always use a blue pencil to rough-up (lay-out) a strip?

JOE: Yes – a special non-reproducing blue. Sometimes, just for a change of pace, I'll switch to pencil. But then it's back to the blue again.

RONN: The photo of you and Norm Maurer in Tor *#1 has you doing the 3 Stooges while Norm appears to be working on Tor; can you explain this?*

JOE: We co-edited each other's work.

RONN: The comic Meet Miss Pepper*; you inked it, penciled, or what?*

JOE: I penciled Miss Pepper – a fellow named Bob Bean inked. Bob is now the guiding hand and power behind "Wylde Studios" here in NY – they produce live and animated ads for TV.

*RONN: Was Viking Prince (*Brave & Bold*) your own creation?*

JOE: V.P. was created and written by Bob Kanigher, who also does Sgt. Rock. He used to write Captain Marvel. He is *the* best, in my opinion.

RONN: Why were you actually pulled off Hawkman? Or is it really true that Sgt. Rock, etc. keeps you too busy?

JOE: It's exactly as I stated before – my commitments on other work made it impossible for me to do Hawkman; as much as I'd've liked to do it! Fact is, the last issues I did were getting close to what I felt

I wanted in the character – when it became apparent I'd not be able to do it.

RONN: Would you like to continue on Hawkman?

JOE: From the preceding answer, what do *you* think?

RONN: What other artists influence you the most?

JOE: Outside of an almost complete art education any aspiring artist can get from Hal Foster – I try to incorporate anything of value that I might see in any artist's work.

RONN: Did you and Maurer create 3-D before it was used in the movies?

JOE: I believe the 3-D movies were out before our comic books. Norm and I were publishing 4 or 5 comics through St. John Pub. Co. when we came up with the idea of employing a 3-D image in comics.

RONN: Have you ever done any art other than comic strips? Your remarkable depth would lend itself well to fine art!

JOE: I've done a considerable amount of painting, including oils and water colors. Portraits and figure drawing in any media are subjects I find most fascinating. I've always thought I'd like to do some carving and modeling, but just never got to it.

RONN: Have you ever considered selling a strip to a newspaper syndicate?

JOE: I've made quite determined attempts at it, but I'm afraid to no avail! I have several weeks of dailies in my closet gathering dust. And, as it happens, Tor is the character I've tried selling. Personally, I feel that Tor – as I've applied him in a syndicated strip – would be successful.

RONN: Is there any chance of your reinstatement on Hawkman now with the editorial change at National?

JOE: No.

RONN: Why did Viking Prince fold in Brave & Bold *after finally winning the entire book to himself?*

JOE: The sales didn't warrant continuation.

RONN: Did you see any/much actual combat action in the Army?

JOE: I was in the army from 1950 to 52. The only action I saw was the GI rush to the chow line.

RONN: Do/did you really draw from models, i.e. *the Tor dinosaurs?*

JOE: I've sketched from models, but not directly for my illos in comics. The sketches taught me my subject (the figure, dinos, whatever), then I tried to apply what I learn to the comics. For me, the amount of time needed to work from models would negate the idea – insofar as its use directly to comics in concerned.

RONN: What type of strip do you prefer – super-hero, war, Viking, Tor?

JOE: I enjoy all subjects – all types of strips – providing that they are well written. By "well written," I mean the writing should utilize the art, rather than use the art merely to enhance the writing. My preference toward Tor is simply because this is my own personal idea and property.

In the Tor books (*1,000,000 Years Ago*), I created the character, wrote it, drew it, lettered it, colored it, and at one point took the original art down to the engraver and set 'em up in front of the cameras, for shots to be set on the metal to be etched.

RONN: Which of the super-heroes did you enjoy doing most?

JOE: Hawkman, Dr. Fate, The Spirit (on which I did inking), and of course, Volton.

RONN: Some readers feel that your art is too dark. What do you think of this?

JOE: I try to draw what seems right to me. Basically, we in comics are working in black and white. I try to use my blacks to gain the "effects" I want. I'm sure I don't succeed all the time, but I *do* try!

RONN: Do you have any personal dislikes associated with comic books?

JOE: The only dislike I have of comics is the type of paper, reproduction, and printing used. This is, of course, due to the cost of producing an article that sells for 12 cents. But within these limitations, I'm gratified at the end results.

Panels from "Black Valley," Tor #3, *taken from one of the many foreign editions which reprinted Tor stories.*

RONN: How far ahead do you work on a strip?

JOE: In comic books, we usually work 2 to 3 months in advance.

RONN: Do you usually adhere strictly to a script?

JOE: No. Bob Kanigher, the editor/writer of most of my work, will allow me "carte blanche" with his script – just so long as it looks good when he gets it!

RONN: Did you originate the panel-within-a-panel method, now used in many DC war comics?

JOE: I may have added slight variations, but fellows like Will Eisner, Simon and Kirby, Lou Fine, Irv Novick, Mort Meskin, to name a few of the real greats, preceded me and others along the lines of "novel" breakdowns.

RONN: What advice would you give pro artist hopefuls other than "Practice, practice, practice!" as stated in the first (and only) lesson of your Comic Book Illustrators Instruction Course, '54?

JOE: I would say that one of the most important things for fellows in our business to learn is anatomy. This is something you cannot learn from comic books, Bridgman's books on anatomy, or "How to Draw," etc. You've got to study from the live figure. Once you have learned the basics, then exaggeration will not look incorrect, but rather an extension of correct drawing.

Watch composition variation – when you jump around from one panel to the next too much, you disrupt the flow of the story – which is all-important!

You may have the most beautiful drawings in the world, but if they don't tell the story, they're worthless, as far as a comic strip is concerned.

I hope my answers will enlighten some of your readers.

by Tom Fagan

Everywhere color. Blacks, golds, blood reds, screaming purples, angry seething yellows. A kaleidoscope of rainbowed fantasies.

Warlock stood alone with the colors swirling about him. His booted feet pressed into the ground. Mailed fists raised in challenge. Dark eyes glinted in defiance from an equally dark form.

IT towered above him. Warlock knew IT from the shadows. Dark hulk, peering eyes and grasping fingers, always searching – always examining him – as if Warlock were a toy and not the mightiest of heroes.

This was not Diablo, not the Talon or Hatpin or Chanticleer. All these Warlock had met and conquered.

Each month a new adversary, or else Talon or Hatpin reappearing for a second, third, or fourth defeat – Warlock had lost track of the times he had been the victor.

Yet, IT was always there. IT watched constantly, studying Warlock's trickery, seeing how each new obstacle was overcome, storing up knowledge of all this, and now IT had decided the time had come for Warlock's survival or death!

A rebel yell from Warlock – anything to attract IT's attention. IT moved curiously above him, bending closer.

Warlock exulted. A strong concentration of mind forces, coalescing together. Warlock's uniform, now red and blue, now cobalt blue and jet black, the domino mask reverting to a bat-eared cowl, chest insignia – first large emblazoned "S" – now winged chiroptera – now death head with evil winking amethyst eye sockets – then lightning-bolt design.

IT watched; IT wondered. Warlock screamed his defiance anew. Wheet! Ten thousand hawks took to the air at Warlock's bidding command; a dolphin army scampered upon Warlock's order, slithering through stormy seas.

Above – a yawn! IT started to move away! Warlock knew he must gain attention. He paused an instant, and then:

Trick arrows, hundreds of them, soared – up – up – toward IT. An ice mountain, torn from icicle roots, hurled heavenward. Firebrands coursed from the hands of Warlock, now suddenly a being of fire.

Super breath blasts blew back the descending hand of IT. An Ibistick twirled, causing illusions; a ring beamed emerald flames.

Within seconds, Warlock became an atom-sized human, then a towering colossus. First speeding through telephone wires, then riding electrical strands on jet-propelled rollers.

Warlock's cape streamed behind dramatically, as befitting one of the mightiest of mortals.

Warlock called the magic name of six letters. Ominous cloud; bolt of golden brightness. New power; new command. New readiness for battle.

IT was tired; Warlock had failed to amuse him or capture continuing interest.

And...

Warlock, like others before him, died the crushing, soul-searing death of a no-longer-read comic book super-hero.

The Inimitable (Who'd want to?) .....
BESTEST LEAGUE of AMERICA
DA Frantic Four
meets...
APPROVED BY THE COMICS CLOD
CA
ATROCITY
GLAD TO MEET YOU AND THE REST OF DA FRANTIC FOUR, READ!
AND IT IS INDEED AN HONOR TO MEET YOU AND THE REST OF THE BLA, GREEN TRASHCAN!
IV
IV
12¢
AND STILL GOING UP!
SCRIPT BY ROY THOMAS
ART BY ROY THOMAS & 'GRASS' GREEN
Featuring Characters Copied-Right 1963 by the Former and the Late TRIAD!

The Inimitable (Who'd want to?).....
BESTEST
LEAGUE
of AMERICA
meets...
Frantic Four
POISON ARROWS
(OKAY, WOMBATMAN, NOW REMEMBER! WHEN I LIGHT THE FUSE, YOU TOSS THE BOMB RIGHT IN THE MIDDLE OF 'EM ALL!)
(RIGHT, SUPE! THEN IT'S BACK TO OUR OWN MAG, WORLD'S SHINIEST COMICS!)
...ALL OF WHICH HAS NOTHING WHATEVER TO DO WITH THIS STORY, BUT READ ON ANYHOW....

OUR STORY BEGINS IN URBAN CITY, HOME OF THE CASH....
HEH, HEH, HEH!
AT SUPER-SPEED I CAN READ ALL THE MAGS ON THE STANDS SO FAST I DON'T HAFTA BUY ANY! I---
OH, NO!
THIS IS A DIRE EMERGENCY! I'LL USE MY TOP-SECRET WAIST-SIGNAL TO CALL A MEETING OF THE BLA!
CARMINE WUZ HERE
THIS URGENT SUMMONS CALLS THE OTHER MEMBERS AWAY FROM VARIOUS TASKS -- FOR EXAMPLE, AQUARIUMAN....
I WAS USING CONDITIONING THERAPY FOR MY AQUAPHOBIA, BUT THE BLA COMES FIRST!
MOTHER
BINGO!
LIFE PRESERVER
-SUPERHAM AND WOMBATMAN...
WE MUST LET THESE VILLAINS ESCAPE AND HURRY TO THE BLA MEETING!
RIGHT!
C'MON BACK, YA FINKS!
PING!
-GREEN TRASHCAN...
I WAS TESTING A NEW TOP-PRIORITY SECRET PLANE OF INESTIMABLE WORTH TO THE GOVERNMENT, BUT... THE BLA OVER ALL!
CRASH!
-WONDROUS WOMAN...
I MUST LEAVE MY FIANCE, STEVE RETRIEVER, STANDING AT THE ALTAR FOR THE 17th TIME THIS MONTH! — THE BLA BECKONS!
AWWWWW
-LEAN ARROW...
I WAS TESTING A NEW, INVALUABLE SUPER-EXPLOSIVE ARROW-MISSILE FOR THE ARMY, BUT WHEN THE BLA CALLS, ALL ELSE FALLS!
BAROOOOM!
-THE IPOM (INFINITESIMAL PARTICLE OF MATTER)....
I WAS GREATLY REDUCED IN SIZE UNDER A MICROSCOPE, FINDING A WAY TO FIGHT A DEADLY PLAGUE GERM, BUT THE BLA WANTS ME, SO--!
OW!
GROW! GROW!
-S'AMM S'MITHH, MANHANDLER FROM MARS...!
AW, NUTS!
GENTS
3

SOON...
...AND SO, FELLOW MEMBERS, I HAVE DISCOVERED THE EXISTENCE OF A NEW SUPER-GROUP CALLED DA FRANTIC FOUR! —AN ENEMY OF MANKIND! —A MENACE TO FLAG! —TO COUNTRY! —TO SALES!
(WHEN HE GETS STARTED LIKE THIS, IT'S BEST TO JUST HEAR HIM OUT!) HEAR, HEAR!
HIT HIT
SEVEN COME 'LEVEN!
WHERE?
BY APOLLO'S SUNBURN! SHOULDN'T WE TALK TO THE FRANTIC FOUR BEFORE WE TAKE ANY ACTION?
YOU'RE RIGHT, OF COURSE, WONDROUS WOMAN! —WE'LL TALK TO THEM...
—THEN WE'LL MOIDER DA BUMS!
HUZZAH!
BUT WAITAMINIT, CASH! HOW'LL WE FIND THIS FRANTIC FOUR'S PAD?
ELEMENTARY, MY DEAR WOMBATMAN!
(NOTICE HOW I MANAGE TO GET IN ALL THE PANELS BY STANDING ON PEOPLE'S SHOULDERS!)
PINK
THEY'VE GIVEN US A MAP OF HOW TO GET TO THEIR APARTMENT PENTHOUSE RIGHT IN THEIR OWN COMIC-BOOK!
HOORAY!! LET'S GO!
WAIT!
F-4 APT.
PLACE TO HIDE ON RENT-DAY
THE WORLD'S GREATLESS COMIC MAG!!!?
Frantic Four
12¢
ARE YOU SURE THE JLA STARTED THIS WAY?
SPLOP!
POUND POUND
BEFORE WE GO, SHOULDN'T WE HEAR A FEW WORDS OF ENTHUSIASTIC ENCOURAGEMENT FROM OUR TEENAGE MEMBER, SNAPPY CARP?
YEAH! WHATCHA GOT TA SAY, SNAPPY?
WELL...
CAPTAIN ROGUE
4

...IN ALL EARNESTNESS, MY EXUBERANT COLLEAGUES, IT IS MY VALUE JUDGMENT THAT LITTLE OF IMPORT CAN BE APPENDED BY MY TEENAGE SELF TO THE SAGACIOUS UTTERANCES WHICH HAVE HERETOFORE TRANSPIRED!
OOOOOOOO! ISN'T HE DIVINE?
AND SO, UNDER THEIR NEW RULE OF OPERATING AS A UNIT ("GANG UP ON 'EM!"), THE SUPER-DOERS SPEED OFF....
BOY, THESE SILHOUETTE SHOTS SURE SAVE A MESSA DRAWIN'!
YOU KNOW, I READ THAT SOMEPLACE!
MUSH! MUSH!
ON, YOU HUSKIES!
AH, HERE WE ARE IN THE FRANTIC FOUR'S HOME CITY OF "NEW YORK"-- A FICTITIOUS NAME IF EVER I HEARD ONE!
WE'LL JUST WAIT FOR A COSTUMED HERO TO COME ALONG AND...
HEY! HERE COMES ONE NOW!
I'M ON MY WAY TO A SUPER-DOERS' MEETING...
SHHHH
NOW! KREEEEGAH! KILL!
NO, WAIT, SUPERHAM! IT'S NOT ONE OF THE FRANTIC FOUR!!—IT'S... THE FLEA!
WHAT'RE YOU DOIN' HERE, FLEA?
BZZZ... I'M ON MY WAY TO THE STARCHIE COMICS COMPANY—BZZZ—TO JOIN FLEA GIRL, THE COUGAR, BLACK HOODLUM, AND THE WINDSHIELD—BZZZZZ—TO FORM OUR OWN SUPER-GROUP! BZZZ-BZZZZ-
WELL, I'LL BE--!
ISN'T HE CUTE?
EVERYBODY WANTS TA GET INTA THE ACT! LEMME CLOBBER 'IM!
5

AW, WE MAY AS WELL LET 'IM GO, GUYS! WE GOTTA GET THE FRANTIC FOUR NOW! WE'LL LET THE METAL MORONS TAKE CARE O' THIS NEW GANG LATER!
AWWWW
YEAH!
BZZ -- GOSH, THANKS, FELLERS!
BZZZ
BZZZ
BZZZ BZZZ
SUCTION
SUCTION
OKAY, GANG! ENOUGH O' THIS "WAITIN' AROUND" JAZZ! LET'S GO UP TO THAT FRANTIC FOUR'S APARTMENT AND TAKE 'EM BY SURPRISE!
THERE'S REALLY NO NEED OF THAT, CASH!
AS YOU ARE PERFECTLY AWARE, I, SUPERHAM, THE MAN OF TIN, COULD DESTROY THE WHOLE KIT'N'KABOODLE WITH A BURST OF HEAT-VISION, OR A FLICK OF MY SUPER TOE-NAIL!
WE KNOW, SUPE...
... BUT AFTER ALL, US OTHER D.C. (DEFECTIVE COMICS) HEROES HAFTA HAVE SOMETHIN' T'DO TOO, Y'KNOW!
YEAH — WHO D'YA THINK YOU ARE, ANYHOW — THE SPECTRAL OR SOME'PIN?
WHEEEE!
SORRY...
HUP, TWO, THREE-
MEANWHILE, IN THE LUXURIOUS PENTHOUSE OF THE WORLD'S GREATLESS HEROES
BOY! THAT HUNK IS SURE A RIDICULOUS-LOOKING CHARACTER! -HOW COULD ANYONE POSSIBLY BELIEVE IN A GUY LIKE THAT?!?
YEAH!
YEAH!
HUNK
YEAH!
HEY! WHATCHA MEAN AGREEIN' WITH ME, THANG? -- DON'T YOU KNOW IT'S YOUR FIGHTS WITH ME, THE FUMIN' SCORCH, THAT MAKES OUR COMIC SO POPULAR?!?
-OH! SURE, SCORCH! -- I FORGOT... IT USED TO BE ME AND MR. FRANTIC!
HELP
BOYS, DON'T FIGHT!
... HERE WE GO AGAIN...
6

WELL THEN, GET WITH IT! CALL ME SOMETHIN'!
OKAY! HOW'S THIS? YOU TEEN-AGE TINDERBOX! YOU BABY BUNSEN-BURNER, YOU! IZZAT OKAY?
YOU TELL HIM SCORCH! (DON'T I REMIND YOU OF ABE LINCOLN'S MOTHER?)
BOYS, STOP THE FIGHTING!
!
YAY! —JUST LIKE OLD TIMES, YOU FUGITIVE FROM A FRANKENSTEIN FILM!
TAKE THAT YOU ACETYLENE ABUSER OF ALLITERATION!
BOYS! STOP 'AT FIGHTIN'!
COMON-N-N, SCORCH!!! (ALL THAT HE IS, OR EVERS HOPES TO BE, HE OWES TO HIS ANGEL OF A SISTER--ME!
?
WHAT'CHA ALLUS STOP-PIN' US FOR, READ?
YEAH, YA KILLJOY!
YEAH! (THAT REMINDS ME OF A LITTLE STORY...)
POST NO BILLS
IT'S JUST THAT... WELL, GEE _I'M THE ONE THE FRANTIC FOUR IS NAMED AF-TER, AND I NEVER GET T'DO NUFFIN'..
WELL WHAT ABOUT ME??? I'VE BEEN A MORE-OR-LESS USELESS MEMBER EVER SINCE OUR COSMIC ACCIDENT FOURSCORE AND SEVEN YEARS AGO...!
THAT'S NOT OUR FAULT, INVISIBUBLE GIRL... IT'S JUST THAT ALL OF THE INVISIBILITY STUNTS HAVE ALREADY BEEN DONE BY CLAUDE RAINS!
PAT PAT
..SNIFFA..
READ!
..SNIFFA..
RUN! RUN! RUN!
IT'S HAPPENED AT LAST--! THE BESTEST LEAGUE IS ATTACKIN' THE BUILDING! RUN FER YER LIFES!!!
RUN!
RUN! RUN! RUN! RUN! RUN! RUN! RUN!
RUN? NEVER!
...THIS WOULD HAPPEN ON THE DAY THAT I'M SUPPOSED TO BABYSIT WITH SPIDERWEBMAN!...
THE FRANTIC FOUR NEVER RUN!
I WILL DISGUISE MYSELF AS A CANDELABRA!
HIDE, YES! BUT NOT RUN!
I GET THE WARM SPOT UNDER THE COUCH!
NOW WAIT A MINUTE, YOUSE GUYS!
OH, DEAR... WHERE WILL I HIDE??
7

YOU GUYS MAY CHICKEN OUT, BUT NOT ME! THERE AIN'T NOBODY CAN BEAT ME BUT SUPERHAM, AN--
GLOW, GLOW!
..BUT THANG-- SUPERHAM ATTENDS THE BLA MEETINGS REGULARLY, NOW!
...HE DO?
_HOPE THEY DON'T LOOK UNDER THIS RUG!
YOU DON'T REALLY THINK THEY'LL FIND US UNDER HERE, HA?
YOU DON'T, DO YA?
HAH???
HOLD IT! NOW IT'S MY TURN TO PLAY THE HERO!
DOWN MIT DER BLA
HOPPETY
ZAZ!
TREMBLE, TREMBLE!
WE GOTTA FIGHT THE BLA OR THE FRANTIC FOUR'LL NEVER BE ABLE TO HOLD UP THEIR CCA SEAL IN PUBLIC AGAIN!
YOU'RE RIGHT, SCORCH! I-- HEY! HERE THEY COME NOW!
AHA!
SLAMMETY!
¡GULP!¡
..AND SUPERHAM'S WITH 'EM ¡SOB¡!
AAAAARGH! I AM TEMPORARILY PARALYZED BY A MINUTE SPECK OF KRYPTONITE DUST SOMEWHERE IN THIS ROOM! --FIGHT THE BRAVE FIGHT WITHOUT ME, O' FELLOW MEMBERS!
YAY! NOW WE GET A CHANCE!
GIT 'EM, THANG!
_WHO??! ..ME ???
HOTEL MARS
NOW I KNOW WHY THEY CALL HIM SUPERHAM!
I WILL FRACTURE THE FLAMING FLEDGLING WITH MY FANTASTIC SMELL-O-RING!
HA! IT IS TO LAUGH, GREEN TRASHCAN! MY ASBESTOS NOSE-PLUGS PROTECT ME!
THANG, YOU AND I WILL LOCK IN SUPERHUMAN COMBAT AS IS THE WONT IN COMIC-BOOK BATTLES OF THIS TYPE!
OKAY, BUT I ALREADY DID THIS A FEW MONTHS BACK-- WITH HUNK, SUNKMARINER AND SPIDERWEBMAN!
(REMINDS ME OF ONE OF THEM RASSLIN' MATCHES ON THE TEE-VEE!)
?
8

I, THE CASH, WILL ENCIRCLE YOU AT SUPER-SPEED!
YOU ARE?? --AN' HERE I THOUGHT I WAS ENCIRCLIN' YOU!
(I WISH GNAT-MAN WAS HERE SO'S I COULD STOMP 'YM!
?
BY PLUTO'S DOG-BISCUITS, MY MAGIC LASSO WILL CATCH YOU ERE LONG, AND THEN -- POW!
-AAH! ..YOU COULDN'T EVEN FIND GLAMAZON ISLAND WITH-OUT YER TALKIN' PLANE TA HELP YOU!
HI!
ACME WATER WINGS
(YOU MAY THINK I WISH SUNKMARINER WAS HERE... BUT YOU'RE CRAZY!)
SINCE THE BESTEST LEAGUE OUTNUMBER THE FRANTIC FOUR...
WE LEFT-OVER MEMBERS'LL DO THE ONE HONORABLE, NOBLE THING..
WHICH IS...
-BLOW UP THE BUILDING!
READY..
SET...
HALT! CEASE AND DESIST!!
IT'S SNAPPY CARP! WHUFFO YOU SAY CEASE AND DESIST, SNAPPY?
BECAUSE IT IS IMPERATIVE THAT THESE AMATEURISH FISTICUFFS BE SUMMARILY TERMINATED!
WHY? WE WAS JUST GOIN' GOOD!
THE BESTEST LEAGUE AND THE FRANTIC FOUR MUST NEEDS COMBINE FORCES TO ANNIHILATE AN ABHORRENT NEW COMMON ADVERSARY, AS HERALDED IN THIS NEW COMIC MAGAZINE!
WHAT?! LET'S SEE THAT COMIC!
YEAH! US, TOO!
..I SHALL STAGGER HEROICALLY TO MY FEET!
HELP
?
NO, YOU IDIOT-THIS IS THE BACK COVER!
NOW, LET'S SEE WHAT.... OH, NO!
GASP
..WE'RE DOOMED!
BY NEPTUNE'S SEASICK PILLS!
!
..HAVE YOU GUESSED WHAT THESE FORLORN FIGHTERS OF FELONS SEE? TURN THE PAGE..
9

DULL
The WORLD'S SWAMPIEST COMIC-BOOK!
THE Glee 'N' Perloo ORGANIZATION of OKEFENOKEE
GOOD GRIEF!
HOW TO SWIM
A. FISH
JES' FINE
SNAP!
SNAP!
-IN THIS ISSUE-
The GOO in another SCAR-SPUDDED SPECTACULAR-
"The INVADERS from FORT MUDGE!"
WALT SILLY
RT
10

JSA AT SF CON

AND ALL IN COLOR – FOR A TIME

by Bruce Pelz

SPECIAL REPORT

In September 1960, at the 18th World Science Fiction Convention in Pittsburgh, Dick and Pat Lupoff of New York handed out copies of their new fanzine *Xero* #1, which featured a long article on Captain Marvel as the first in a series called "And All in Color for a Dime." With this, SF fandom was launched into a spate of nostalgia – radio programs, comics, old pulps – which has not yet abated. At the Pittcon, too, the Lupoffs appeared in costume at the masquerade (a standard part of SF World Cons) as Captain and Mary Marvel – the Big Red Cheese and Cheesecake, come to life. This also set off a chain reaction in SF fandom, but it took two years to materialize.

Although only a few of the L.A. fans collect comics, most all of them are comics fans in that they read or have read comics and enjoyed doing so (though a large number would refuse to admit the fact). The idea of going to the 1962 convention as comic characters was bound to come up, as several of the group remembered the Lupoffs at the Pittcon and thought about going as his or her favorite costumed comic character. So before the Seacon (Seattle) masquerade had even been held, we decided to go to Chicago in 1962 as The Justice Society of America.

Late in the spring of 1962, Bjo Trimble of Long Beach took a stack of colored ditto carbons and copied full-page illustrations of the JSA characters, which I duplicated so we would have work-sheets to build the costumes from. For those such as myself who are quite incompetent at making costumes, or even knowing where to purchase the materials, Bjo included a checklist of costume materials and suggestions of where they could best be located. As the end of July came, with less than a month to go before we left for Chicago, we started work on the costumes. As it turned out, Bjo made two of the costumes and advised us on a couple more. Dian Girard, who joined the group as Wonder Woman, made two others besides her own.

When the masquerade at Chicago finally came around, we had eight JSA members with our group: Hawkman, Green Lantern, Wonder Woman, Dr. Fate, Flash, Sandman, Dr. Mid-Nite, and the Black Canary. It turned out that others had decided that comic characters were "in" for that masquerade, too, as other fans came as Batman, Robin, Prince Ibis, Taia, and another Flash, as well as a Flash Gordon group that took the "Best Group" prize that we were trying for. It was a good year for comic heroes.

Bjo's husband, John Trimble, went as the Sandman: a double-breasted green suit from a rummage sale, an old hat sprayed orange, a gas mask left over from his time in the service. All parts of the costumes were in the original comic book colors. As someone said: "All these old comic heroes had some weakness – the Sandman's must've been that he was color-blind!"

All in all it was fun to do. At the Chicon, since all of us normally wear glasses except for Black Canary, most of us were semi-blind during the masquerade. (Fred Patten complained that the Other Flash wasn't authentic, since he wore his glasses.) This prevented the taking of pictures during the masquerade, and post-convention efforts have failed to get shots of either Dr. Mid-Nite or the Sandman. The Canary has moved out of state, so photos of her aren't available, either.

The remaining five were taken at the annual Halloween Party of the Los Angeles Science Fiction Society, after which the costumes were rather completely disassembled. The standard parts we'll keep for future costumes, the specialized ones will be disposed of – though I suspect the Green Lantern will want to keep his ring. (At Chi's masquerade, during the Grand March, Ted Johnstone found himself following a huge Luna Moth costume, and the wings kept flicking him in the face. He turned around and raised his ring, saying: "Watch – I'm going to make the biggest damn green fly-swatter you ever saw!")

Abridged from AE *#6*

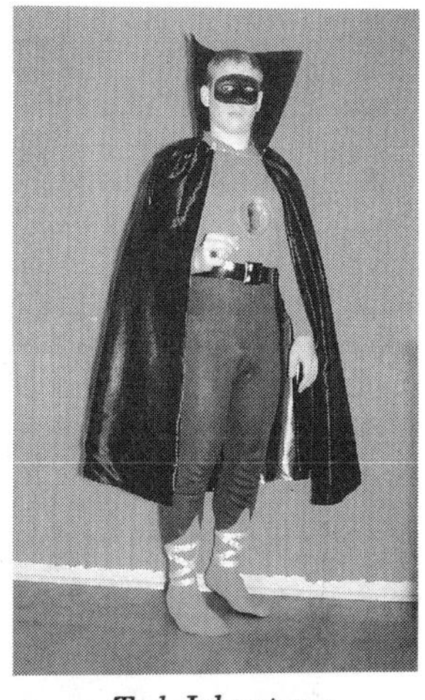

Ted Johnstone

Dian Girard

Bruce Pelz

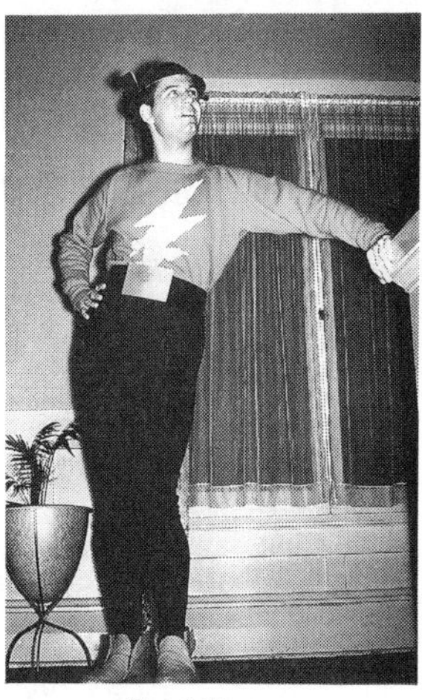

Fred Patten

THE ACADEMY OF COMIC BOOK ARTS AND SCIENCES

presents:

The ALLEY AWARDS for 1962

PRO DIVISION

I. Best Comic-Book of the Year:
Fantastic Four

II. Best Editor of a Comics Group:
Julius Schwartz

III. Best Script Writer:
Gardner Fox

IV. Best Pencil Artist:
Carmine Infantino

V. Best Inker:
Murphy Anderson

VI: Best Hero:
Hawkman

VII. Best Group of Heroes:
Fantastic Four

VIII. Best Villain:
Sub-Mariner

IX: Best Supporting Character:
The Thing

X. Best Short Story:
"Origin of Spider-Man"
(*Amazing Fantasy #15*)

XI. Best Book-Length Story:
"The Planet That Came to a Standstill"
(*Mystery in Space #75*)

XII. Best Single Comic-Book Cover:
Brave and Bold #42
(Hawkman)

XIII. Comic Book Most in Need of Improvement:
Batman

XIV. Hero(ine) Most Worthy of Revival:
The Spectre

[illo by Vosburg]

THE ACADEMY NOMINATING COMMITTEE

Jerry Bails, Nelson Bridwell, Dale Christman, Richard Durell, Tom Fagan, Donald Foote, Ronn Foss, Paul Gambaccini, Steve Gerber, Don Glut, Richard Green, Ron Haydock, Parley Holman, Robert Jennings, Howard Keltner, Richard Kyle, Ed Lahmann, Gordon Love, Douglas Marden, John McGeehan, Raymond Miller, Fred Norwood, Frank Nuessel, Bruce Pelz, Howard Rogofsky, Bill Sarill, Paul Seydor, Roy Thomas, Don Thompson, Mike Vosburg, Bill White

AMA DIVISIONS

Entries in all categories were rated according to the following 5-point scale:

5 - Excellent
4 - Very Good
3 - Good
2 - Fair
1 - Poor

XV. Comic Fanzines of 1961 and 1962

PLACE - FANZINE / EDITOR	RATING
1. Alter Ego #1-4 (Jerry Bails)	4.79
2. Comicollector #7-8 (Ronn Foss)	4.49
3. Xero Comics #1-9 (Dick Lupoff)	4.43
4. Komix Illustrated #1-16 (Bill White)	4.40
5. The Comic Reader #4-14 (Jerry Bails)	4.25
6. Comicollector #1-6 (Jerry Bails)	4.17
7. Comic Art #1-3 (Don Thompson)	4.13
8. The Komix #1 (John Wright)	4.01
9. The Comic World #1 (Bob Jennings)	3.96
10. Spotlite #1-2 (Parley Holman)	3.80
11. Masquerader #1-2 (Mike Vosburg)	3.51
12. Super-Hero #1 (Mike Touhey)	3.30
13. The Rocket's Blast (G.B. Love)	3.19
14. Skybird #2 (Ron Haydock)	3.02
15. Comic Collector's Handbook (Love)	2.98
16. Bullseye #1 (Fred Bronson)	2.87
17. The Comic Fan #1 (Buddy Saunders)	2.71
18. Fan to Fan #1 (Bob Butts)	2.71
19. Headline #1 (Steve Gerber)	2.70
20. Comic Heroes Revisited #1-2 (Bernie Bubnis)	2.61
21. Comic Heroes Unlimited #1-2 (Love)	2.47
22. The Comicscope (Walt Taylor)	1.80

XVI. Special Projects

1. Index to All-Star Comics (Jerry Bails)	4.64
2. 1961 Alley Poll and Report (Roy Thomas)	4.22
3. Alley Trophies for 1961 (Ronn Foss)	4.21
4. Photos of 1st Issue Covers (Kenny Heineman)	4.05

XVII. Articles

1. "The Light of The Green Lantern" (Jerry Bails)	4.47
2. "MLJ Leads the Way" (Howard Keltner)	4.31
3. "The Education of Victor Fox" (Richard Kyle)	4.02
4. "Capt. Billy's Whiz-Gang" (Roy Thomas)	3.87

XVIII. Features

1. "Profiles on Collectors" (Bill White)	4.29
2. "On the Drawing Board" (Jerry Bails)	4.05
3. "Hall of Fame" (Raymond Miller)	3.99
4. "SERIALously Speaking" (Ron Haydock)	3.88

XIX. Strips

1. Bestest League of America (Roy Thomas)	4.19
2. Frantic Four (Richard Green)	4.05
3. The Viper (Ronn Foss)	3.72
4. The Fog (Bill White, R. Green)	3.49

XX. Fiction

1. "The Reincarnation of The Spectre" (Roy Thomas)	4.13
2. "The White Dragon" (John Wright)	3.96
3. "The Case of the Misplaced Super-Hero" (Al Kuhfeld)	3.31
4. "Wot Me Wikes 'bout Wonda Tot" (F.T. Frost)	2.69

READERS Write

FEMININE MYSTIQUE

We keep getting these letters – "Who is she?" The only answer can be: She has no pseudonym... her real name is Joy Holiday!

I want to thank you for sending me the Alley Awards results, even though you robbed me of the pleasure of swiping Stan Lee's copy as I do with all the fanzines that are sent to him.

Spider and Strange are happy about the favorable comments and hope we will do better next year – without having to threaten anyone or have Strange put a spell on fandom. Thanks again.

Sincerely, Steve Ditko

Stan Lee
Editor: Marvel Comics Group

We're very pleased to learn that *The Fantastic Four* was voted Best Comic Book of the Year. It was also most gratifying to learn that the fans seemed to favor Sub-Mariner and the Thing. And of course we're proud that the "Origin of Spider-Man" won the Best Short Story Award.

It seems that the Academy of Comic-Book Arts and Sciences is doing a most commendable job, and although a number of categories seem to have gotten away from us, we still applaud the diligence and sincerity of all you "academicians."

In all fairness, though, I wonder if the name of the Academy shouldn't be changed to the Academy of Super-Hero Arts and Sciences, as they are the only type of magazines you people seem interested in. That's all well and good, and I am quite in agreement with you, for certainly the super-hero magazines have the most color, glamour, and fan following. However, how do I ever explain all this to poor Millie the Model or Patsy Walker?

Anyway, the only thing spoiling my complete satisfaction is the fact that the Thing keeps yelling at me, "Why dont'cha go see Gardner Fox and have 'im teach ya how to write?!"

All the best,

Stan Lee

DEAR RONN—

THE DRAWING BELOW DOESN'T NECESSARILY CONTAIN A PARTICULAR MESSAGE — PERHAPS A PSYCHIATRIST WOULD FIND A HIDDEN MEANING. HE MIGHT GET THE IMPRESSION I'VE BEEN FLOORED BY THE 'COMIC MONSTER' WHO REPRESENTS THE MANY YEARS I'VE BEEN DRAWING PANEL AFTER PANEL, DAY-IN AND DAY-OUT. YET I FEEL FRESHER TODAY THAN EVER BEFORE AND MORE OFTEN THAN NOT, TRY MY DOGGONDEST TO DO BETTER. IF YOU FIND IT SUITABLE TO USE IN YOUR MAG- FEEL FREE.

THANKS FOR YOUR VERY NICE LETTER AND KIND THOUGHTS

ALL THE BEST,
Curt Swan

Don & Maggie Thompson
Editors: *Comic Art*
29 College Place
Oberlin, Ohio

Your idea of printing the names and addresses of article writers after each article is a good one, as is the suggestion that comment on articles be made directly to authors. But (1) I haven't time to write short notes of comment to each, and (2) this could lead to a pretty dull lettercol for *AE*. Not only do the photo and drawings of Infantino make your repro process worthwhile, but the letter was interesting, amusing, and valuable to a comic fan. More of this sort of thing in the lettercol, please! Justified margins are not, in my opinion, worth the trouble – and as you know, it *is* trouble. Better spend the time on proofreading than have to worry about such hyphenations as "evol-ved" and "co-ntinued." And the use of 2 columns per page just complicates the problem. It would seem more profitable to work on content. You know, collectors do not necessarily write good articles (contrary to what JBPhD seems to be indicating); there are too many poor articles now, to my way of thinking. It was a fine inspirational piece, but I'd like to have seen one suggestion included – that is the notion of collaboration on an article; Don couldn't have written his *Xero* articles without the very kind help of Bill Thailing.

Mike Vosburg
Editor: *Masquerader*
3040 Avalon
Pontiac, Michigan

"JLA - Overcrowded?" was much better than the Wonda Tot mess in *CC*. I really enjoyed this article. Too bad National doesn't have their eyes open to these events. Biljo's illos were simply beautiful. My Spider-Man looked halfway decent, but the Torch was a real mess. I probably could have and should have done much better on these. I like Weiss' work, but don't care much for his inking... reminds me of a sketch; but it looks quite good. Haydock, Woolston, Lahmann – all good articles. I suppose I'm not a Thomas fan, but to me the BLA pin-up was a waste of space. Something by Grass would have been much better, if you wanted something funny. Your Eclipse was excellent; the best I've ever seen by you. I looked in vain for a Kubert influence. Hope you have much more of this type of thing in the future.

John Ryan
11 Reginald St.
Abbotsford, N.S.W.
Australia

Many, many thanks for *AE* #5. I only wish I could pass on to you a small portion of the sheer pleasure it gave me. I read and re-read it until I could almost quote you the line and page of the entire contents from memory. Congratulations to all concerned! I enjoyed The Eclipse, and you're to be commended for resisting the temptation of using his "solid-passing capabilities" in the opening stories. The list under "Recommended Reading" really staggered me. Never, in my wildest fancies, did I imagine there was such an active interest in comics and their creators. To be perfectly honest, for years I've always regarded myself as being slightly "odd." Who ever heard of a man collecting comics and locking them away for safekeeping... or telling people that the highlight of his trip to England was discovering a 1st edition of *Marvel Comics*? I tell you, Ronn, it's a wonderful feeling to find out you're not the only square peg in the round hole. Your comments regarding the task facing anyone searching for a name for a new hero were right on the button... it's darn near impossible!

Russ Manning

AE #5: Fine editorial. Woolston's article is *good* ... of a type too often missing in other fanmags ... solid analytical thought. Too many articles on comic books and/or heroes are of the complete rehash of plot only slightly abridged type. Lahmann: Infectious! I wanted to rush out and get every one of the overpriced things he listed! Very informative and enthusiastic. Haydock: Half-and-half. Some information, then a plot-rehash of something I haven't seen ... guaranteeing boredom. ECLIPSE: More of this! More original strips ... just as wild, flashy, and off-trail as you can draw them, or inspire them from other contributors. Few will be as well done as your Eclipse, but all comic books, amateur and pro, will eventually benefit from such a transfusion of imagination and enthusiasm. The biographies of Bails and White are very welcome. These are truly the meat of fanmags for me. Where else can I learn so much, so quickly, about all the people who create comic books and those who collect them? This includes the Infantino bit, of course. Lettercols rate the same as above, for the same reasons. The I'D LIKE TO SEE MORE OF IN YOUR MAG dept.: More original strips, more drawings, and more photos. Your lay-out is more than adequate, and the cover well designed, so in truth, one can only ask for more of the same.

My special love in comic books has always been the reprints of the very fine comic *strips* from the newspapers. Here, I feel, one can have the very best of illustrated strip artwork *plus* fine stories. The EC things in the fifties qualify here (*excluding* the Ghouls), as do a good portion of the Julius Schwartz mags at DC. I balk at the prices being asked for mags these days, however, and find that there is enough demand for my artwork that I can trade drawings for the mags I want.

Gardner F. Fox

Just a few lines to say many thanks for the high tribute you and your fellow members of the Academy of Comic Book Arts and Sciences have paid me by naming me as best script writer for the year 1962. It is an honor to which I will devote my very best efforts to live up to in 1963, 64, and so on.

I was especially tickled to see that my story, "Earth's First Green Lantern" won second place in the Best Short Story division. According to my records it is the *first* Green Lantern story I ever wrote. Since that time, of course, I have written a number of GLs, necessitated by John Broome's illness in Paris. Also many thanks for the honor paid to "The Planet That Came To A Standstill," which (as you know) I authored.

And a sigh for the good times I had writing about Adam and Alanna on Rann. I just turned in the last script (sigh) I will do about them.

E. Nelson Bridwell
1010 N. Quapah
Oklahoma City 7, Oklahoma

"The Eclipse" was well done, and shows the real possibilities for a Dr. Mid-Nite revival. The only change I'd have made was in the idea of having the crooks after radium; it's overdone. Narcotics is what they'd be more likely to be after. After catching those two, the Eclipse would track down the pushers and suppliers, and vow to dedicate his powers to war against those who prey on human misery. But I can't agree with your statement that "nearly all the likely names for a hero (and gimmicks incorporated in an exceptional idea) have been more than well covered through the course of the past 20 years." This reminds me of the lawmaker who wanted to close the patent office in 1830 because there was nothing left to invent. I personally have enough original ideas to supply a publisher with a full stable of costumed heroes. Ed Lahmann's article on collecting was informative, but hardly all-inclusive. How about the Quality group, for example?

Narcotics is what Dru's script called for; I changed it to avoid nasty letters about "contributing to the delinquency of minors." My humble apologies for the gross exaggeration of the lack of original characters; here's hoping you have the opportunity to display your ideas... you'd make a fine editor!

About the cover of* Alter Ego *#7 (October 1964): *Biljo White's cover stands as one of the highlights of what Bill Schelly christened "The Golden Age of Comic Fandom." This image is reproduced from the original art, with which Biljo gifted Roy in 1964.*

Self-portrait by Roy Thomas

Alter Ego #7 – Notes & Commentary

In early 1964 Roy Thomas became Alter Ego*'s third editor/publisher, but the precise chain of events by which that happened is something of a minor mystery, at this late date.*

In the editorial leading off AE *#6, and elsewhere in that issue, Ronn Foss indicated that Biljo White had volunteered to assume the role of publisher. (In these and other references, if Roy was mentioned at all, it was as a contributing or co-editor only.) Roy, too, vaguely recalled Biljo's having planned to edit AE. Invited by Roy to clarify the matter, Biljo graciously responded:*

"On Ronn's only visit with me during this time, I recall sitting on the living room floor while he laid out the pages he had prepared of AE *#6 for publication. I found it most fascinating to see what he'd accomplished. Whether it was a feeling of being overwhelmed by the responsibility of continuing such a fine publication, or my desire to try other things, I don't believe I ever really considered being its editor and publisher. I felt being an art director was more to my liking, and working with you on later issues proved me correct.*

"My association with Alter Ego *was one of the truly high points in my years of comic fandom, and it was a real thrill to see my work appear within its pages. I'm particularly proud of my covers, as experience picked up working at the American Press (in Columbia, Missouri) allowed me to produce the proper color layouts. I feel fortunate that you became* AE*'s new editor, since we both lived in Missouri, and not too far from each other. This allowed me to work more closely with you, and complete the art assignments in the way you visualized."*

However it occurred, by summer of '64 Roy was readying AE *#7 for printing in his hometown of Jackson, Missouri, 100 miles south of the St. Louis area where he'd been teaching high school English for the past two years. He wanted the issue in the mails by October, to be eligible for that year's Alley awards, since a nomination or two might help sell copies.*

Pauline as Joy

Not only did that issue sell out its print run of approximately 1000 copies, but it was later reprinted in an edition of several hundred copies by G.B. Love, publisher of The Rocket's Blast/Comicollector, *who had also reprinted* AE *#5.)*

This issue introduced a new model under the Joy Holiday garb: Roy's friend Pauline Copeman. Her portrayal, with the trademark "upswept" hair, appeared in photographs through issue #9.

Richard Kyle, one of the best fan-writers, contributed "And That Was the End of Solomon Grundy?" – a minor but well-written piece Roy billed as "The First of an Important New Series under the Direction of Jerry G. Bails, Ph.D." It was "important," of course, mostly because the JSA was and would always remain of paramount importance to Jerry and Roy.

To Roy the brightest single spot of the issue was Biljo's agreeing to be art editor, meaning primarily that he supplied much of the art for the next three issues. (Jerry was listed as "editor emeritus.") For, despite an occasional reprinted actual comics cover or page in earlier offset issues of AE, *it was a chancey thing to deliver a copy of a vintage comic into the hands of a printer and pray for it to be returned intact after photographing.*

Nor were fan-publishers of the day at all certain that DC, Marvel, et al., *might not object to actual reprinting of their copyrighted art, while they seemed quite tolerant of drawings done by fans, even those that were virtual tracings. Fan-publishers could certainly have claimed "historical usage," but out of a combination of preference and ignorance they did not.*

Besides his cover and spot illos, Biljo contributed a seven-page comics story, "Alter and Captain Ego." Because it utilized the name of the fanzine itself, it seems likely this feature was at least begun during the brief period when Biljo was flirting with the notion of publishing AE. *Since both in art and concept it was a partial homage to Captain Marvel, the strip fit perfectly into the issue.*

Roy wrote two articles for AE *#7 – "A Hot Idea!" about the early days of the original Human Torch (for which Roy used as a pseudonym the name of a fellow teacher), and "One Man's Family," about Captain Marvel and his friends and relations, both researched using Biljo's huge collection. In retrospect, Roy winces to recall that in the Marvel piece he neglected to mention Magnificus, Sivana's first boy-child, and that the text gives the impression that Cap Jr. and Mary debuted before the Lieutenants Marvel, when it was the other way around. All the same, the article is one of the best-remembered features in* AE*'s long history, and won a 1964 Alley (as did Biljo's sterling cover and* AE *#7 as a whole).*

In addition, Roy drew nine "Gilded Age of Comics" cartoons in the style of Shel Silverstein, popular for his work then appearing in Playboy *(and indeed Silverstein himself was caricatured in the final cartoon).*

E. Nelson Bridwell, shortly before becoming assistant editor on DC's Superman titles, contributed an article called "The Tragic Monster," which traced the roots of Marvel's ever-lovin' blue-eyed Thing to ancient Sumer, Greek myth, Shakespeare, Mary Shelley, and elsewhere. Roy welcomed this piece, as he wanted to place the super-hero in an historical and social context, rather than pretend the concept had totally originated with Superman.

For the past year or so, Roy had been corresponding with longtime Captain Marvel/Marvel Family *writer Otto O. Binder. At Roy's request, Otto sent a long letter detailing his memories of the Big Red Cheese. All this emphasis on Captain Marvel and his over-extended Family made* AE *#7 virtually a "theme issue."*

But when he announced that AE *#8 would feature a never-published* Marvel Family *script written by Otto in 1953, just before Fawcett canceled its comics line, Roy inadvertently carried that "theme" over into* AE *#8, in a way he could never have envisioned. More on that in a few pages....*

The Editors

BESTEST LEAGUE DEPT.
"With Apologies to Mike Vosburg" Division

Introducing:
ALTER and CAPT. EGO
WRITTEN and DRAWN by BILJO WHITE
WHILE CAPTAIN EGO COMBATS THAT FLAMING ROBOT MONSTER, THE BOY WILL BE LEFT UNPROTECTED! BY OVERPOWERING HIM I CAN TAKE THE TELEPATHICONTROL HELMET AND GAIN CONTROL OVER EGO'S AMAZING STRENGTH!
CLANK!
WHAT IF YOUR FRIEND BECAME ILL EVERY TIME YOU DID? —IF HE LAUGHED AND WAS HAPPY WHEN YOU WERE? — OR IF WHEN YOU WERE SAD—HE WOULD CRY? THIS STORY IS JUST SUCH A TALE... A MOST UNIQUE ADVENTURE IN WHICH A YOUNG BOY GAINS A RE-MARKABLE POWER OF MAGIC & SCIENCE! ... BEGIN NOW, THE 1ST EXCITING STORY OF A GREAT NEW TEAM...
"ALTER MEETS CAPT. EGO!"
1.

BOY—LOOK AT THOSE JETS GO!

BOOM!
GOSH! IT ALWAYS SHAKES ME WHEN THEY BREAK THE SOUND BARRIER!

SAY!—THAT WAS AN EXPLOSION!
—AND THOSE AREN'T JETS! THEY'RE ROCKETSHIPS!

HIGH ABOVE, A STRICKEN SPACEMAN STRUGGLES WITH THE CONTROLS!
IT'S NO USE, I C-CAN'T MAKE IT!
CRUNCH!
THE WOUNDED CRAFT, ITS GLEAMING SURFACE IN FLAMES, SLIDES INTO THE SOFT EARTH AND SKIDS TO A STOP!

GRAVELY HURT, THE TALL, BLOND PILOT SHAKILY PULLS HIMSELF FROM THE WRECKAGE!
A STRANGE HELMET IS CLUTCHED TIGHTLY IN HIS ARMS!

BEFORE HE FALLS TO THE GROUND, HE MOTIONS THE BOY TO DON THE WEIRD-LOOKING HEADPIECE...
GULP! I'M GETTING SOME KIND OF THOUGHT EMISSIONS! THE WOUNDED MAN IS TELLING ME HE'S COME FROM FAR AWAY—ON A MOST URGENT MISSION....! NOW—HIS THOUGHTS ARE INSTRUCTING ME TO WILL HIM TO GET WELL!..?
2

I **ALONE** WAS ELECTED TO TRY AND REACH EARTH TO WARN **ITS** INHABITANTS THEY NEXT ARE SCHEDULED FOR **EXTERMINATION** BY **TIGRIS**! IT IS HOPED THIS DEVICE WILL THWART HIS EVIL INTENTIONS!

"ONLY BY TEAMWORK CAN WE HOPE TO DEFEAT TIGRIS! AFTER HE DESTROYED THE ZIRCON CIVILIZATION, HIS BAND TRAILED ME HERE TO EARTH! HE WILL STOP AT NOTHING TO GET THE TELECO HELMET—OR TO DESTROY IT!

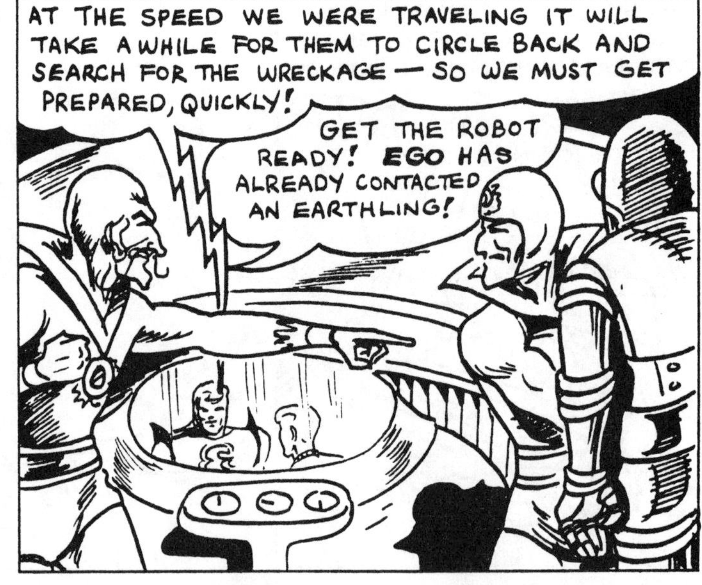
AT THE SPEED WE WERE TRAVELING IT WILL TAKE A WHILE FOR THEM TO CIRCLE BACK AND SEARCH FOR THE WRECKAGE — SO WE MUST GET PREPARED, QUICKLY!
GET THE ROBOT READY! EGO HAS ALREADY CONTACTED AN EARTHLING!

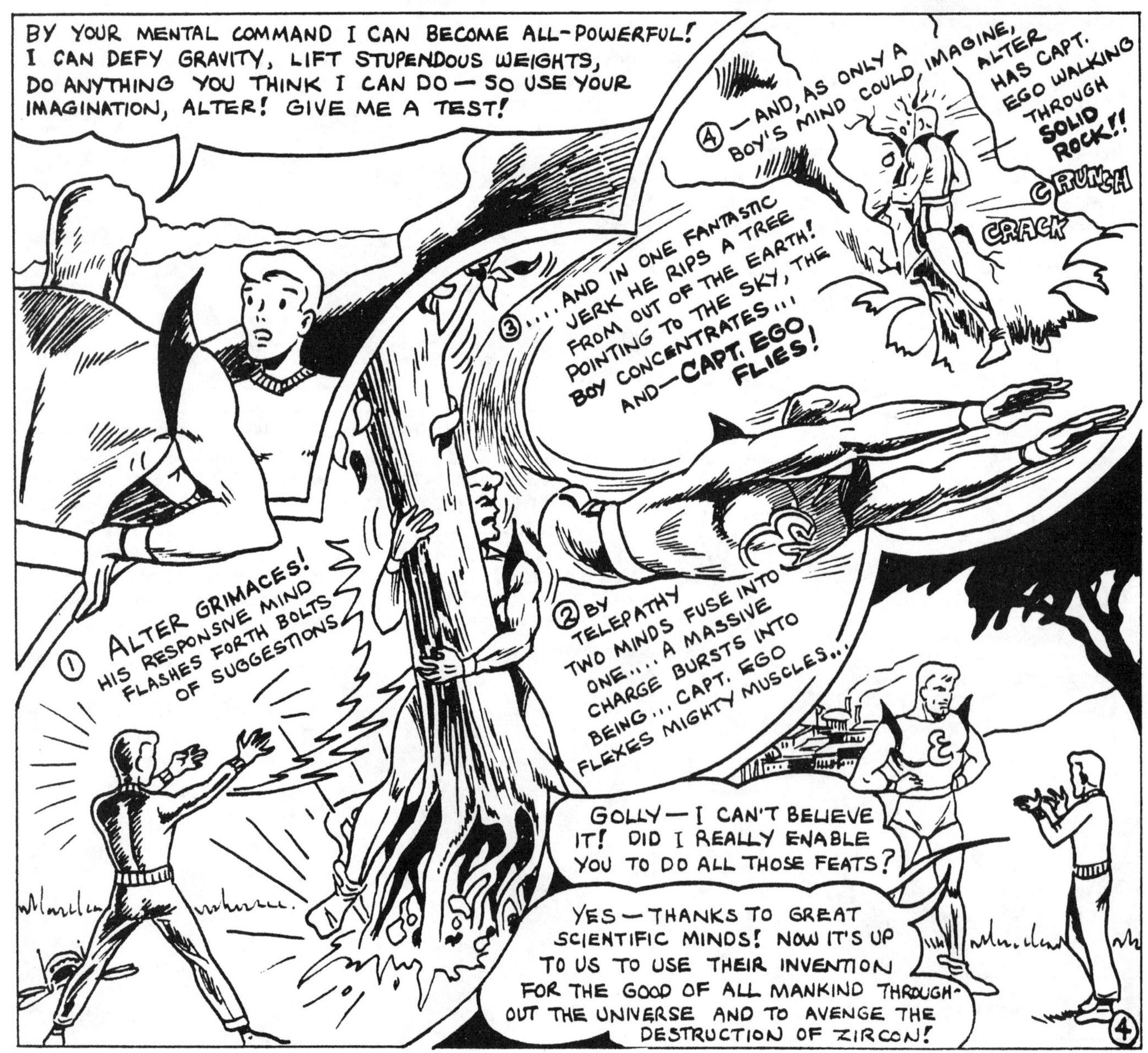
BY YOUR MENTAL COMMAND I CAN BECOME ALL-POWERFUL! I CAN DEFY GRAVITY, LIFT STUPENDOUS WEIGHTS, DO ANYTHING YOU THINK I CAN DO — SO USE YOUR IMAGINATION, ALTER! GIVE ME A TEST!
① ALTER GRIMACES! HIS RESPONSIVE MIND FLASHES FORTH BOLTS OF SUGGESTIONS
② BY TELEPATHY TWO MINDS FUSE INTO ONE... A MASSIVE CHARGE BURSTS INTO BEING... CAPT. EGO FLEXES MIGHTY MUSCLES...
③ ...AND IN ONE FANTASTIC JERK HE RIPS A TREE FROM OUT OF THE EARTH! POINTING TO THE SKY, THE BOY CONCENTRATES... AND—CAPT. EGO FLIES!
④ —AND, AS ONLY A BOY'S MIND COULD IMAGINE, ALTER HAS CAPT. EGO WALKING THROUGH SOLID ROCK!!
CRUNCH
CRACK
GOLLY — I CAN'T BELIEVE IT! DID I REALLY ENABLE YOU TO DO ALL THOSE FEATS?
YES — THANKS TO GREAT SCIENTIFIC MINDS! NOW IT'S UP TO US TO USE THEIR INVENTION FOR THE GOOD OF ALL MANKIND THROUGHOUT THE UNIVERSE AND TO AVENGE THE DESTRUCTION OF ZIRCON!
4

WHAT SHALL WE DO WITH THE HELMET?
IT MUST BE PROTECTED, HIDDEN IN A SAFE PLACE DUE TO TWO WEAK-NESSES AS YET UNPERFECTED! THE HELMET MAY BE NEEDED TO RE-CHARGE YOUR Z-BEAM CONTACT....

"IF TIGRIS SHOULD STEAL THE HELMET, CHANCES ARE THE Z-BEAM WOULD GIVE HIM THE POWER OF THOUGHT CONTROL AND HE'D USE ME AS A TOOL FOR CONQUEST OF THE UNIVERSE! WITHOUT ME, HIS EVIL HORDES WOULD PROBABLY OVER RUN EARTH IN LESS THAN A MONTH, BUT BY USING TELEPATHIC SUGGESTIONS HE COULD COMMAND ME TO INFLICT DRASTIC DAMAGE TO...
..YOUR PEOPLE AND THEIR POSSESSIONS!
SO BE PREPARED! TIGRIS IS A TRICKY AND DEADLY ENEMY!"

YOUR EVERY THOUGHT WILL RE-SULT IN INSTANTANEOUS OBEDIENCE BY ME — EVEN WHEN YOU ARE SICK, HAPPY, OR MAD, I WILL BE INFLU-ENCED IN SOME WAY, SO REMEM-BER TO KEEP YOUR HEALTH AND SPIRIT IN TOP SHAPE!

COURAGEOUSLY, YOUNG ALTER ALBRIGHT ACCEPTS HIS FATE!
GOLLY — I WONDER WHERE THOSE ALIENS ARE, ANYWAY?
5.

THEY COULD BE ANYWHERE! WILL ME TO FLY!... FROM A HIGH DISTANCE I MAY BE ABLE TO SPOT THEM!
SSHHH! IS THE ROBOT SET?
YES, AL-MIGHTY!

BEFORE CAPT. EGO CAN TAKE TO THE AIR—THEY HEAR A METALLIC ROAR.... THEY FEEL A BLAST OF FURNACE-LIKE AIR AND THE LIGHT IS BLINDING AS A HUGE FLAMING ROBOT MONSTER LOOMS BEFORE THEM!!
W-WHAT IS IT!?
TORNO!-THE DREADED ROBOT THAT HELPED TIGRIS DESTROY ZIRCON!
WILL ME THE POWER TO COMBAT IT!-QUICKLY!
READY NOW!... DON'T SHOOT! I WANT THAT HELMET ALL IN ONE PIECE!
REGAINING HIS COMPOSURE, ALTER GESTURES AND CAPT. EGO JUMPS TO THE ATTACK!
THEN...
MY ARM! A STABBING PAIN! THAT MEANS...
IT'S A TRAP! THEY'VE GOT ALTER! ... BY HURTING HIM... IT-IT'S CAUSING ME TO LOSE MY STRENGTH...!!
I-I CAN'T HOLD OUT MUCH LONGER! TIGRIS WILL GET THE TELECO HELMET AND EARTH IS DOOMED!!
CONCENTRATE, ALTER! CONCENTRATE!!
6

JUST AS THINGS LOOK BLACKEST... ALTER BREAKS FREE AND SCOOPS UP A HAND FULL OF DIRT.....
COUGH!
DIRECTED BY THOUGHTS OF UNLIMITED STRENGTH, CAPT. EGO SMASHES THE ROBOT INTO FRAGMENTS!
POW!

REALIZING TIGRIS HAS THE TELECO HELMET, CAPT. EGO WHIRLS AND CHARGES AT THE SURPRISED TYRANT!
INCREDIBLE! THIS INVENTION IS EVEN GREATER THAN I GUESSED!

ASSISTANTS TRY TO HALT CAPT. EGO — ONLY TO MEET SUDDEN DISASTER!

ONE CRUNCHING BLOW ENDS TIGRIS' MARCH TO CONQUEST OF THE UNIVERSE! ZIRCON'S DEFEAT IS AVENGED!

WE'VE WON THE FIRST ENCOUNTER, ALTER! BUT THE OTHERS, THOUSANDS OF TIGRIS' FOLLOWERS, WILL SWARM OVER EARTH LIKE LOCUSTS! IT'LL BE A RACE AGAINST TIME, SO WE MUST PREPARE—NOW!

EARTHMEN! THIS IS A WARNING! YOU AND YOUR PLANET ARE DOOMED! I, TIGRIS, SHALL DESTROY YOU—DESPITE CAPT. EGO AND THE BOY! BECAUSE SOMEDAY, SOMEHOW I WILL GET THE TELECO HELMET! THEN YOU ARE DOOMED!!
BILJO WHITE '64
The END
7

SHEL SILVERFISH
LOOKS AT
THE GILDED AGE OF COMICS

EVERY CITY, EVERY COUNTRY, EVERY BUSINESS SEEMS TO HAVE HAD A MYSTICAL "GOLDEN AGE" AT SOME TIME IN THE VAGUE, INDEFINITE PAST! FOR THE COMICS, THAT "GOLDEN AGE" WAS THE LATE 30'S AND EARLY 40'S! THIS WAS THE TIME OF IDEALISTIC SUPER-DOERS IN COMICS PUBLISHED BY PUBLISHERS WHOSE ONLY CONCERN WAS FOR THE ENTERTAINMENT AND WELL-BEING OF THE CHILDREN OF AMERICA....

Conceived and Executed by

Roy Thomas

TODAY'S COMIC BOOKS ARE PUBLISHED WITH THE SAME CREATIVE FLAIR! THE EXISTENCE OF DOZENS OF SUPER-HEROES ON THE MARKET HAS LED TO A CLOSE RELATIONSHIP BETWEEN EDITOR, WRITER, AND ARTIST TO CREATE COSTUMED CHARACTERS UNIQUE TO THIS ATOMIC AGE....

"We'll admit that your picture of Superman battling a gigantic blue-and-green speckled dinosaur antedates ours of Captain Marvel combatting an enormous green-and-blue spotted dragon, but we have an even *earlier* one showing Captain Marvel fighting a tremendous bluish-green polka-dotted sea serpent, and...."

"Now, Steve, I *know* you stayed up all night trying to come up with a truly good sketch of an original hero, so I'm afraid you're not going to like what I'm going to have to tell you...."

"Er... Sid... I, uh, understand this quirk of yours about always pencilling your women in the *nude*... but you're doing *inks* now... Er, Sid... Sid...."

"Yes, Bob... The splash panel for the latest 'War That Time Forgot' story is almost finished."

"Now look, you guys, this is the graceful effect I want you to achieve as Thor rescues the nurse from Loki's magic tornado...."

"Looks like another one of those days -- four fan letters and 321 requests for fanzine plugs...."

"Now here's the plan, Russ.... As soon as *Tarzan* sales pick up and *Korak Son of Tarzan* is a big hit, we hit them with *Borax Son of Korak Son of Tarzan*. Then, when *that* catches on, we...."

IN THIS SECOND HEROIC AGE OF COMIC BOOK SUPER-DOERS, HIGHER STANDARDS OF PRODUCTION HAVE RESULTED IN A CORRESPONDINGLY HIGHER SET OF VALUES ON THE PART OF TODAY'S COMIC FANDOM, THAT GROUP OF HYPERCRITICAL AND DISCRIMINATING READERS WHICH MAKES AND BREAKS COMIC BOOK PUBLISHERS IN CASTING THEIR CAREFULLY CONSIDERED ECONOMIC VOTES!

"Gimme a copy of *Little Lulu*."

One Man's Family

THE SAGA OF THE MIGHTY MARVELS

by ROY THOMAS
Illustrated by BILJO WHITE

One dark night in 1940, a lonely newsboy stood on a corner, hawking his journalistic wares. It was late, and not a soul remained on the street to buy a newspaper. Suddenly, he heard a "Hist!" from the shadows. Turning in surprise, the newsboy spotted a mysterious dark-clad figure beckoning to him from the entrance of an abandoned subway. His curiosity thoroughly aroused, he followed the sinister shape into the subway.

Inside, he found himself in a dark passageway lined with grotesque sculptures representing the Seven Deadly Sins: Lust, Envy, Greed, *et al.* Further on, the passageway opened into a large room, in the center of which stood a marble throne. Seated on the throne was a bearded patriarchal figure in a long flowing mantle. Over the man's head, though the newsboy did not notice it at once, was a large stone block suspended somehow by a single thin strand.

Abruptly belying his statue-like appearance, the robed figure spoke, informing newsboy Billy Batson that he was Shazam, a wizard from the Egypt of 3,000 BC. Billy had been summoned, he learned, to be given miraculous powers in the service of humanity.

"Billy Batson, speak my name!" the youth was ordered.

"Shazam!" Billy obliged, and immediately the most unrealistic lightning ever to appear in a comic book transformed him into a sort of muscular Fred MacMurray, dressed in a red suit trimmed in gold (or yellow, if you will), complete with a lightning-bolt insignia on his chest and a short white-and-gold cape.

A moment later, the thin strand supporting the stone over Shazam's head snapped in a pre-ordained manner, and SPLAT! – no more wizard!

And so Captain Marvel was born.

It cannot truly be said that he was the most invincible super-hero ever invented. Superman, the adventure character that Cap alternately imitated and parodied, was at least as powerful and later became even more so, since Kryptonite (whether of one color or 37) is a relatively late creation. And then there was the Spectre, whose powers – as Jim Harmon once wrote – were roughly equal to those of God.

Perhaps a better comparison than either of these is available in today's Thor, whose powers are great but indeterminate. The Mighty One, also, utilizes magic lightning of dubious realism to turn from human to super-human. Thor is, as everybody knows, the Norse god of thunder; Captain Marvel got his powers from the name of Shazam, an anagram composed of the initials of various gods and heroes of Greco-Roman mythology, with Solomon tossed in for good measure. Thor, however, having evidently never heard of the Teutonic myth of Ragnarok (the day on which all the gods will be killed in a battle with the Giants), is constantly called immortal; one of the most common epithets applied to the Big Red Cheese was that of "The World's Mightiest Mortal."

And he was, at least, a reasonably strong contender for that title, since the Spectre was a ghost and therefore not a mortal. In another sense, Cap became the World's Mightiest Seller, also. Quickly outgrowing his mere cover-feature status in *Whiz Comics*, Captain Marvel branched out in 1941 into his own monthly magazine. (For a short time in the middle 40's, *Captain Marvel Adventures* was even a biweekly. And, of course, there was the Republic serial....)

An equally significant facet of Cap's tremendous growth in popularity was his fantastic progeny. The Big Red Cheese proved to be such a gold-mine to Fawcett Publications that he was almost immediately cut into several profitable slices.

The best of these occurred in *Whiz* #25, when a villain named Captain Nazi permanently crippled and almost killed another poor newsboy, one Freddy Freeman. (Symbolism, anyone?) Captain Marvel saved the lad and took him before old Shazam's spirit, which could be conjured up at any time simply by lighting a torch next to his vacant throne. Shazam told Cap that he would give the boy powers comparable to those of the Mighty Mortal himself.

On awakening, the boy saw Captain Marvel standing near him. On gasping out the super-hero's name in surprise, Freddy was turned by magic lightning into Captain Marvel Jr., a blue-clad counterpart of Cap. Unlike the original Marvel, however, Junior remained a teenager, identical in facial features to the newsboy he had been. Evidently Junior didn't have as much on the ball as his mentor; while Billy Batson rose quickly from newsboy to radio

newscaster, Freddy Freeman remained to the end of his teenage days at the corner newsstand, yelling "Extry, extry!"

Junior was not the only spiritual offspring of Captain Marvel, however. Indeed, as has been observed before, almost all the Superthis and Superthat characters introduced by National Comics were done years earlier by editor Wendell Crowley's similarly inventive associates, namely artist C.C. Beck and writer Otto Binder. Just as Superboy was preceded by Captain Marvel Jr., so did Cap Sr. gain a sister long before Cousin Supergirl was even a twinkle in Mort Weisinger's eye.

In her origin in *Captain Marvel* #18, a dying nurse informed Billy Batson that he had a long-lost twin sister, and he immediately launched a nationwide search for her. As it turned out, she was much nearer at hand than he suspected – a quiz-kid on a radio show at his own Station WHIZ, as a matter of fact. He found her just in time, too. Later in the story, Billy and Freddy were knocked unconscious by criminals holding Mary for ransom, and in consternation she cried out: "Billy! Freddy! Speak your magic words! Oh, they can't! They're gagged! Billy can't say SHAZAM...!"

BOOM! ZAP! Instantly, in Mary Batson's place stood Mary Marvel, identical in physical appearance to her predecessor but garbed in a short-skirted version of Capt. Marvel's famed costume.

The new Miss Marvel was understandably upset about the treatment of her brother and his friend, and dealt one of the crooks a gentle slap – which sent him reeling twenty feet against a wall. While she stopped momentarily to admire the lovely outfit she was so suddenly wearing, another felon smashed a chair over her pretty head – ineffectually, of course.

The crooks' last resort was guns, and Mary squealed in terror as the remaining kidnapers opened fire on her. But naturally the bullets bounced off. Realizing now to some degree the extent of her powers, she smashed the two remaining crooks and freed Billy and Freddy.

Later, Shazam's spirit explained that, because she was Billy's twin, the power of changing into a superbeing was inherent within her, as well. This makes no logical sense, of course, since Billy's own power was only a relatively recent gift from the late Egyptian mage; but this was in those happy, carefree days before editorial footnotes and "explanations" for every use of a hero's power. After all, Cap and his brood were magical, not logical.

At any rate, logical or not, Mary Marvel at once zoomed from this issue of *Captain Marvel Adventures* to join Batman-type Mr. Scarlet in *Wow #9* and future issues for years. To poor Scarlet she must have been about as welcome as a bath in red ink remover, for she immediately knocked him off the cover of that magazine. And of course she and Junior both had their own comics ere long, Junior in 1942 and Mary in 1943. (Junior was also in *Master*.)

After that, you would think that old Shazam had virtually subdivided his powers into nothingness, but not so. One day, after Billy's regular radio broadcast, three more Billy Batsons showed up – Tall Billy, Fat Billy, and Hill Billy. In this adventure (*Whiz* #21), all four were captured and tied to a log pointed nervously at an unfriendly buzzsaw. In order to yell above the noises of the saw (a problem that didn't bother him in subsequent tales), our Billy Batson had his three new friends shout "Shazam!" with him. Result: they, too, were transformed into adult superbeings – Lieutenants Marvel or the Squadron of Justice, as they alternately called themselves.

Enough? Uh-uh. Fawcett also planned to start a Disney-type comic entitled *Funny Animals.* Its cover feature? "Hoppy the Marvel Bunny," what else? It seems that this little rabbit was sitting under a tree one day, kiddies, and this mean bully was trying to steal his girl friend. Reading an issue of *Captain Marvel*, he remarked wistfully that he wished he could become strong just by saying "Shazam!"

BOOM! ZAP! Another member of what could have justifiably been called the Merry Marvel Bullpen! From that time on, no Nazi funny-animal was safe! Hoppy, too, got his own comic, but not till a much later date and not for very long. And, in one memorable if especially unrealistic tale, he and Mary Marvel teamed up in an other-dimension adventure.

There were a couple of non-super Marvels along the line, too. Billy's Uncle Dudley, who first appeared in *Captain Marvel* #43, claimed to share the powers of his nephew and niece and would shout "Shazam" while struggling out of his street clothes to stand decked out in a poor man's version of Cap's uniform. The others liked "Uncle Marvel," however, and pretended to believe he had Shazamic powers like their own. He generally "flew" by clinging tenaciously to Captain Marvel's cape. A teenage girl named Freckles appointed herself the cousin of Mary Marvel, also, but she didn't claim extra powers because of it.

A few *villains* followed the Shazam tradition, as well. There was Levram, which is "Marvel" spelled backwards. And in *Captain Marvel* #8 a milquetoast crook named Stinky Printwhistle was given by Lucifer the power to pronounce the initials of Ivan (the Terrible), Borgia, Attila, and Caligula and become Ibac, a muscular do-badder.

The most memorable of the Marvel *crooks*, however, appeared in December of 1945, when the first issue of *Marvel Family Comics* appeared. That first beautiful cover (and the stories inside, as well) featured Cap, Junior, Mary, Uncle Marvel, and Shazam himself – or at least his never-say-die spirit.

It seems that 5000 years before, in Egypt, old Shazam (who was probably *never* young) had decided to pass on some of his power to supposedly worthy Teth-Adam. The venerable sorcerer called the selectee before him and commanded him to pronounce his name (something that is still disputed among Captain Marvel fans). Upon doing so, Teth-Adam instantly became Mighty Adam, who was dressed in a black-and-gold, capeless edition of Cap's suit.

The color black proved to be rather prophetic. Either Shazam was wrong from the start about the purity of soul of Teth-Adam, or else in old Egypt power corrupted more quickly than it does *today*, because Mighty Adam immediately raced to the pharaoh's palace, broke the royal neck, and proclaimed himself ruler of the land.

He was destined for a short reign, however. Appearing before the new pharaoh and addressing him now as Black Adam (the name that finally stuck), Shazam proclaimed that, although he could not destroy the receiver of so many of his powers, he *could* still banish him to the farthest star, which he proceeded to do. At once Black Adam was hurled far out into space and it took him 5000 years to get back.

When he finally arrived, he found Cap, Junior, and Mary unable to stop his rampage of terror. It was a stalemate. However, while the other three Marvels tried their luck with Black Adam, Uncle Marvel tried a more laudable approach – that of using his head. He lit the magic torch that summoned the spirit of Shazam. The late wizard advised Dudley to get the evil Marvel to say the magic word, which would defeat him.

Quickly, Uncle Marvel threw himself into the fray between Black Adam and the confused Marvel Family (as they were now officially known). "Stop, kids," he shouted. "He's so strong, let's make him a member of the Marvel Family. After all, he got his powers from old Mazham. I mean... Hamshaz. No, I mean Shamhaz... er, uh..."

"You sputtering old fool," sneered Black Adam. "You mean *Shazam*!"

BOOM! ZAP! The magic lightning turned the evil one back into Teth-Adam, whom Captain Marvel instantly clobbered. Moments later the unconscious Teth-Adam crumbled into dust. (After all, he *was* 5000 years old.)

Marvel Family Comics #1 was the first of a quite successful series of comics, which was declared to be a monthly from the start. However, issue #1 was dated December 1945, and #2 didn't come out until June 1946. The first issue was 36 pages long and contained the foregoing origin tale, if such it can be called, and another one in which the Marvel Family temporarily adopted a "Baby Marvel" who was left on Billy Batson's doorstep.

Unfortunately, *Marvel Family Comics* #2 did not quite live up to the promise of the fine first issue. It featured only one Marvel Family tale, a rather short one which covered a "family reunion" of the original four members with the Lts. Marvel thrown in. The other stories in the issue were individual adventures of Cap, Junior, and Mary such as could be seen in any of the half dozen other comics starring these three characters.

This issue, regrettably, set the pace for the next several years, so that the most interesting thing about most of those very early *Marvel Family* comics was the back cover, featuring as it often did many Marvel items for sale. For prices ranging from 10¢ to 50¢, Fawcett offered readers Captain Marvel felt hats, magic folders, pennants, statuettes, felt emblems, and an overseas cap. If you preferred Junior, there was a felt emblem which pictured him instead of Cap. And the girl readers could send off for Mary Marvel novelty pins and – you guessed it – felt emblems. You got a free Captain Marvel pencil clip with your order, too.

The back of #3 pushed Marvel Family games, featuring eight items (a $2.10 value, the reader was assured) for $1. This set of items included tattoo transfers, a Shazam game, and various other games. And you got free a magic lightning box, comic clock, Captain Marvel's magic eyes (whatever *they* were), C.M. buzz bombs, as well as iron-ons of Cap and other Fawcett heroes such as Spy Smasher, and don't we all wish we had them today!

There were a number of goodies *between* the covers as well, however. This writer's personal favorite is the

tenth issue of *The Marvel Family* (as the comic was called starting with issue #3).

It featured an action-packed cover in which Cap, Mary, and Junior were slugging it out with their most consistent and malevolent foes, the Sivana Family, therein united together for the first time. Old Thaddeus Budog Sivana himself, the self-styled World's Maddest Scientist, was more or less a deliberate Fu Manchu type at the start (as writer Binder himself has admitted), who appeared in the very first Captain Marvel story and who was easily the most popular of Cap's many intriguing foes.

When success caused Cap to be amoebaed into several subsidiary characters, Sivana followed suit, and out of nowhere appeared his equally evil and buck-toothed progency, Junior Sivana and Georgia Sivana.

In regards to the latter, however, it should perhaps be stated here that she was not the *first* daughter of Sivana. There was another, earlier child, Beautia, who appeared in some of the very early *Whiz* tales and who fell in love with Captain Marvel; but she was the lovely black sheep of the Sivana clan and was dropped after a few stories. Georgia herself, as was explained when she first appeared in *Mary Marvel* #1, spent all her early life on the planet Venus. *Why*, I don't know.

Part of my interest in the story in *Marvel Family* #10 ("The Sivana Family Strikes at the Marvel Family") lies in the fact that its basic format is similar to that of the famed Justice Society tales. There is an introductory chapter in which the Marvels (and the Sivanas as well) appear together, then a separate chapter for each of the three major members, and of course a slam-bang let's-get-together-and-polish-'em-off ending.

This 1947 tale of tales began with a scene from the famous Marvel Family television show, a round-table affair presided over by Uncle Marvel (who was, incidentally, appearing in his last issue of *Marvel Family*). Watching the program from his floating laboratory was Dr. Sivana himself, who had decided it was time for *his* family to join forces likewise. He had built a giant machine which he was convinced would utterly destroy the Marvels forever, but no further work could be done on it until he and the kids could measure the voltage of the Shazam lightning.

Accordingly, the next day the three Sivanas let themselves be seen on the roof of Station WHIZ, and moments later Billy, Mary, and Freddy said the magic words which turned them into the Cheeses. (It was Sivana, by the way, who invented and popularized Captain Marvel's most persistent nickname through the years, the Big Red Cheese.)

As the enchanted lightning bolts thundered down from the heavens, however, they proved to be so powerful they exploded Sivana's meter, and he and his offspring were forced to use a smokescreen to escape from the Marvels. (Well, what could Thaddeus expect, anyhow? The meter had only been designed to measure 6,000,000,000,000,000,000 mega-volts!)

At this point Junior came to the aid of his insidious papa with an old manuscript from ancient Atlantis which mentioned an element named Protium. Patterned after uranium, this fictitious element took 10,000 years to turn into Neutrium, and 10,000 more to become Electrium. A bomb in which these three elements were combined, Sivana thought, would give him the power he needed for his mysterious Marvel-mashing machine.

In today's comics there are a number of pseudo-scientific explanations as to how the super-heroes travel to other times. Superman flies counter-clockwise around the earth or some such nonsense, Flash runs on a souped-up treadmill, and the Atom goes fishing.

But not in a Fawcett comic! The Binder-Crowley-Beck theory of the universe held that at its center was a gigantic peak called the Rock of Eternity (not to be confused with the Rock of Ages). From here it was possible to travel almost anywhere – including into the past and future – instantly. From his long "association" with the Marvels, Sivana had learned virtually all their secrets, so he naturally knew of this Rock. And furthermore, he possessed a rocketship capable of space-warping its way there in minutes.

However, Dr. Sivana had overlooked one little detail. Dwelling in a castle on the Rock of Eternity was Shazam itself; this was evidently where good little ancient wizards went when they died. Telescope in hand, Shazam spotted the Sivanas' rocket and immediately used his ethereal form to contact the Marvel Family. Cap, Junior, and Mary zoomed at once to the Rock, but arrived only in time to follow their respective worst enemies into various historical periods.

In the second chapter Georgia Sivana arrived in the Atlantis of 8000 B.C., whose language she instantly comprehended because "we Sivanas are a family of brilliant geniuses." Finding the home of Chal-Patzun, the Atlantean scientist who had discovered Protium, she found to her dismay that he had developed a machine he declared would save his supposedly doomed continent, which he claimed would soon sink because of an earth fault.

Gaining his confidence, however, Georgia discovered that he merely meant that his machine would make Atlantis rise again from the sea in the far future. For this purpose he had sent his only son to another land with instructions to keep alive the memory of the sunken continent for 20,000 years.

When Chal-Patzun showed her various lead test tubes filled with samples of the radioactive Protium, Georgia revealed her true nature and conked him from behind. However, as she was about to flee with the Protium, Mary Marvel swooshed in and knocked her unconscious. She awoke, bound, to see the World's Mightiest Girl conversing with the recovered scientist.

Then suddenly the ground began to shake; the earth fault in Atlantis was finally cracking. In a last-ditch attempt to speed up the changing of Protium to Neutrium, Mary said the magic word which brought a "KARASH!" of lightning. She changed into Mary Batson, but the Protium remained Protium.

To make things worse, an extra-strong rumble at this moment knocked her and Chal-Patzun off balance

THE MARVEL FAMILY vs. THE SIVANA FAMILY
(FROM COVER OF MF #10)

while freeing Georgia. The daughter of Sivana tied and gagged Mary and lugged her into her miniature rocket, leaving the Atlantean scientist to die for and with his country. She had her Protium.

In the third chapter Dr. Sivana himself shrewdly deduced that any descendant of Chal-Patzun would probably be a scientist, so it was no trouble (at least in a Fawcett comic book) to locate his little home "out here in the suburbs" and kidnap him at gunpoint. His name? Charles Patterson, of course. However, the clever good scientist managed to scrawl the location of sunken Atlantis on the wall, and when Captain Marvel arrived he was soon hot on Sivana's trail. He succeeded in rescuing Patterson, but Sivana escaped.

Inside the water-proof dome which Chal-Patzun had built to protect his pet machine, Cap and Patterson found the original Protium changed to Neutrium. However, at this moment, Sivana returned to the attack in his rocketship, which doubled as a submarine. He had brought back a giant harnessed electric eel, whose shock – magnified by water pressure, it says here – changed Cap back into Billy Batson, who was half drowned at once. Sivana promptly shot Patterson in cold blood, took a vial of Neutrium, and fled with Billy in his rocket. And so the plot thickened.

In the future world of 12,000 A.D. it seems that the Atlantean tradition was still being carried on, and scientist Chass Passon had just used the Electrium still in his father's dome to raise the lost continent to the surface when Junior Sivana arrived.

In a scene perhaps too reminiscent of the first two individual adventures, Captain Marvel Jr. arrived just in time to rescue the future Atlantean from the young Sivana's clutches, although the wicked Junior escaped by tossing seaweed into the other Junior's face. But when the World's Mightiest Boy introduced himself to Chass Passon and thereby changed automatically back into Freddy Freeman, Junior Sivana took advantage of the situation to strike from hiding and K.O. the crippled newsboy. Then guess what – he killed Charles Passon, took the Electrium and Freddy, and rocketed back to the twentieth century. Surprised? Likewise.

In the fifth and final chapter (entitled "The Battle of the Age"), the three Sivanas reunited and congratulated each other in front of the bound and gagged teenagers. Dr. Sivana took the Protium, Neutrium, and Electrium and tossed them (rather haphazardly, I thought) into his beloved machine. It was turned on and began to go WHIR-R-R and HMMMMM and other comic-booky noises. "The world is ours – all ours!" Sivana chuckled.

Then, sharp blade in hand and world's wickedest gleam in eye, he approached Mary, Billy, and Freddy, who were understandably terrified, though helpless. However, to their utter amazement, all he did was cut their bonds. Convinced that old Thaddeus had finally popped his cork once and for all, they immediately yelled out their words – but nothing happened!

Obligingly, Sivana explained. His machine had created a vast amount of free electrons, which had instantly formed a shell around the earth. These special electrons, he informed them, repelled lightning as like repels like, so that the famed Shazam lightning bounced harmlessly off. Understand?

"So now you see," he chortled in his glee, "why we went to all the trouble to get Protium, Neutrium, and Electrium. For as long as this machine operates, you kids can never again change to the Marvel Family! *Heh heh!*"

"H-Holy M-Moley!" exclaimed Billy.*

Convinced that the final barrier was removed from his becoming the Rightful Ruler of the Universe, Sivana took the de-Marveled teenagers (as well as his own evil brood) to a palace he had built in the middle of nowhere. In it were huge thrones for "King Sivana," "Princess Georgia," and "Crown Prince Junior." And, being royalty, the Sivanas decided to indulge at once in the sports of kings, fox-hunting – with the kids as the foxes.

The ending of the story, unfortunately, was not quite up to the rest. Billy utilized the oldest of foxy tricks, walking backwards in one's own footprints, and managed to double back to the unlocked rocketship. Since all intelligent teenagers can pilot evil scientists' private rockets, Billy flew Mary and Freddy back to the floating lab of the Sivanas, where they turned off the machine and Shazamed at once into the mighty Marvel Family.

There were five more clashes with Dr. Sivana and his brood. In issue #16 the Sivana Family, to stop the Marvels from winning a $25,000 "best family" prize, put an "Emotion Emulsion" into their water so that they would quarrel on the air. However, while battling their way across the countryside, they were accidentally rescued from the spell by the soothing harp-playing of none other than Miss Georgia Sivana herself.

In #23 the Sivana Family bought a newspaper and attempted unsuccessfully to use yellow journalism to ruin their foes. In #68 they conquered the entire universe by holding old Shazam as hostage in his Rock of Eternity castle; they attacked the Marvel Family with bolts of magic lightning before finally being defeated. In 1952, in issue #75, the Sivana tribe journeyed into the far future of the year *1960*, when space ships were zooming from planet to planet, to capture a Marvel-less universe. And in their final joint appearance (though Sivana starred many other times as a lone villain) they set a "Triple Trap of Terror" by land, sea, and air that almost finished off the Cheeses.

---

*Moley (or *Moly*, the usual spelling) really *was* holy, by the way. In Greek myth it was a plant with magical powers. In the Odyssey the god Hermes gave some to Odysseus to prevent him from making a pig of himself over the witch Circe.

The "family" motif proved to be a very popular one in the comic, as a perusal of titles will show. In the 89 issues of *The Marvel Family* there appeared space-squatter families, netherworld families, future families, hermit families, and the most interesting of all (excluding, of course, the Sivanas), which appeared in issue #20.

It seems that in the "hill country" a unique situation had occurred. One family, the Kruggses, had disposed completely of all its traditional feudin' rivals. The McCorns, the Batfields, the Nayleys – there just warnt none of 'em left.

Finally, in consternation, they turned to old Granny Kruggs. "Ain't there nobody nowhere fer us to feud with, Granny?" they implored earnestly.

"Wal," drawled Granny, "a long time back a feller named William Batson opined it was agonna be good weather, when gran'pappy said it was agonna rain. So nacherly he shot the Batson feller like a dawg, fer argying with him."

So the Kruggses started off after Billy Batson, whose picture they saw in a newspaper. It took more of a struggle than you might imagine for even the Marvels eventually to round them all up and slap them in jail.

Another predictably common theme, which we have already encountered, was the "trio" motif. Titles like "The Triple Trap of Terror," "The Trio of Terror," and "The Triple Time Plot" are indicative of this formula. After Unc dropped out of the picture – and since none of the Lieutenants Marvel ever appeared after #2 – the World's Mightiest Family was especially suited to this type of format.

There were few recurring villains aside from the Sivanas. King Kull, the beastman enemy from *Captain Marvel Adventures* whose *raison d'être* was to destroy all humankind, held forth in such epics as "The Democracy Smasher" (#67), "The Crust Cracker" (#73), "The Threat to the Junior U.N." (#77), and "The World Wrecker" (#86). The titles of these stories pretty well indicate their contents, but I always found King Kull an entertaining adversary for the Cheeses.

Other interesting one-shot villains: Zonga, leader of intelligent apes in #85; Mr. Power, who absorbed kinetic energy to become stronger each time the Marvels struck him, in #26; the Amoeba Men in #27; and Abigail Archibald, "The Earth Changer," who in issue #37 came up with the charming idea of rearranging the positions of all the earth's continents in the interest of easing world travel.

Contents-wise, *The Marvel Family* had a rather spotty history. First of all, it was impossible to guess how many pages it would contain from one issue to the next. Issues #1-4 contained 36 pages due to the wartime paper shortage.*

With #5 it became a 52-page comic, and it hopped back and forth between these two sizes for several years before finally shrinking to the 36-page format that most comics have today.

Even more confusing to the regular reader was attempting to guess what those contents would be. *Marvel Family Comics* #1 contained two stories of the combined Cheeses; #2 had one family story and three individual adventures of Cap, Mary, and Junior. This was at least a common format for some years, although #10 and a few other early issues contained several-part serials. And, just to make matters more confusing, #11 boasted *three* Marvel Family stories, while #12 contained two MF tales and one in which Captain Marvel graciously aided Ulysses in regaining his lost kingdom of Ithaca.

Happily, the format established by the feature-length story in #10 seems to have caught on; it became increasingly common as the comic's life wore on. For example, issue #36 featured a "novel" in which the Marvels fought living meteors, "The Invaders from Infinity." In #48 they battled reincarnations of the Four Horsemen of the Apocalypse. In #56 they embarked on "The World's Mightiest Project," creating a duplicate earth for inhabitants fleeing a dictatorship at the center of our planet.

---

*This was Fawcett Publications' answer to the shortage. National solved this same problem in an intriguing manner; it published a number of its monthly comics only six times a year. If that puzzles anyone, just remember that this is the same company which now publishes several Superman annuals a year.

But, as the magazine neared the end of its long and checkered run, a subtle change crept over it, as well as over others in the Fawcett line. Wm. Gaines' Entertaining Comics (or was it *Educational* Comics?) had set the industry on its ear with its "realistic" war and horror comics, and even Shazam's magic lightning couldn't stop the Marvel Family from being infected.

The Marvels began to take an active part in the Korean War, just as they and other early super-heroes had fought superhumanly against the Japs and Nazis. Villains like the Red Vulture (in #78), the Great Red Brain (#80), and the Mightiest Mongul (#81) began cropping up in *The Marvel Family*. Even worse for their effect on the Cheeses were EC's horror comics. Fawcett (like most other comic companies) never really got the hang of publishing readable horror stories, but it tried. And, to inject life into its apparently sagging sales, it even began to toss monsters into its remaining super-hero magazines with depressingly increasing regularity.

There were the Hissing Horror in #74, the Mad Mummy in #79, the Space Ghoul in #80, and the Flying Skull in #83. Not all of these monsters took themselves too seriously, thank Shazam, but their mere presence seemed a detriment to the Marvel Family reputation.

And, as the last straw, there were even occasional combinations of the war *and* horror motifs – for example, in issue #82 where a story of "The Beast Batallions" dealt with communist attempts to win the Korean War by sending giant serpents and other enlarged creatures against the United Nations forces.

Fawcett also began again to carry two or three Marvel Family tales per issue in a futile attempt to please every type of reader possible. In this regard, *Marvel Family* #80 seems especially symbolic. It contains three Family stories: "The Space Ghoul" for the science fiction and horror fans, "The Great Red Brain" (also with SF overtones) for all the little warmongers, and "The World Jumbler" with Sivana for the decreasing few who still enjoyed the type of story that had once put Captain Marvel on top of the super-hero heap.

But it was no go. The super-doer comics were doomed, at least temporarily. And as if the sales picture alone weren't bad enough – for other comics as well as ones with costumed heroes – Fawcett still had the lawsuit with National hanging over its bowed head.

As virtually everyone knows by now, DC had sued Captain Marvel as a "direct imitation" of Superman – a charge which I will leave it to the readers of this article to debate – while the first issue of *Whiz* was still warm. The case had been argued out of court for years, enriching no one but an army of lawyers. In 1953 it suddenly occurred to Fawcett that maybe it was time to give up, so they paid National an "unspecified sum" and haven't published any comic book but *Dennis the Menace* since.

The last published story of the Marvels, in issue #89, was fittingly though not purposely titled "And Then There Were None." On the cover a boy looked amazedly at blank white outlines of the Marvels and exclaimed, "Holy Moley! What happened to the Marvel Family?"

What, indeed?

But, although it becomes increasingly difficult to find a teenager who has the vaguest idea of who Captain Marvel was, the Cheeses have never really been completely forgotten. The serial is still around, ready to be resuscitated – and a very good one it was, too. And several years ago Charlton, the company which took over many non-super titles from Fawcett, used a number of old Marvel Bunny strips as secondary features in *Atomic Mouse Comics*. Charlton changed his magic word to "Alizam," his costume to blue (without the lightning-bolt insignia), and his name to Hoppy the *Magic* Bunny, and they were in business. And nobody sued, either.

Recently it has also been brought to my attention that a television guide carries a semi-direct copy of Captain Marvel (or perhaps of Junior) called Captain TV. The stories aren't much, but they do call forth some of the old nostalgia.

No, Captain Marvel will probably never return. Prospects for a revival are virtually nil, though Fawcett has many other excellent super-heroes it could restore to the newsstands at will.

But to those of us who still daydream at least once in a red-cheese moon about a magic lightning bolt that will change us into the world's mightiest mortal, "Shazam" is our favorite word!

READERS WRITE...

[A portion of the portrait of Otto Binder that originally appeared in AE #9.]

SPECIAL! -- A LONG, LONG LETTER FROM MR. MARVEL FAMILY HIMSELF -- OTTO BINDER!

EDITOR'S NOTE: Ordinarily, the "Readers Write" section is devoted to letters from fans, with a sprinkling of responses from pros. However, I would like to depart from this established policy this issue to print the following letter from Otto (Eando) Binder, who was kind enough to answer my request for information on Fawcett artists with a lengthy but welcome letter which is virtually an article in itself. I trust that *AE*'s readers, especially those who were and are Captain Marvel enthusiasts, will not mind the deviation.

Dear Roy,

I'll start now, and see how far I get in giving you some of the information you wanted.

First of all, I wrote a total of 152 stories of all types for *Marvel Family Comics.* If you know the total number of issues and stories, you can figure out what percentage of the total I did.

As for artists, I'll have to go only by my notoriously non-photographic memory....

C.C. Beck did most of the Marvel Family and Captain Marvel stories, although at the start my brother Jack's art shop did MF stories. His chief layout man was Ken Bald (yes, the same artist now famed for a couple of syndicated strips and much top commercial art and advertising). Inkers were legion: Bill Ward, Pete Costanza, etc.

Most, if not all, of the Mary Marvel stories were done either by Jack's workshop or by Jack himself (after his art shop fell apart through the draft and post-war headaches).

Captain Marvel Jr. stories were, I believe, all done by Mac Raboy, although there may have been an alternate artist.

George Tuska and a few other independents may have filled in with odd stories or issues, but I believe that 95% of the art was done by the above art staff.

Regarding *Mr. Mind,* the evil worm from outer space who plagued Captain Marvel for two years, there is not much to say except repeat what was said in *Xero*, which went out, unfortunately, primarily to science fiction fans.

Mr. Mind wasn't a worm, at least not for the first half dozen chapters. The *CMA* (*Captain Marvel Adventures*) brain-trust composed of Wendell Crowley as editor, Charles Clarence Beck as artist, and myself as scripter, got our heads together to figure out just who or what Mr. Mind should be, after I invented him as a disembodied voice.

We undoubtedly went through a hundred concepts, until somebody (and, frankly, in those skull sessions, I have no idea who *first* thought of any particular gimmick)... somebody said, "Why not take the most *unusual* thing we can think of? Not the traditional human or galactic villain, nor robot, nor this nor that of the routine masterminds, but just the goofiest of all things – maybe a *worm*!"

I vaguely recall that this was enthusiastically endorsed by us with much laughter and a tongue-in-cheek attitude; we had no idea that *thing* would become POPULAR!!?? We truly were amazed at the electrifying response... letters pouring in... and believe me, with a readership of over *one million* as we had in those days, the mail can become pretty imposing. A rousing consensus simply *loved* Mr. Mind! Why? We never figured it out. *You* figure it out, you researchers today into the mysterious hypnotic power that comic characters had on readers.

The flood of letters, as a matter of practicality, set us to dreaming up new and more *outre* situations between the World's Mightiest Mortal and the Universe's Weakest Creature (which may have been the genetical thought that conjured up a worm).

Of course, the sheer poles-apart contrast made for a wealth of ideas (as inspirations always do), so that the serial ran for 24 chapters before we decided, perhaps wisely, that too much of a good thing is bad.

I won't exactly say tears were in our eyes that day we worked up the final chapter and executed Mr. Mind; but, in all honesty, I think we all felt a "loss" of some kind. You can't write about *any* character for a length of time – worm or warm-blooded man – without a sense of sadness at "killing him off."

[Mr. Mind by Biljo White à la *Beck*]

The only other *CMA* serial that approached Mr. Mind – and quite closely, as a matter of fact – was the Tawky Tawny Tiger non-serial succession of sequels. Response was also overpowering for him, and, because he lent himself more to orthodox concepts, it was Tawny that Beck and I chose as a possible syndicate newspaper strip.

This was after the Superman suit which ended the career of Captain Marvel and his gang in 1953. The incomparable Beck (a vast talent, in my opinion, that by bad luck never reached the acme of his peers such as Ray Alexander and the guys whose names I can't remember who do Buck Rogers, Li'l Abner, Popeye, etc.) and I did up a series of Tawny strips tailored to the daily syndicate (with Fawcett's blessings), but it came to nothing.

In answer to your question regarding the Mr. Mind serial, Roy, the "Monster Society of Evil" had no slightest connection with DC's "Justice Society of America," either by intent or accident.

I say the latter because, with the first announcement of a Superman suit against Captain Marvel, back around 1944-45, Fawcett's upper offices wisely suggested that all writers and artists completely avoid looking at DC publications so as not to "subconsciously" utilize or dress-up a plot or situation or gimmick of theirs, which could be damaging in court. I honestly doubt if I ever knew of the Justice Society, or else it was in such vague and remote terms that it had no remotest bearing on Mr. Mind and his organization.

Let me add one word here about that famed but non-earth-shaking event, the Superman vs. Captain Marvel suit and its allegations.

First of all, I myself did not originate the character (that was the doing of Beck and Bill Parker); and, secondly, I did not read Superman stories (even before the Fawcett ban), except at rare times. Each time I did, I felt it was *not* for Captain Marvel, who was developed into a wholly different area of humor, fantasy, and "whimsy," you might say – not the dead-serious grimness and plodding "consistency" of Superman.

In my opinion, my development of Captain Marvel and his "family" (I was chief writer and idea-man from mid-1941 till the end) was entirely my own, and, if anything, it avoided any of the "tone" of Superman completely. This I can state categorically – *not one story idea was ever "lifted" from Superman!*

A curious thing came out in the pre-settlement era, when we Fawcett people were asked to help compare hundreds of Superman and CM stories, ideas, even individual panels; for as many as "copied" Superman, even more appeared in Superman as if copied from CM! I'm not saying they "stole" from Captain Marvel! I'm simply bringing out the simple fact (which I'm sure the Superman lawyers knew) that by sheer *coincidence*, when you have dozens of writers and artists on either side producing massive material following the same general idea of a "super character," literally *hundreds* of panels and sequences would be almost *identical!*

The reason Fawcett withdrew from a court hearing and settled the suit has nothing to do with the above "rebuttal evidence" against imitation, plagiarism, or whatever they called it. It was because dropping sales and profits by 1953 convinced the Fawcett money-counters that the comics had had their heyday and why not quit while ahead?

The fact that they killed *all* their comics (the Superman injunction killed only the Marvel series) is proof enough to the fair-minded observer that Fawcett's giving up was not an admission of guilt, just canny business, saving enormous court costs if they had stubbornly fought out the case to save a "dying cause."

– MR. TAWKY TAWNY –
the TALKING TIGER

But enough of that long-gone event. At the invitation of *Alter Ego*'s publisher, Roy Thomas, let me ramblingly reminisce about the "Golden Days" of comics, in a completely random manner....

I had some two million words of science fiction pulps published between 1932 and 1945. The comics bug had already bitten me as early as 1939. For one Harry Chesler, among the pre-comics pioneers who first put out picture booklets using only newspaper strips at first, I was asked to write some new and original features – a really great innovation at that time. I did write up the following comics-type scripts for him:

"Dan Hastings," adventure character; "Scott Rand," ditto; "Astounding Man," a scientifically "super" hero; and "Iron Munro," space explorer; all from early 1939 into 1940, after which the big publishers lured me away.

My first comics scripts among the big publishers (Chesler never followed through to produce all-new comics mags) were for "The Black Owl" in *Prize Comics*, starting in late 1940.

In March 1941 I first wrote for Fawcett with the "Mr. Scarlet" assignment. After Ed Herron, then chief editor, saw my stuff, he began "grooming" me for the big boy (Captain Marvel) by having me do Captain Venture, Spy Smasher, Minute Man, Bulletman, El Carim, Golden Arrow, Ibis, and Dr. Voodoo, all through 1941.

Oddly enough (not so oddly, since I was a pulp writer), my first CM story was in prose form – the *Captain Marvel Storybook* series, including *The Scorpion* in August 1941.

My first *Captain Marvel* comics script was written in December 1941 and appeared in the ninth issue, April 1942. The end result of this, some 12 years later in 1953, was a total of 529 stories about the Big Red Cheese alone, for earnings of $37,358. My present-day home in Englewood, New Jersey, was dedicated at a Fawcett party as being "The House That Captain Marvel Built." Truer words were never spoken. He paid for it twice over.

In that fabulous period, as the comics phenomenon rose and expanded with a greater rapidity, I think, than any other literary "fad," the rates to writers and artists exploded at astounding speed.

The earliest rate I recall in 1939 was $2 per page (5 to 8 panels), which became $3 in 1941 when I began with Fawcett, then kept shooting up through the wartime (I was first OWI-deferred, then 1-B for a

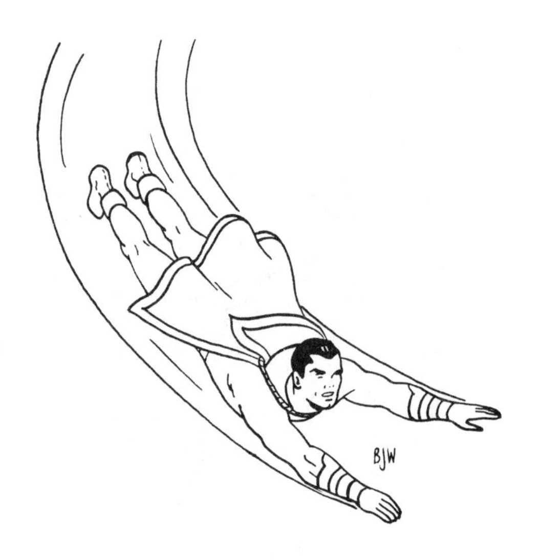

hearing defect, then 3-A married man deferred, finally 4-A over-age), to reach a standard rate of $10 a page – with higher exception for special short-lengths or characters, up to $15 per page. All of us writers at that time called it "The Golden Rut" with a sneer, all the way to the bank.

New titles were launched in that dizzying period with machine-gun rapidity. I personally launched (by writing the original scripts) *Mary Marvel, The Marvel Family*, and others for Fawcett, not to mention a dozen or more for other publishers, such as *Young Allies* for Goodman.

My most stunning surprise came when I sold a science fiction pulp story to *Fantasy & Science Fiction* mag in 1953 and received an acceptance letter from one of the co-editors, Anthony Boucher, who added a paragraph: "I am a great Captain Marvel fan, along with my two boys. We know by heart most of the Captain's adventures over a great many years, with their ingenuity of plot. A lot of your Jon Jarl short-shorts have very nice gimmicks too."

But even more dumbfounding to me was some three years ago when, through Dick Lupoff, I was first introduced and invited to a comics-fan club meeting and learned the Cap'n was far, far from forgotten... not by thousands of one-time avoid fans and readers now grown up into the Roy Thomases, Bill Spicers, and all others who contacted me.

And *this* was most incredible of all – they were *decent, law-abiding citizens* rather than unspeakable degenerates (as the Comics Code people and their ilk preached far and wide in the old days).

In fact, the comics "fans" were serious, often scholarly, researchers, many of them sporting engineering degrees and professional honors, all far more important and promising first-class people overshadowing the anti-comics crowd who today no doubt have some other scapegoat to hound down – perhaps *motherhood* by now! And who are, mercifully for America, obscure and impotent to have any slightest power to block young minds charging eagerly into the future.

I always stoutly maintained, to all and sundry in those days who sometimes quite viciously attacked the comics (even neighbors and friends) that red-blooded adventure (which comics were) was almost a *necessity* for the young, or at least was less harmful than such things as *phonetic spelling* in our school system, which today has proven itself the monstrous thing it was.

I don't know how much credit goes to the powerful groups that opposed comics, for the decline that set in, bankrupting dozens of publishers and murdering deathless characters. But if I ever saw anything close to a book-burning witch hunt, that was it.

So, all of you comics readers of years gone by who are today, as a matter of inevitable course, degenerates, rotters, addicts, adult delinquents, *liberals*, and *worse*. Then how come so many of you are Ph.D.'s and other types of professional men? I rest my case!

Enough philosophy or social comment. One more anecdote of the Comics Age: Just before the ax fell in June 1953, I was working on a *Marvel Family* script, whose outline is before me as I write this letter. It was titled "The Seven Marvels" – *a new serial.* Only the first chapter of six pages was completed, for which I was paid; then Fawcett announced the demise of the Marvel books, and all the other comics they had published.

If you like indigestible facts, my *total* comics output – all publishers and all characters – up to the end of 1957 was 2,227 stories for 18,100 pages, or approximately 100,000 panels.

After that, I wrote many more for DC's Superman mags from 1957-60. I dropped comics entirely from 1960 to 1964 while switching to full-time editing/writing for *Space World Magazine*. Then, after this was sold to another publisher (Ray Palmer of science fiction and flying saucer fame), I resumed with Mort Weisinger, chief of the Superman group at DC, as a fill-in for my non-fiction books and my NASA-contract space writings.

The above reminiscences, disjointed and seemingly narcissistic, are offered only with the thought of shedding some insight on those days of yore when comics were in flower. To attempt any sweeping, definitive picture is madness. Only in the tiny flashes of light given by individual anecdotes and recollections of those of us in the field as pros at the time can come any rational picture of what to me is still an incomprehensible rise-and-fall of a great empire -- the world of picture-story heroes whose peers will never again be seen.

Roy, you will be dismayed to hear that I have barely begun the reminiscences I have in store (which are triggered whenever I look through my voluminous files and records of those days), and that therefore when you send me the next issue, it will probably start me off on another tirade that you will wincingly receive and wonder what to do with.

You see, it isn't you readers that became degenerates; it's us writers and artists! The Comics Code crusaders never thought of *that* one!

Best Luck,

Otto

Otto Binder

To quote the liner notes from his most recent book, *Riddle of Astronomy* (1964: Basic Books, Inc., New York), "Otto O. Binder, former editor-in-chief of *Space World*, is a leading authority and pioneering writer on space topics, with over four hundred published articles and twenty-seven books to his credit." To comics fans, of course, Otto is known primarily as the brain behind Captain Marvel for many years. *Alter Ego* is proud to announce that an illustrated version of that last, previously unpublished Marvel Family story will appear in *AE* #8. Also, a near-future issue will feature some of the original "Tawny Tiger" strips conceived by Otto and executed for *AE* in the grand manner of the great C.C. Beck.

Sid Greene
Inker: *The Atom*

In answer to your question as to why I don't include Julius Schwartz in my inking jobs -- I don't feel it's fair to the penciller. I had done so on the first two Atoms I inked, which created a great deal of confusion amongst readers, to judge from the letters the editor received. I feel that, where inking is concerned, my job is to complement the pencils with my inking according to the penciler's technique. If you'll notice, my inking of Elongated Man or Batman is, in my opinion, different from the Atom inks.

Frankly, I would like to get back to penciling. But I like working for that taskmaster Schwartz! However, I've been promised pencil work at the first opportunity that comes along.

Please forward *AE* when it's available. I enjoy reading it. I'll sign off now as I have to take my pain-killer.

By way of explanation of artist Greene's closing sentence, be it known that he was undergoing dental surgery at the time he wrote the above letter. We sincerely hope that by this time he has fully recuperated and that he is again "up and Atom."

Bill Spicer
Editor: *Fantasy Illustrated*
418-H W. Stocker St.
Glendale, California

Dear Ronn:

The Kubert interview was probably the highlight of the issue. Somehow I had never figured that Kubert was the one responsible for *Tor* from beginning to end – and certainly not for the coloring of the pages! The coloring, in fact, was yet another of the standout features of *Tor* that caught my eye. I don't think I've ever seen better, more imaginative use of color in any comic book, and that would include (gnash, grind) the EC's.

The best piece of original writing in *AE* #6 was not Glassman's or Thomas' but Tom Fagan's "Warlock." It seems to take an uncommon effort just to get Fagan to write something, but when he does, it's generally of Alley Award quality. The Warlock piece is so short, however, that it probably won't even receive more than a handful of votes, if that many.

Best part of the BLA/F4 strip was Roy Thomas' script; concept and construction of the gags, for the most part, came off really well. I think Thomas' artwork might have been more effective if his cartoons bore some resemblance to the original heroes being depicted. This is where Grass' art came through better -- his caricatures are closer to the real thing. (Thang?)

You'll find no argument in this corner concerning the quality of "Warlock." As to the lack of similarity of the BLA to the JLA, the reason is simple: the BLA was created some weeks before *Alter Ego* was conceived, and was not originally meant to be seen by anyone but yours truly. I hoped to make each member a character in his own right, not just a parody of *a* JLAer. Maybe I should have left well enough alone?

Ronn Foss
Former Editor
924 George
Van Wert, Ohio

Dear Roy:

It is with some regret that I take leave of my position as publishing editor of *Alter Ego*. However, I am glad to be able to turn it over to you, as I feel that there is no one who could do a better job.

It is also a source of comfort to me to know that the fabulous Biljo White, one of the most talented cartoonists in or out of fandom, will be around as art editor. I feel certain that the two of you will make a great team, one that will keep *Alter Ego* flying high!

Many thanks for the vote of confidence, Ronn. Biljo and I will try to fulfill your expectations. You neglected, though, to mention one item that Bill and I feel will be a major factor in any future success that *Alter Ego* may have – the promise of more artwork *à la* the Hawkman/Grundy and Joy Holiday drawings this issue) by one Ronn Foss. No one who read the great Moroz-Foss "Eclipse" script in *AE* #5 will want to miss the next *Alter Ego*, which features the return of the Master of the Midnight Hours.

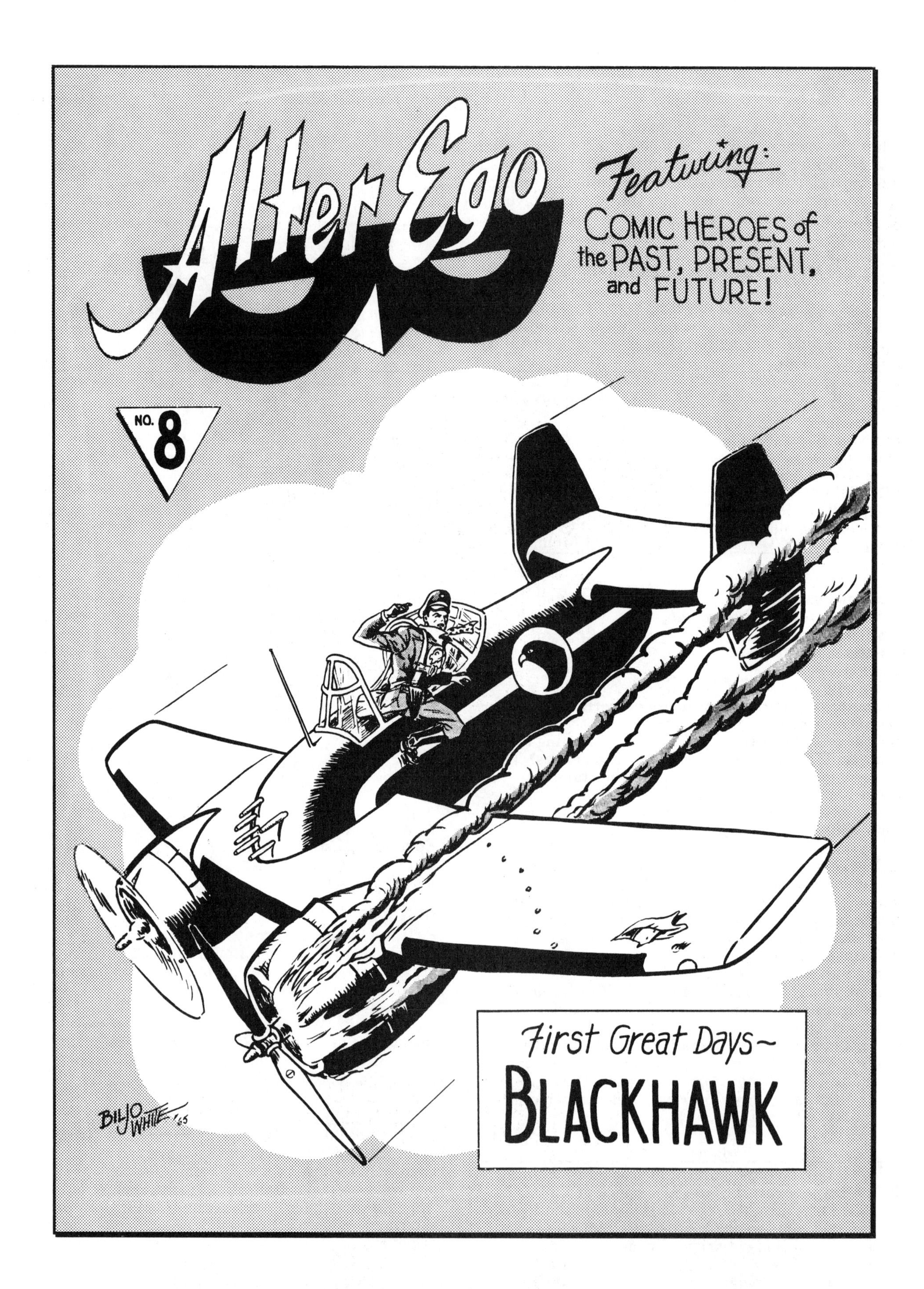

About the cover of* Alter Ego *#8 (March 1965): *The cover of* Alter Ego *#8, a powerful image by Biljo White of Blackhawk's modified Grumman Skyrocket plummeting earthward, won a 1965 Alley for "Best Offset Cover" of a fanzine. (The issue itself received the award for "Best Fanzine" of that same year.)*

Alter Ego #8 – Notes & Commentary

Like Ronn Foss before him, as soon as he took over as AE *editor, Roy Thomas hatched plans to publish related magazines as well. In* AE *#7 he had announced projected monthly (!) publication of* Alter Ego Comics, *to be entirely devoted to printing comics material by himself, Ronn, Biljo White, and others.*

But in AE *#8 (dated "Winter 1965") Roy had to report that "various fan and pro projects" had forced the cancellation of plans for* AE Comics, *with its stories re-scheduled to fanzines such as* Star-Studded Comics, Fantasy Illustrated, *and* Alter Ego *itself. Though not revealed in* AE *#8, Roy had been approached to edit (with help from young Steve Gerber and others) a new* Mad*-type magazine, an offer which lasted just long enough to torpedo* AE Comics*; while Biljo had become more and more involved in his own fanzine* Batmania *and felt he couldn't obligate himself to produce strips for* AE Comics *on a regular schedule.*

To replace it, Roy announced a photo-offset special to be called The Bestest from Alter Ego Nos. 1-3, *which would be published "as soon as 300 orders are received." Response was good, and for it Roy started writing* "The Alter Ego Story," *tracing the birth of the fanzine based on his memory and on letters saved by Jerry Bails; the bulk of what Roy completed is reprinted earlier in this volume. However, largely because by summer Roy moved to New York City to work in the comics industry,* Bestest *never saw print – except to the extent that this book, nearly a third of a century later, contains much of the material planned for it, and then some!*

AE *#8 further demonstrated Roy's desire to widen the horizons of both his fanzine and of fandom itself. He enlisted a fellow English teacher, Bob Hopkins, to write an article on Doc Savage, the influential pulp hero whose vintage exploits were just starting to be reprinted in paperback.*

When Biljo White sent this photo to Roy Thomas several years later, he inscribed it: "When it was all a lot more fun."

Also, during a month-long drive through Mexico the previous summer, Roy had added to his small collection of Mexican comics acquired in Puerto Rico, and now wished to initiate an on-going series on super-heroes of other countries. Feeling ill-prepared to do the research himself, he turned to Fred Patten, a comics and science fiction fan in Los Angeles, who wrote the first of two projected articles on Mexican comics, to be illustrated (as was most of AE *#8) by Biljo White.*

Glen Johnson, who taught Navajo children near Crownpoint, New Mexico, contributed the issue's JSA piece, "Two Cases of Conscience," about a pair of socially relevant issues of All-Star Comics.

Derrill Rothermich, a student at the School of Mines and Metallurgy in Rolla, Missouri, wrote a piece on the formative early days of Will Eisner's brainchild, Blackhawk – except that in 1964-65 fans had no idea that the creator of The Spirit had also conceived the Military Comics *hero. Deciding the article needed sprucing up, Roy made the drive to Biljo's "White House of Comics" – a small concrete block building behind his home in Columbia, Missouri, which housed Biljo's collection – and re-wrote the article. It was published under both writers' names.*

Spread throughout the issue were various cartoons-- "Famous Blast Words" – written by Roy and drawn by Jay Kinney (later a well-known underground cartoonist), in response to a cartoon in Don and Maggie Thompson's Comic Art *#5.*

FAMOUS BLAST WORDS (thomas/kinney)

Drury Moroz and Ronn Foss came through with their second (and best) "Eclipse" story, which we've reprinted in its entirety. In the letters section Ronn related how their projected revival of DC's Dr. Mid-Nite metamorphosed into a new hero. It turned out that "The Reincarnation of the Spectre" in AE *#1-2 had been both the first and the last of a breed.*

Otto Binder contributed another informative letter – and another arrived from Wendell Crowley, a Fawcett editor from 1941 till the end, in 1953. The memories expressed in the two letters contradicted each other on several key points, indicating that piecing together the history of American comic books was not going to be quite as simple as might have been hoped.

On a page donated to the fan organization which had been grandiosely re-christened the Academy of Comic-Book Fans and Collectors, executive secretary Paul Gambaccini announced that ACBFAC had taken over the Alley Poll, and that Glen Johnson would now publish The Comic Reader, *the Academy's official newsletter. Gambaccini also announced a new tradition: "an official annual Comic Fan Convention (Comicon)," the first of which was to be held that summer in New York City under David Kaler.*

When Roy printed that announcement, little did he imagine that not only would he be attending that convention, but that by then he'd be briefly living at Dave Kaler's Lower East Side apartment – and that he'd be on staff at Marvel Comics....

The Editors

[Above: Two examples of artwork from AE *#8 by Biljo White, demonstrating how his talents contributed so much to the impact of these pieces which (unfortunately) could not be included in this book.]*

The Eclipse
MASTER OF THE MIDNIGHT HOURS... SILENT, SWIFT AS A SHADOW SENTINEL OF A GREAT CITY... CAT-LIKE NEMESIS OF INJUSTICE!
WHEN NEWLYWEDS ALICE AND JOHN PHELPS MOVED INTO THE ANCIENT MALIMOOR MANOR THEY KNEW FULL WELL THE LEGEND SURROUNDING ITS WARPED AND DECADENT HALLS... BUT THEY DIDN'T SUSPECT THAT THE LEGEND WAS TRUE— OR THAT THE WONDERFUL NONSENSE OF THEIR "HAUNTED HOUSEWARMING" WOULD BE INTERRUPTED BY STARK TERROR- ONLY THE ECLIPSE DARED BRAVE THE SUPERNATURAL TO FIND THE SOLUTION TO...
the MYSTERY of MALIMOOR!
Uhn... THAT-THAT GHOSTLY FIREBALL! IT KEEPS GROWING LARGER- WEAKENING ME!! CAN IT BE THAT MALIMOOR MANOR IS TRULY HAUNTED?
Script by DRURY MOROZ Art by RONN FOSS
AT A NOVEL HOUSEWARMING, GUESTS ARE TREATED TO A GLOOMY LEGEND...
"THIS IS THE MELANCHOLY HISTORY OF PRE-COLONIAL ELEGANCE... ALONE AND UNLOVED LIVED ITS MASTER, KEMMET MALIMOOR"-

"THEN CAME THAT FATEFUL YEAR OF THE GREAT FAMINE — WHEN CROPS FAILED, MAN COULD NOT LIVE..."
"THE WEALTHIEST MAN IN THE VILLAGE OF CRESCENT WAS KEMMET MALIMOOR, WHO MADE A FORTUNE SPECULATING IN BRITISH TRADE - BUT MALIMOOR WAS A PENNY-PINCHING MISER..."
OUT WITH YOU— ALL OF YOU! I WON'T LEND A CENT!!
"TIS SAID THAT PLAGUE AND PESTILENCE WERE RAMPANT IN THE VILLAGE... HALF ITS POPULATION WERE TAKEN — AND ONE OF THE SICKENED, AN AVOWED WITCH, PRONOUNCED A CURSE..."
YER EVIL HAS CONDEMNED YE—DEATH SHALL BE YER REWARD, AND THE DEVIL HIMSELF YER EXECUTIONER! YE SHALL NOT DIE, BUT A SPIRIT BE—DOOMED TO EARTH ALL ETERNITY!
"THAT NIGHT, AT MALIMOOR MANOR—"
AIIEEE!!
"AYE, KEMMET MALIMOOR DIED... OR DID HE? NO ONE EVER REALLY KNEW! SOMETIMES AT MIDNIGHT, ON A MOONLESS, DARK NIGHT, A GHOSTLY FIRE-BALL CAN BE SEEN FLOATING ABOUT MALIMOOR!!"
AMONG THE GUESTS ARE DR. CRAIG (THE ECLIPSE) PIERCE AND HIS 'PERSONAL NURSE', TERESA ASTER—
ISN'T THAT JUST TERRIFYING, DR. PIERCE? TO THINK THE GHOST MAY STILL EXIST!
2

IT MIGHT AT THAT, MISS ASTER- AND I WOULDN'T BE SURPRISED IF IT VISITED US TONIGHT!
I SHOULDN'T HAVE LET YOU COME HERE... YOU'RE STILL IN DELICATE HEALTH AFTER THAT AWFUL LAB EXPLOSION*!
*SEE ALTER EGO-5: ORIGIN

I DON'T KNOW WHO SHE'S TRYING TO CONVINCE -HERSELF OR ME! BUT IT'S MY OWN FAULT, I SUPPOSE... WHEN I THOUGHT I'D BE BLIND FOR LIFE, THE HOSPITAL SENT ME A WELFARE WORKER -MISS ASTER!

I'D DISCHARGE HER IN A MOMENT IF IT WOULDN'T CREATE SUSPICION OF MY ALTER EGO OF THE ECLIPSE! BESIDES, I'VE GROWN A BIT FOND OF THIS ENDEARING LITTLE SCATTER-BRAIN!
HERE COME OUR HOSTS, THE PHELPSES!!

SO THERE YOU ARE, DR. PIERCE - AND THIS MUST BE YOUR RECEPTIONIST, MISS TERESA ASTER?!
ENJOYING THE PARTY, DR. PIERCE?

THE NIGHT IS YOUNG - JUST REMEMBER, WE AREN'T RESPONSIBLE FOR GUESTS' SAFETY! THOSE WHO CAME DID SO AT THEIR OWN RISK!!

LATER, AS CRAIG SURVEYS THE GATHERING-
THERE'S ENOS CRAMER, THE BANKER - MR. PHELPS IS HIS CHIEF ACCOUNTANT, YET HE SEEMS TO BE AVOIDING THE PHELPSES... Hmm -

AS THE BUTLER AND MAID ENTER-
THAT'S ODD... SAM BORDEN AND LUCY KNOWLIN! THEY WERE DOING TIME FOR A GOLD SWINDLE THE LAST I HEARD OF THEM - WONDER IF OUR HOST KNOWS!

SUDDENLY, THE LIGHTS DIM-
MUST BE GETTING CLOSE TO MIDNIGHT - TIME FOR THE GHOST OF MALIMOOR MANOR...

AND OUT OF THE DARKNESS-
YIIEEE!
FLAP FLAP FLAP FLAP
THUMP!
'GHOSTLY' SOUNDS - MUST BE ON TAPE
OOHHHH
Uh-Oh! THAT LAST ONE SOUNDS TOO REAL!!
ARGH
3

CATLIKE EYES PIERCING THE GLOOM, CRAIG MOVES THROUGH THE DARKENED HALLS UNTIL—
IT'S CRAMER, NEAR DEATH— AND THERE GOES HIS ASSAILANT!

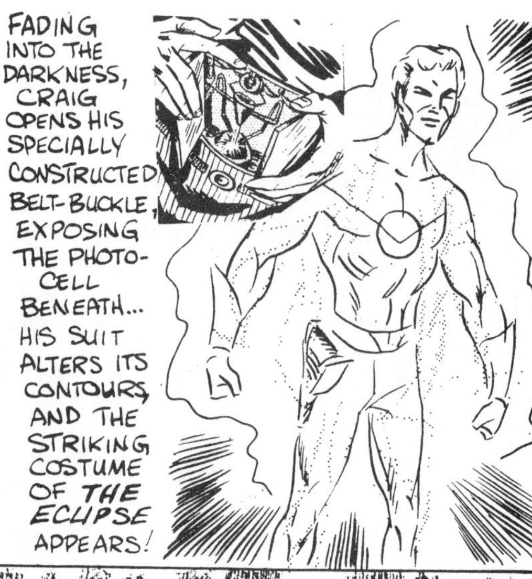

FADING INTO THE DARKNESS, CRAIG OPENS HIS SPECIALLY CONSTRUCTED BELT-BUCKLE, EXPOSING THE PHOTO-CELL BENEATH... HIS SUIT ALTERS ITS CONTOURS, AND THE STRIKING COSTUME OF THE ECLIPSE APPEARS!

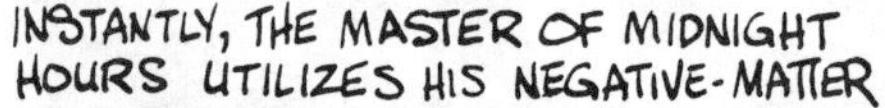

INSTANTLY, THE MASTER OF MIDNIGHT HOURS UTILIZES HIS NEGATIVE-MATTER ABILITY—

WHA! THROUGH THE WALL-?

NOW WE'LL SEE WHAT YOU LOOK LIKE—UHN!

SECONDS LATER—
ESCAPED! I MIGHT'VE KNOWN THERE'D BE TWO OF THEM! I'D BETTER TAKE A LOOK AT CRAMER AS DR. PIERCE!!

SHIELDING HIS EYES FROM THE SUDDEN GLARE WHICH HE KNOWS WOULD BE DISASTROUS FOR HIM,* CRAIG TURNS ON THE LIGHT—
UHN—FIREBALL... GHOSTLY FIREBALL —HARD TO BREATHE!
EASY, CRAMER—YOUR PULSE IS WEAK, BUT WE'LL GET YOU TO A HOSPITAL!
4
*DR. PIERCE IS A VICTIM OF CHRONIC LIGHT-SENSIVITY, A TYPE OF BLINDNESS!

LATER, AS DAWN STREAKS THE SKY—
I'M LT. JAMESON, HOMICIDE! WE LEARNED THAT SOMEONE TRIED TO SUFFOCATE CRAMER WITH POTASSIUM OF CYANIDE! AND, HAMILTON GLENN, ONE OF YOUR GUESTS HERE WHO WORKS FOR THE TREASURY DEPT., FOUND THERE'S A HALF MILLION DOLLARS MISSING FROM CRAMER'S BOOKS!!

YOU'RE CRAMER'S ACCOUNTANT, MR. PHELPS, SO I'M ARRESTING YOU ON SUSPICION OF ATTEMPTED MURDER!

LATE THAT NIGHT, A STRANGELY GARBED FIGURE POURS OVER OLD NEWSPAPER FILES IN THE CRESCENT CITY LIBRARY—
Hmm- WHEN 'CRAIG PIERCE' VISITED JOHN PHELPS IN HIS CELL TODAY, HE MENTIONED THAT ENOS CRAMER HAD WANTED TO BUY MALIMOOR... NOW I CAN SEE WHY!
CRESCENT CITY TIMES
CRESCENT CITY TIMES

SHORTLY, AT THE MANOR—
UNLESS I MISS MY GUESS, THIS OLD RELIC IS PROBABLY HONEY-COMBED WITH SECRET PASSAGES!
PASSING THROUGH—
Hmm- SOMEONE ELSE IS ALSO INTERESTED!

ALL RIGHT, YOU- LET'S HAVE AN EXPLAN... WHA? MISS ASTER!!
Ohh- LET ME GO, YOU... YOU BRUTE!

Y-YOU! YOU'RE THAT CRIME FIGHTER, THE ECLIPSE... I'VE READ ABOUT YOU IN THE NEWSPAPERS! I CAME TO LOOK FOR DR. PIERCE- HE FANCIES HIMSELF A DETECTIVE OF SORTS... HAVE YOU SEEN HIM?
NO, I'VE NEVER EVER MET THE DOCTOR!

WELL, AS LONG AS I'M HERE, I MAY AS WELL HELP YOU! NOW, IT'S OBVIOUS THAT MR. PHELPS WAS FRAMED, SO, THERE HAS TO BE SOMETHING THE CULPRIT WANTS! BUT, WE'RE GOING TO FIND IT FIRST, RIGHT?!
5

A HIDDEN PANEL! IT-IT'S AWFULLY DARK IN HERE!!
Shh- JUST HOLD MY HAND, DARKNESS IS NO PROBLEM TO ME!

HOWEVER, AT THAT SAME INSTANT-

RECOVERING CONSCIOUSNESS, THE PAIR FIND—
A-A SHIMMERING FIREBALL... IT KEEPS GETTING LARGER, MAKING ME WEAK!
THE MALIMOOR LEGEND... IT— IT'S *TRUE!*

MEANWHILE, NEAR THE HIDDEN DOORWAY LEADING OUT OF THE PASSAGE—
WE WON'T NEED THESE ANYMORE, CYNTHIA, M'DOVE! AS SOON AS OUR 'FIREBALL' HAS DONE ITS JOB, I'LL GO BACK AND GET IT!!

NO ONE WILL EVER FIND THEM... NO ONE ELSE KNOWS OF THIS PASSAGE!
RATHER CLEVER OF US, ISN'T IT, HAM — JUST THINK, ONE MILLION DOLLARS IN PRE-COLONIAL GOLD COINS, AND IT'S ALL OURS!

HA-HAH! THAT'S THE ADVANTAGE OF WORKING FOR THE TREASURY DEPARTMENT — ONE GETS TO KNOW THESE THINGS! OF COURSE, I DIDN'T ELIMINATE CRAMER'S RIVALRY AS I'D PLANNED, BUT AT LEAST WE HAVE THE GOLD TO CONSOLE US!!

AS HAMILTON GLENN AND HIS WIFE PREPARE TO LEAVE —
THERE THEY ARE!

THE MODIFIED LASER BEAM EMITS OPAQUE BLACKNESS —
7

THROUGH THE MURKY DARKNESS, ECLIPSE... *AND* TERESA ASTER – STRIKE!

OH, DARN–THERE GOES MY *OTHER* HEEL! BUT IT'S WORTH IT JUST TO PAY MRS. GLENN BACK FOR THAT CRACK ON THE HEAD SHE GAVE ME!

SPIKED HEELS ARE THE HANDIEST THINGS EVER INVENTED, AREN'T THEY, ECLIPSE?! I SHUDDER TO THINK WHAT WOULD'VE HAPPENED TO US IF I HADN'T WORKED MY SHOE OFF IN TIME TO WEDGE THE SPIKED HEEL INTO THAT CYANIDE-LOADED 'FIREBALL' SMOKE-GENERATOR!!

THE NEXT DAY, A BLISSFUL REUNION TAKES PLACE AT MALIMOOR MANOR–

RIGHT, DR. PIERCE! AND ENOS CRAMER FACED RUINATION DUE TO EMBEZZLING A HALF-MILLION FROM HIS OWN BANK, WE LEARNED, TO INVEST IN ONE OF SAM BORDEN'S FAKE 'TRIPLE-YOUR-MONEY' SCHEMES! CRAMER WILL BE ALL RIGHT, BUT HE FACES PRISON FOR EMBEZZLEMENT! WHEN HE LEARNED OF THE MALIMOOR GOLD, HE ASKED HAMILTON GLENN WHAT IT'D BE WORTH *NOW* – WHICH NATURALLY MADE GLENN INTERESTED, AND...

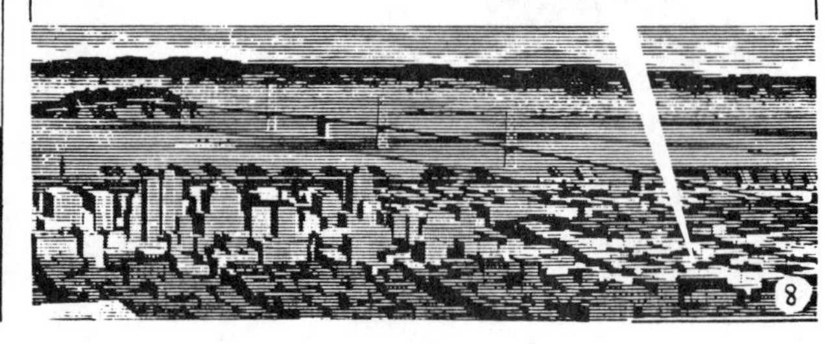

—AND HE SEIZED UPON THE 'GHOSTLY FIREBALL' IDEA TO DISPOSE OF HIS COMPETITION! FAILING, HE AND HIS WIFE TRIED TO MAKE OFF WITH THE GOLD BEFORE CRAMER COULD RECOVER AND TALK!!

SORRY WE THOUGHT YOU WERE INVOLVED, MR. PHELPS!

FORGET IT, LT.! I'M HAPPY NOW THAT MALIMOOR IS CLEARED OF THE LEGEND! ALICE, DARLING, WHAT'S WRONG?

The comic book super-hero is usually considered a uniquely American phenomenon; nor does one often see much to change this impression. The super-heroes we read about are all 100% American, from the Fantastic Four *et al.* in New York to Green Lantern in "Coast City" by the blue Pacific.

Is someone threatening to blow up the Eiffel Tower in Paris? The Flash will take care of it. Are the Commies getting especially active in Vietnam? Everybody from Capt. America to Magicman seems to be on hand to push them back again. If there's trouble anywhere in our world, our comics proclaim, one of *our* super-heroes will buzz right over to set things aright.

This picture of a complete U.S. comics monopoly is enhanced if you read the letter columns, too. I'm sure you've all seen the letter from some boy in a South Pacific nation, who has just found an isolated two-year-old copy of The Comic on his newsstand and wants to know if anybody in America will send him more issues so he won't continue to be culturally deprived. Or the one from the American serviceman stationed abroad who's just come across The Comic in the Base PX, and, boy, does it remind him of the good old days of comicdom!

The implications are clear: the whole world would be in a mess if it weren't for the American super-heroes, and obviously no other nation is capable of producing such Men of Might. (Though some of these foreign places manage to come up with a colorful super-*villain* every now and then.) Furthermore, the U.S. seems to be the only country that publishes these comics; any copies to be found in foreign lands are either exported American issues, or, at best, sloppy reproductions of U.S. comics in the quaint local tongue.

'Tain't so! Granted, there are a lot of exported U.S. comics and reprints of same. But other countries also have their *own* super-heroes, who combat mad villains and natural and extraterrestrial disasters in their own right. Comic fandom has spent several years now discussing the American comic book in great detail; it's time we broadened the field to take in the comics output of other nations.

The acme of desirability would be a sort of comic book Baedeker, in which any comic fan could look up in an instant the information as to what comic books and which super-heroes are available in any given country. To commence such a project, let's look into the comic book situation just across the Rio Grande.

The Mexican super-hero and science fiction comics can generally be divided into three broad fields: straight reprints of U.S. comics; original comics based on American titles; and entirely original comics with their own heroes and villains. As this is too large a subject to cover thoroughly in one article, it will be broken into two parts: Part I, following, will discuss the first two of these fields lightly; and Part II, in *AE* #9, will go into the original Mexican costume-hero comics in much greater detail. Onward, then!

Part One

The reprinting of U.S. comic books in Mexico is largely in the hands of two publishing companies, both located in Mexico City. These are "Organización Editorial Novaro, S.A. de C.V." and "Editora de Periodicos, S.C.L., 'La Prensa.'" Of these, Novaro has by far the largest percentage of U.S. reprints, consisting of all Mexican publication of National Periodical (DC), Gold Key, and Dell titles: super-hero, Disney, and otherwise. La Prensa has just the Marvel titles, of which they reprint only four.

La Prensa's main line is in original comics based on U.S. titles (not always with permission to use the U.S. characters) and completely original Mexican comics drawn in the "American" (*norteamericano*) style. Indeed, La Prensa's comics seem to be produced for sale in the United States as much as for Mexican sale. The cover price reads: "$1.00 [*i.e.*, one peso, or 8½ cents in our currency] en la Rep. Mexicana; 0.10 dolares en el extranjero." A note inside confirms that the price "in foreign lands" is in U.S. money.

Incidentally, the peso price-tag (and yes, that $1.00 startled *me* the first time I saw it, too) is unanimous on all regular Mexican comics, though the newsstands here in Los Angeles charge 15 cents apiece for them. All in all, Novaro and La Prensa take up about equal amount of space on stands with their titles, though La Prensa doesn't have nearly so many in the adventure-hero line.

The bulk of Novaro's super-hero comics lies in its reprints of the DC issues. These are usually reprinted six months to a year after their original appearance in this country, and they pretty well cover the entire DC output. The biggest difference lies in the number of titles appearing, because Novaro generally combines two or more U.S. titles into only one Mexican title, leaning heavily toward "presentations" in the *Brave & Bold* and *Showcase* manner.

Most of the DC comics edited by Mort Weisinger are reprinted under the single title of *Supermán*, which appears weekly. For instance: *Supermán* #466 (Sept. 23, 1964) is a reprint of *Jimmy Olsen* #71 (Sept. 1963); *Supermán* #467 (Sept. 30, 1964) is our *Superman* #170 (July 1964); *Supermán* #468 (Oct. 7, 1964) is *Lois Lane* #46 (Jan. 1964); *Supermán* #469 (Oct. 14, 1964) is *Adventure Comics* #316 (Jan. 1964); and *Supermán* #470 (Oct. 21, 1964) is *Superboy* #109 (Dec. 1963). The *80-Page Giant* "annuals" appear as "Numeros Extraordinarios" and are not numbered, though they are dated.

Batman, also a weekly (issue #254 is dated Jan. 21, 1965), reprints in the same way *Batman, Detective Comics,* and *World's Finest Comics* (a holdover from when Jack Schiff edited the U.S. version). In addition, *Batman* also "presents" Flash (*The Flash*), Linterna Verde (*Green Lantern*), and Campeones de la Justicia (Champions of Justice – the *JLA*). Thus, under these two weekly titles are reprinted twelve of the DC Comics.

Other DC reprints are lumped together in lesser amounts. *Historias Fantásticas* is published on the first and fifteenth of every month and consists of reprints of *Tales of the Unexpected, Rip Hunter, Sea Devils*, and *Brave & Bold* (the issues featuring super-heroes, anyway). *Marvila*, a monthly, is *Wonder Woman*, who "presents" *Showcase* (the Tommy Tomorrow issues) and *Metal Men. Relatos Fabulosos*, also monthly, runs *Aquaman, The Atom,* and *House of Secrets. Titanes Planetarios,* a semi-monthly, is for some reason publishing 1951 issues of *Strange Adventures* (Captain Comet and all) with the new *Hawkman*.

Three straight monthly reprints are *Mi Gran Aventura*, which is just *My Greatest Adventure* (now *The Doom Patrol*) running under the same old title; *Tomajauk (Tomahawk);* and *El Halcón de Oro (Blackhawk).* That's right, Spanish-speaking readers; Blackhawk is translated as *Halcón de Oro* – I'll get to that one later.

As for the Gold Key reprints, these all appear in the weekly *Domingos Alegres*, which means "Merry Sundays" – presumably the day on which it appears in Mexico (#567 is dated for Feb. 7, 1965). This takes in *Magnus, Dr. Solar, Space Family Robinson, Turok*, and *Twilight Zone,* as well as other non-science-fiction titles. The only other Gold Key reprint of note is the monthly *Tarzan*, which also guest-stars *Korak*. There is one Dell reprint I know of: *Space Man*, which appears in something called *T.V. Mondial,* along with other adventure strips.

This covers Novaro's contributions to the Mexican comics field, insofar as costumed heroes and science fiction are concerned. La Prensa's Marvel reprints come in two parts, which are both bi-weeklies. *Los 4 (i.e., Cuatro) Fantásticos* alternates reprints of *Fantastic Four* with *Strange Tales*, while *El Sorprendente Hombre Araña* switches off *The Amazing Spider-Man* with *Tales to Astonish*. Both of these are fairly new titles, of course; *Fantásticos* is only up to #37 (Jan. 31, 1965) and *Hombre Araña* to #26 (Jan. 15, 1965).

◆

That's it as to what there is, and how often it comes out. Now, how do these translated reprints compare to the U.S. originals?

Not quite as good, but not too much worse. Their biggest faults are that they "lose something in translation," as the saying goes, and that they lack the continuity of the U.S. versions.

This latter shows up most clearly in the reprints of the Marvel titles. Stan Lee's comics are all so tightly woven together that you have to read *all* of them in order to fully understand everything that goes on in *any* of them. But the Mexicans are getting only *four* of these; so when an issue of *Fantastic Four* guest-starring the Avengers is reprinted, for example, I imagine a lot of Mexican readers are going to be wondering who these "Vengadores" are and where they suddenly came from.

Things aren't quite so bad with Novaro's DC reprints, both because the DC titles aren't so closely connected and because they are *all* being reprinted. But there is still likely to be some confusion, for the chronological order of the different original titles has been lost. The drastic extreme is seen in the case of *Hawkman*; reprints of the *Brave & Bold* tryouts, the *Mystery in Space* stories, and the first issue of the *Hawkman* comic are appearing simultaneously.

Reproduction? Novaro's reprints are as good as the originals, though occasionally the colors will be a little more washed out. La Prensa, unfortunately, doesn't produce nearly so good a product. The color is faded and sometimes blurred, the pages are often cut crookedly so that the panels at the top or bottom are almost running off the paper, and the dialogue is almost always off-center in the speech balloon, sometimes running up into the black line of the balloon itself, which makes for difficult reading. It's all too obvious that the original text has been cut out here and something else put in its place.

Things get interesting in the translation department.

By and large, the Spanish text follows the English one rather closely – after all, it's so connected with the art that it can't be altered too greatly. What textual change there is tends toward simplification. For instance, in *Action Comics* #304, "The Interplanetary Olympics," page 6, panel 1, reads: "Come now, Superman, we expected more competition from you than this! Where are the mighty super-powers I heard so much about?" The same panel in Mexico's *Supermán* #454 reads simply, "¡Esperabamos una actuación mejor de ti, Supermán...!" (translation: "We expected a better performance from you, Superman...!")

This simplification sometimes has a strong effect on the conclusion of a story. In *The Doom Patrol* #90, "The Spy within the Doom Patrol," Madame Rouge, who has just gained the power to mold herself into a duplicate of anyone else's body, has substituted herself for the Chief and is about to shoot Larry (Negative Man) Trainor on the grounds that, since he "forgot" his code word, *he* must be the deadly spy. Larry defeats her, and when the real Chief later asks him how he knew the apparent Chief was actually an imposter, Larry replies, "When Madame Rouge referred to 'Elasti-Girl,' I knew that wasn't you speaking – because you never call Rita by that freak name! So I *pretended* to forget my code word -- just to see how far she'd go!" To cut down this speech in *Mi Gran Aventura* #54, it was rewritten to become, "Me pareció extrano que ella sacara un arma para acabar conmiga, sélo porque yo había olvidado la contrasena" ("I thought it was funny that you'd pull a gun to shoot me, just because I'd forgotten the countersign").

Because of this pruning down of the original dialogue, much of the natural flavor of the speech – and sometimes a detailed explanation at the end of a story – is lost. The whole effect is similar to that in the case of literary classics, such as *The Count of Monte Cristo* or *Ben-Hur*, which are abridged from their original 900-page lengths to 400-page "popular editions" for easier reading.

The one area in which the translators have given themselves free rein is in the translation of the proper names of characters, both their secret and public identities. Here, strangely enough, Novaro and La Prensa take opposite extremes. Novaro will seldom change a super-hero's name, but his secret identity – or the name of the group – is something else again. Batman remains Batman, even though a subtitle has to be added (*El Hombre Murciélago*) to tell the Mexican readers what the name means. But Bruce Wayne has become Bruno Díaz. (And, interestingly, Steven Dayton – Mento in *The Doom Patrol* – has become *Sergio* Díaz. I wonder if the translator felt that, since they are both among the wealthiest men in the world, they should be related to each other.)

[Not from AE #8]

The Challengers of the Unknown – Prof, Rocky, Red, and Ace – have become Los Temerarios (The Reckless Ones) and are now Uriel, Lino, Mauro, and Efrén. Barry Allen is Bruno Alba, and Jay Garrick is Jorge Luna (the JSA, by the way, are now Los Defensores de la Justicia). And though J'onn J'onzz retains the same weird combination of letters, his later alter ego has been known as Julio Jordan; now, of course, he has been replaced in the *Detective* reprints by "Rafael Rivas, El Hombre Elástico."

Long names tend to be shortened into one-word names. In La Legión de Superhéroes, Ultra Boy is Ultra, Phantom Girl is Fantasma, Saturn Girl is Saturna, Cosmic Boy is Cósmico, etc. (Here, of course, Spanish can show gender by utilizing Latin suffixes, a device immeasurably preferable to the rash of "Boys," "Girls," "Lads," "Lasses," "Kids," *et al.* in English-language comics.

Even in the case of a proper name, the cognomen is seldom used. Barry Allen is just "Bruno" throughout most of the Flash issues of *Batman*. In the Hawkman reprints, Carter and Shiera Hall are almost universally referred to as "Carlos y su esposa Mirna" ("Carlos and his wife Mirna"), though if you look hard enough, you'll finally discover that Carlos' last name is Lara. In his identity as El Hombre Halcón, he is usually just Halcón (and so is Blackhawk, in the Mexican edition of that comic).

On the other hand, in La Prensa's reprints of the Marvel comics the personal names remain untouched, even in the case of Johnny Storm, though the Mexicans have their own diminutive of John ("Juanito"). But the public name of the super-hero is much more apt to be revised. The Hulk is La Mole (mass, bulk); the Thing is El Coloso. Daredevil has become El Dynamo, and Dr. Strange is now Dr. Centella (Dr. Lightning, or Dr. Spark).

Outside of the stories themselves, almost everything in the Mexican magazines is original. Novaro reprints a few of the one-page filler comics, such as Prof. Eureka and Charlie Cannonball; but, for the most part, it has its own supply of strips, such as Patachín (a robot), Milocho, Lucas, etc. These run throughout the Novaro comics, including the Gold Key and Dell reprints.

The advertisements are, of course, entirely original and for Mexican products. La Prensa's comics carry ads for their other comics (*revistas*), "Enciclopedia Popular" information on nature topics, crossword puzzles, pencil mazes, connect-the-dots, and that sort of thing.

El Sorprendente Hombre Araña is the only comic book in Mexico, so far as I know, that carries a letter column. As to credits, most of these have been deleted. The loss of the letter columns in the DC reprints means that most of the information as to writers, artists, etc., is gone. Novaro *does* leave credits in when they are printed on the first page of the story, as in *The Atom* and *Hawkman*. La Prensa, though, has cut out all of Stan Lee's wacky credit statements, as though it is trying to give the impression that the comics are entirely original with the Mexican edition; the blank boxes on the first page are now filled with a note saying to "Ask for magazines edited by 'La Prensa'!"

A final, minor difference between the Mexican and U.S. editions of a comic is that, in the Spanish-language text, the exclamation point is seldom used. An ordinary period suffices. Unforgivable, no?

There is a reason for this besides common sense. In Spanish an exclamatory or interrogative sentence is always preceded by an inverted version of the closing punctuation mark; this would tend to give all generally doesn't know whether a sentence is declarative or exclamatory until he comes to the end of it, at which time it is too late to make much difference.

◆

Between the above-mentioned direct reprints of American comics and the completely original Mexican costume-hero books comes a small intermediary class of original Mexicomics featuring U.S. comic book characters. There are only a few of these, and they aren't particularly noteworthy in art or plot quality when compared to the original American titles, but they are distinct enough that they cannot be ignored and should not be lumped together with any of the other categories of Mexican comics.

Most of these are published by La Prensa, and the most popular of these is apparently *El Halcón Negro*, featuring our old friends the Blackhawks. This is a decidedly different set of stories from those published in the present U.S. comic, corresponding more closely to the old Quality *Blackhawk* issues than to the modern DC ones. What is even more unusual, though, is that there is another Mexican Blackhawk comic, Novaro's *El Halcón de Oro*, which is the reprint edition of the current DC magazine. It would be interesting to know how *two* Blackhawk comics came to be.

Apparently La Prensa began its original adventures first, patterned after the U.S. *Blackhawk* comic as it then was. When Novaro started its series of DC reprints, it came up against the fact that the Spanish translation of Blackhawk – *El Halcón Negro* – was already being used, and was forced to settle for a poor substitute – *El Halcón de Oro*, or "The Hawk of Gold." While Novaro's monthly reprint is only up to issue #84, La Prensa's comic (which comes out twice a month) is already up to #221 (February 15, 1965).

That La Prensa's original comic is an unwelcome interloper to both Novaro and DC can be seen from a notice (translated below) which is printed on the first page of each issue of Novaro's *El Halcón de Oro*: "We remind our readers that only in *El Halcón de Oro* will they encounter the sensational adventures of the *authentic Blackhawks*, and that the Organization Novaro, S.A. de C.V., editor of the magazine that you now hold in your hands, is the *only one authorized* to publish them, in Spanish, by National Periodical Publications, Inc., holders of the literary and artistic rights to Blackhawk (El Halcón Negro) in the whole world."

Actually, La Prensa's *El Halcón Negro* has made a number of definite and important changes in the Blackhawks. Its version has dropped Chop Chop entirely, and changed the names of the rest of the group, so that Olaf is now Lars, Hendrickson is Henrik, Andre is Pierre, Chuck is Jock, and Stanislaus is Stanley. As in the Novaro comic (where Chop Chop is just "Chop"), Blackhawk is called just Halcón, but in this case he also has a *real* name which is no secret; the newspapers run stories about "Liam O'Hara, known as Blackhawk...." They still wear the old uniforms, and its clear that these *are* uniforms, not just costumes. Which brings us to the major change in emphasis:

These Blackhawks are not nearly so much a band of roving costumed heroes, as the American ones are, as they are a special military group. The American comic has tried to return to the semi-military tie-in lately, as evinced in the recent issue which had them serving under the United Nations. But in the La Presna *revista* they are definitely a military squad, directly under the orders of the Army's Department of Security (though whether this is the U.S. or Mexican Army isn't made clear). Blackhawk Island is still the base of their operations, but it is just another military outpost, rather than a secret lair.

Possibly the best example of this is given in issue #219, in the story "Los Proscritos" ("The Exiled"). The Blackhawks are flying to Ciudad Centro (Central City) when a robot bomb homes in on them and explodes. Though none of them is hurt, they are all covered with a radioactive material. Blackhawk contacts his superiors in the Department, who order him not to return to the island, as "the island and the equipment on it belong to the government." It all turns out to be a trick at the end, but it is easy to see the change in status that the Blackhawks have undergone in this Mexican comic.

Weird creatures are out; their adversaries are usually either the Red Chinese or mad scientists – but no costumed super-crooks. Lady Blackhawk is gone; in her place is Vanessa, a lone-wolf agent who may seem to have sold out to the enemy but who is usually just working as a spy in their camp.

El Halcón Negro consists of 24 pages, not counting covers, as do all the original La Prensa comics. These are divided into three stories, generally of eight pages each, though there will occasionally be an advertisement on page 24 instead. No other interior ads or one-page cartoons are used and, unlike in U.S. comics, there is no need for a page of text anywhere in the issue. The art (unsigned) is in the style of the U.S. comic but is distinctly inferior, with nothing like the fine-line detail of the work of Richard Dillin and Charles Cuidera. Unlike La Prensa's Marvel reprints, however, it *is* clearly printed, the pages are cut correctly, and the dialogue is properly centered in the speech balloons.

Interesting to the many admirers of the artwork of Joe Kubert is La Prensa's *Azor el Primitivo*, which is based on his

Tor comic published by St. John in the mid-50s minus the "Danny Dreams" and "Wizard of Uggh" features. The art in most issues, though not in *Azor* #2 or house-ads in other La Prensa mags, is divided between thick-lined tracings and mimicking of Kubert's *Tor*. Original drawings and/or poses of Tor have been reworked into original stories, usually three to an issue. Azor goes on sale at the end of every month, and the latest issue as *AE* #8 goes to press is #10 (Feb. 27, 1965). Strangely enough, "Tor" has evidently proven more popular in Mexico than he did in the U.S. original.

The principal difference between Tor and Azor seems to be that the latter-day caveman has a steady mate, Rhea, who follows along in his adventures -- though both Rhea and Chi Chi (the Mexican version of Tor's pet monkey Chee Chee) are being played down in recent issues. Aside from that, it's the same battling with dinosaurs, invading tribes, etc. – coupled with the invention of such things as music long before any other human thought of them – that *Tor* and other caveman comics have presented.

Skipping over the original La Prensa editions of *Robin Hood, Davy Crockett, et al.*, which have no place in an article on costume-hero comics, there is one other that should be mentioned at least briefly. Those of you who followed the cowboy comics of a dozen years ago, notably Magazine Enterprises' efforts, may remember a masked avenger called the Ghost Rider (created by Gardner Fox, incidentally), who regularly caught villains by making them think he was a spirit, "come from the depths of the grave – summoned by the screams of your victims" (as he put it in *Best of the West* #4), and terrorizing them into publicly revealing their crimes. He appeared in his own comic as well, where he superseded Rex Fury, "The Calico Kid," taking the latter as his own secret identity.

Well, the Ghost Rider, now known as El Espectro (literally, *the Spectre*), can be found occasionally today in Editora Sol's *Aventuras-Vaqueros Intrepidos*, a bi-monthly novel-lengther of 36 pages (counting covers and ads). The art (signed by Ram Zittie) is more detailed than anything Dick Ayers ever contributed to the old series and the ghostly tricks are played up less, but otherwise it's the same comic, complete with plots and art that would never make it by the CCA today. The Ghost Rider's secret identity of Marshal Rex Fury has now become Rojo (Red) Perez, and his Chinese sidekick Ming now talks in broken Spanish instead of broken English.

This, then, should cover virtually the entire subject of Mexican reprints of U.S. costume-heroes and Mexican comics which utilize characters from American magazines. Next issue, we'll get into what most of you are really waiting to hear about – the original Mexican super-hero comics. Perhaps I'm wrong and today's American comics readers have become so used to the styles of National and Marvel that they will find little to appreciate in the somewhat unusual characters and approaches of the Mexican publishers. However, I'd prefer to think differently and that a perusal of the more original Supermen South will leave more than one reader with a desire to take up the study of Spanish.

I guess we'll just have to wait and see.

AE #9 would spotlight such original Mexican super-heroes as Santo, Relámpago, El Piloto Fantasma, and Neutrón. Roy Thomas acquired these comics – and his interest in the subject matter – during trips to Puerto Rico and Mexico in 1963 and 1964. [Reproductions not from the original fanzine.]

A Few Notes on Lightning Bolts and Litigation ...

When Dick Lupoff wrote the first installment of the comics-related series "And All in Color for a Dime" for his fanzine Xero *in 1960, he chose as his subject "The Big Red Cheese" –* i.e., *the original (or, as he prefers to say, "the real") Captain Marvel.*

Because Xero *was a science fiction fanzine, Lupoff soon learned that Otto O. Binder had been the major (if uncredited) writer of* Captain Marvel Adventures *and* The Marvel Family *from 1941 through the demise of the Fawcett comics line in 1953. Otto had been well known to readers of SF pulp magazines in the 1930s under the name "Eando Binder" (and indeed later wrote many two-page text stories about Jon Jarl of the Space Patrol for* CMA *under that name, his only overt credit in the comics).*

Otto quickly became a sort of third patron saint – after his longtime friends Julius Schwartz and Gardner Fox – to early comics fandom. SF and comics fan Bill Spicer skillfully adapted Binder's pulp tales "Adam Link's Vengeance" and "The Life Battery," among others, into comics form for his excellent fanzine Fantasy Illustrated.

Roy Thomas soon began a lively correspondence with Otto, who took a personal, almost avuncular interest in Roy, as he did in Bill Spicer. On several occasions in 1964-65, Otto also sent Roy materials which he was invited to use in Alter Ego.

Among other things, this treasure trove included six dailies each of "Mr. Tawny" (the Talking Tiger from CMA*) and two other comic strips done by Binder and* CMA *artist C. C. Beck; comics-style Christmas greetings sent out by* Marvel Family *artist Kurt Schaffenberger and by Fawcett itself in the late 1940s; photos of Otto and other Fawcett pros taken during that period; concepts and even leftover scripts of Otto's that could be used (and even continued) in* Alter Ego *and/or* Fantasy Illustrated *–*

– plus Otto's 1953 synopsis for a never-printed issue of The Marvel Family *(whose last published issue had been #89, cover-dated January 1954)!*

Roy was naturally flabbergasted when he opened that particular package in 1964. Only the Mr. Tawny originals could have made more of an impact on him. For here, on the front and back of three sheets of typing paper, were actually four different and exciting items:

(1) A two-page single-spaced typed synopsis for a 17-page Marvel Family story titled "Seven Modern Wonders," complete with penciled crossings-out and handwritten corrections;

(2) Two additional pages of typed and hand-written notes re the above, mostly story changes (perhaps made at the behest of editor Wendell Crowley) – plus red-circled notes handwritten by Otto in '64: "MF serial - 17 pages - which was started - first chapter of 6 pages done & paid for - June, 1953. - End of Fawcett comics - MF serial never used";

(3) Page 6 of a Marvel Family story (also evidently unpublished), wherein Cap, Mary, and Junior pursue a shape-changing villain called "Mr. Alias," who eludes them by changing Plastic-Man-like into a lamppost;

(4) A one-page single-spaced synopsis for a CMA *story entitled "Captain Marvel's Apprentice!" – likewise apparently unpublished.*

Talk about your comic book cornucopias!

FAMOUS BLAST WORDS (thomas/kinney)

unabashedly inspired by a cartoon in a comic art fanzine which wishes to remain anonymous

With Otto's permission, Roy announced in Alter Ego #7 that the very next issue would contain a special bonus: "The Last, Previously Unpublished Adventure of the MARVEL FAMILY by Otto Binder!" – accompanied by several illustrations by Biljo White.

Alas, it was not to be.

In mid-December, some weeks after AE #7 had gone out in the mails, Roy received a letter from an attorney for Fawcett Publications; for, though Fawcett had discontinued its comics in 1953, it was still a major publisher of magazines and paperback books.

That letter is long since lost, but the gist of it was that not only did Fawcett intend to sue Roy if he went ahead with plans to publish that MF synopsis (or even any future articles or drawings dealing with "Fawcett's copyrighted characters"), but that he was to immediately cease distributing copies of AE #7. More: he was ordered to (somehow) retrieve all previously-mailed copies and destroy them!

Roy was, to say the least, taken aback.

Financial insolvency, if not a prison cell, suddenly seemed to loom large on the horizon.

Roy isn't certain at this late date if he wrote Otto at once for advice, or if the name was mentioned in the attorney's letter, but Roy soon exchanged letters with Ralph Daigh, a Fawcett vice president.

Daigh explained, firmly but civilly: "Such use as you have made... would tend to permit the characters to go into public domain.... It is my recollection that, as a result of [the law suit with National/DC], Fawcett agreed not to publish, and also not to give anyone else permission to publish, material of or concerning the Marvel Family."

Roy at once acquiesced (like, he had a choice?) and dropped all plans to publish any further Marvel Family material, ever. Fortunately, this done, Fawcett ceased to concern itself with whether he mailed out any more copies of AE #7, let alone whether he retrieved ones already mailed out. In fact, Roy had given fan-publisher G.B. Love his blessing to reprint several hundred copies of AE #7, and even advertised that reprint in AE #8, with no complaint from Fawcett.

(Of course, Roy's announcement in AE #8 of Love's reprint did state that "Alter Ego #7 is no longer available from Roy Thomas!" G.B. was taking his chances, and he escaped unscathed. No doubt all Fawcett had ever wanted to do was to keep DC's lawyers off its back. Understandable, since Fawcett had already had a decade of litigation with DC from the early 40s through 1953!)

And so matters stayed, from 1964 until 1997.

Then, as he and Bill Schelly were readying the contents of the volume you hold in your hands, Roy suddenly got an inspiration:

For two decades it had appeared that "Shazam!" was a magic word that would never again be uttered by anyone more heroic than TV's Gomer Pyle or Ed "Kookie" Byrnes, or a lazy newspaper headline-writer. That's why Roy had proposed in 1970 that the awards given out by the comics industry's own Academy of Comic Book Arts be called the "Shazams."

Then, in 1972, DC publisher Carmine Infantino shocked an ACBA meeting in New York by announcing that he had made a deal with Fawcett for DC to publish comics starring Captain Marvel and company. Because Marvel Comics had pre-empted the name "Captain Marvel" for a hero of its own (mostly to keep anyone else from doing it), DC's comic would be called not Captain Marvel but – Shazam!

Soon the Marvel Family was back. And there's never been a time since when Cap and his kinsmen haven't been appearing somewhere in the DC line. Indeed, Roy's first story for DC in 1981 was a Superman-Captain Marvel battle in which the two heroes exchanged powers (inspired by a cartoon by Steve Stiles in the Thompsons' fanzine Comic Art, as a matter of fact – which in turn had inspired the "Famous Blast Words" cartoon reprinted on page 131).

Back to 1997: Roy realized that, since DC now controlled the Marvels, Fawcett could no longer object to publication of Otto's 1953 material; it was just a matter of seeing whether DC Comics would oppose its being printed.

DC publisher Paul Levitz, an old friend and longtime fan, had already graciously arranged for this book's cover to be able to feature the Alter Ego covers which had depicted Green Lantern, Blackhawk, and the Marvel Family. And now, in answer to a fax from Roy, Paul sent back word that DC had no objections to the Binder material being printed in this volume.

Thus, we're proud to showcase, on the next three pages, Otto Binder's actual synopsis (with notes) for what would have been the lead feature in a never-published Marvel Family #90 or later, as well as the Captain Marvel synopsis and the page from the "Mr. Alias" MF story (which might well have also been slated for #90-91). Pay no attention to the big "X's" through the latter pages; Otto merely crossed them out to indicate that they weren't a part of the "Seven Modern Wonders" story.

And now, as we were about to say 33 years ago, before we were so startlingly interrupted ...

The Editors

[From Comic Art #5, October 1964]

RAINBOW BRIDGE

oob

MF - 17 - Seven Modern Wonders.

Chap one---Story begins in future, 3000 A.D., where a "MARCHMONT Morris" of that time has big dispute with Emil Judd. Morris "owns" the "seven wonders" (all in one mountain country), due to MF, in 20th century, bequeathing it to him as "public domain". But Judd says that's a "fairy-tale" (MF stuff sounds that way) and that his family should own them. To settle dispute, they take time-trip back to 1953.

Meanwhile, in 1953, Sterling Morris of Whiz has traced his genealogy back to these mountain people (indefinite locale or nation). Just then, big news flashes from that same place---in big danger.

Morris all perturbed, so MF fly him there. Huge glacier is crunching down into this valley. Morris's relatives will be killed. But all people in valley stubbornly refuse to move. (Why? Same reason people along Ohio, who get flooded often, stick and start over. Or people near volcanoes etc. Briefly, how people "love" their homeland, no matter how "harsh", etc).

MF can't talk people out of leaving, so must save the valley (now the most dangerous land on Earth). MF construct first wonder---giant pyramid, blocking the creeping glacier for all time.

But meanwhile, a Jason Judd of valley raids town, a hill "bandit" type. MF also stop him, but he escapes. However, this is being observed now by the future-Morris and future-Judd...and it is the future-Judd who helps his ancestor escape MF. And meanwhile, the future-Morris meets Whiz Morris, and they greet each other fondly.

MF think their job is done---but one thing leads to another. The reason the glacier started sliding down was because underground heat has been building up. Now whole valley gets steamy hot---MF find huge coal-bed on fire under valley. People soon to be roasted alive. Cliffhanger.

Chapter two---MF do second "wonder", making big hollow under burning coal, letting it drop, filling space with asbestos. Then, third wonder, pipe up steam and make giant power-plant.

Meanwhile, the future-Judd sees the "fairy-tale" is true---of MF action. But schemingly, he and Jason Judd join forces now, to pull biggest "robbery"---of the rights to these wonders. All they have to do is kill off the past Morris, ending his line---so there will be no future-Morris. Then future-Judd will have sole claim to these "wonders".

Danger pops up, and again (CAUSED) it's a natural "follow-up" of before. The terrific heat a wide chasm in the valley, suddenly opens up CRACK. Rescue work first, and then MF build giant bridge across chasm, 4th wonder. Meanwhile, this gives the Judds chance to nab the two Morrises---to bump them off.

MF receive "ransom-note"---sign over all rights to "wonders" to Judds, and have kids deliver it to hills. Thus kids captured, and with the signed-papers, Judds can kill them all and cover trail completely. Cliffhanger.

Chap three---Kids escape trap, with Morrises, but Judds escape, to now organize big "feud" between Judds and Morrises (Dozens of both families (OVER)

by rapidly building huge "dyke" of stone 100 feet high. (5th wonder)

MF quash this, but Judds go free again when in valley). new big danger pops up in sequence---a mountain splits off and crashes---except MF prevent avalanche etc. But this was only and main road out of valley, destroyed. Only straight cliff there. So MF build mile-high elevator as easy exit from valley (for buying supplies etc). 6th wonder. TUNNEL THRU MT.

Finally, in desperation, the two Judds sneak to steam-plant and release scalding steam which will kill everyone in valley.

Last big feat by MF, as they fly to nearby mountain-lake, WHIP up tidal-wave whose terrific spray wets down steamed valley, cooling steam to harmless water. And thereby proving they themselves are the seventh wonder.

Judds now caught. 1953-Judd jailed there. Future-Judd taken back in time-ship as prisoner of future-Morris. Judds' claims all forfeited for good. Morris's claims proven, so that future-Morris can continue letting 7 wonders serve the valley for free, in 3000 A.D.

Main points---

Seven Wonders now all tied together, a sort of "chain-reaction" of dangers resulting in one thing after another for MF.

Sterling Morris directly involved, as this personally concerns his relatives of past, present and future.

Judd family villains have strong motivation to win "rights" to wonders, and then charge exhorbitant fees etc.

MF have two "jobs"---one of making seven wonders to save valley. Other of saving Morrises and nabbing Judds.

MF doing seven wonders will make good pix, but now have integral part in story, not thrown-in for their own sake.

OPENING - DEED - JUDGE - IN ENVELOPE - JUDDS OF FUTURE LEAVE DURING TRAP AFTER SIGNING - BUT MF DESTROY DEED (ESCAPE TRAP) + IN FUTURE ENVELOPE EMPTY

SEVEN MARVELS

Opening---Judd in 3000 has deed in envelope, will open it in court. Just found deed in family-papers.

Marchmont Morris into past via time-ship, with Judd as stowaway. Judd wants to kill Morris, in past, etc.

Story follows, to point where ~~Marrisxxxx~~ Sterling Morris trapped, plus kids, and Morris must sign over all rights to Judd.

Then future-Judd leaves, thinking his job done, with deed in hands of past-Judd to be duly passed on in family. (so all can benefit) But kids escape trap---and finally get deed and rip it up.

In future, finally, as Judd opens envelope---empty.

Change seven wonders, like ~~brainbox~~ rainbow bridge, solidifying rainbow. Vast tunnel through mt (instead of elevator). "sky"hook for glacier, or giant anchor with cable to mountain top. Hot geyser bursts forth (creating original heat) and MF cap it with ~~xx~~ steam pipe to ~~xiantxx~~ power plant.

Two more needed. (MF 7th).

MF SERIAL - 17 PAGES - WHICH WAS STARTED — FIRST CHAPTER OF 6 PAGES DONE + PAID FOR.
JUNE, 1953

END OF FAWCETT COMICS -
MF SERIAL NEVER USED

"SKY HOOK" - GIANT ANCHOR TO HIGH PEAK

(1) GEYSER HAS BURST FORTH - MF CAP IT + PIPE IT STRAIGHT UP — MILE HIGH STONE PIPE (HIGHER THAN MTS LONG SIGHT) (STEAM CAN BE USED FOR HEATING)

(2)

(4) CHASM - RAINBOW BRIDGE - SOLIDIFY RAINBOW TO REACH

(3) GLACIER COVERED ROAD SO MF MAKE TUNNEL THRU MT. - UPHELD BY COLUMNS

(5) LAVA UP FROM CHASM - MF SHAPE IT INTO SUSPENDED ROAD INTO AIR — TO BRIDGE

(6) FUMES - ~~MAGNETIZED~~ ~~IRON FAN~~ HUGE BALANCING STONE TEETERS UP + DOWN, FANNING IT AWAY.

(7) MF (STATUES)

1.
/MM chasing and woman points ahead/

WOMAN: THE crook went that way!

MM: No place for him to hide!

2.
CAP: But again...

/MM leans against lamp-post/

MM: He just vanished in thin air!

3.
/MM leaving, and lamp-post thinks/

MM: Did he turn into a ghost?

POST(T): No, a lamp-post, my dear! Haaa! (ONE OF MY BEST ALIASES YET, I'D SAY!

4.
CAP: But later, a grim trio joins together as the famed, mighty Marvel Family, with a new plan!

/They cruise over city/

CM: Cruise the city! The moment we spot him, we've got a surprise ready!

BELOW: Help! Mr. Alias! MM---Dive!

5.
Ffdive around him from three sides/

CM: The Marvel Dragnet! Try and escape it, chum!

ALIAS:(t): Curses! No chance to run and change!

6.
/Shoots gun at ground/

ALIAS: But listen, fools! I've set my Earthquake Gun to send shock-waves through the ground to a distant point! A whole town, one hundred miles away, will be wrecked by an earthquake NOW!

CM: Holy moley! Is it a trick?

7.
/Hear radio from window nearby, zoom off, with Alias running/

RADIO: Flash! Earthquake struck Midville!

JR: No! He wasn't vluffing! Save the town!

ALIAS: And I escape!

CAP BELOW: Ruthless Mr. Alias escapes by the brutal ruse, for SAVING human lives (ALWAYS) come first to the merciful Marvel Family! But can they speed to the scene of disaster swiftly enough? Already disaster overwhelsm Midville!

/Scene of town cracking up, earthquake/

CHAP

[There! *Now we feel all better! Thanks again, Paul!*]

CMA---Captain Marvel's APPRENTICE/ ASSISTANT (FIRST), WHO GRADUALLY GETS BIG IDEAS TO REPLACE CM.

Story stype---Cm problem story, limelighting CM himself.

Villain---an old-time bad god, Satyr, who was driven from Earth long ago, but is now back seeking again to be "worshipped" and "idolized". This is his motivation, since that is what "gods" thrive on.

General theme---his plot is to replace CM---the most "idolized" man on earth today. Thus, he would gain his craving desire, with millions of people once more fawning at his feet as in days of lost glory.

Background---that long ago, Old Shazam himself, the good wizard, drove him and all bad gods from earth. Thus, if Satyr can take CM's place, he is not only gaining his goal but also having "revenge" on OS.

His method---by the use of powerful evil magic, in the form of pinches of magic dust, he convinced CM himself that he should "retire". He uses Slow Dust, Weak Dust, Fat Dust, Age Dust (borrowed from other plot) on CM---but note, they only affect CM in small degree, not sweepingly. Slow Dust on CM doesn't make him real slow in flying, but just a little slower than before. Weak Dust only takes away a small portion of his strength. Fat Dust makes CM look a bit heavy with a slight paunch. Age Dust makes him look a bit older.

All for the purpose of making CM himself think such thoughts as---Am I slowing down? Am I getting weak? Am I gaining weight? Am I growing old? So that at the ripe moment, CM himself is ready to step down and let a new CM take his place---for the good of the world.

Satyr has to play this subtle game in order not to arouse the attention of OS to what's going on at Earth. (OS at Rock of Eternity is busy keeping eye on whole universe and won't pay any attention to Earth as long as Satyr plays his cards right, so that neither CM nor B summon OS himself, and complain).

Satyr himself becomes the new CM, using Marvel Dust on himself, giving him flying power, strength etc. Also---a key thing---Satyr poses as Old Shazam as the final clincher, telling CM he is being replaced, which lulls CM's suspicions entirely.

And cleverest of all, after CM "retires" and Satyr replaces him as the new CM (identical in appearance and all) he does only good deeds. Exactly like CM. No evil deeds, to arouse CM or OS against him. And as the new CM, the whole modern world of billions will "idolize" him---his goal attained. This is what makes it all very insidious for CM, utterly duped,

In short, and I think this is a good twist, the villain for once is not going to stupidly grab for "power" or "rule" or anything, overplaying his hand. He's using the old maxim---if you can't lick 'em, join 'em. So as the new CM, doing blazing good deeds, he's won all he needs and wants---the new "god" of the 20th century, in a secure safe position. He's licked his "exile" and "banishment" from Earth, by OS, and has the laugh on him.

Development---Satyr first deliberately gets CM on his trail by openly forming a "Satyr Cult", dedicated to obvious evil. BB would hear of it, go to meeting, ku-klux-klan atmosphere etc, presided over by black-robed evil Satyr (goat-like hooved god, as per Greek myths).

Doubtless every editor has his own favorite title for the letter column (if any) of his magazine. In the case of *Alter Ego*, founder Jerry Bails had his "Conversations" and Ronn Foss his "Readers Write," a title which I decided to keep until I found one which particularly appealed to me. Having found same in the abbreviation "re" which frequents business communications, I rest content.

Without further delay, we now begin with an open letter from *AE* editor emeritus Ronn Foss, whose information re the creation of the Eclipse would seem to be of "especial interest":

Ronn Foss
1624 N. French
Santa Ana, California

The limitless conglomeration of comic heroes necessitates some gimmick or otherwise outstanding variation to differentiate one character from all others. When Dru Moroz and I collaborated on a hero with the intention of submitting him (or her, as the case might've been) to one of the NYC publishers, we fully realized this, hence spent many months of correspondence strictly anent all possibilities which could be incorporated into a "new" hero.

About six months before I assumed editorship of *AE*, we had settled on a hero whose forte was super-psyche: a mentalist, normal except for his hyper-sensitive mind whose powers were limited only by his ability to apply concentration. Shortly thereafter, Dell beat us to the proverbial punch with *Brain Boy*; our hero was to have been DynaMan, and I still feel he'd have offered better sales potential.

Faced with this, we began anew. At that time (late 1962), adventure-heroes were just getting re-established in reading popularity, so we decided upon a revival attempt. Discarding this character and that, we settled upon a "new" Dr. Mid-Nite, which Dru scripted in short order. With all due respect I submitted the fifty-plus-page story (which amounted to thirteen pages of art) to editor Julie Schwartz for his sanction for presentation in *AE* #5. Mr. Schwartz replied, after "glancing over" the script, that he himself was not in control of the copyright, but that he was given to understand that we could use neither the name "Dr. Mid-Nite" nor the crescent moon which had been his symbol. Personally, this suited yours truly just fine, since I preferred modernizing the character anyway – not only by way of the dialogue and plot which Dru had done, but the name and costume as well.

Thus we spent another month

Dr. Mid-Nite à la *Stan Josephs (Asch) flanked by two of Ronn Foss' developmental versions of Mid-Nite / Eclipse*

hashing over titles... some unique name which would convey a similar (midnight) impression, yet not be quite as obvious as such references as "moon" and "darkness." Eventually we came up with "Eclipse," which in itself suggests victory over lawlessness, and I redesigned the costume – several dozen times in all manner of variations – adding appropriate symbolisms as he began to take on depth and significance.

I don't know whether or not the pros spend as much time and care developing their characters (though I suspect, as is too oft apparent, they don't) as we did, but I earnestly recommend that amateurs with hopes of prodom consider every aspect of what they present. Not only must a hero provide some spark of originality (an obstacle in itself), but it should also be fully developed and highly polished into a smooth, genuinely appealing and individually unique characterization. Only through trial and error before publication can an amateur hero become successful upon initial circulation, and only the best of these will be strongly unusual enough for repeated publicity.

My thanks to all of fandom that the Eclipse has become one such.

Wendell Crowley
Former Editor:
***Captain Marvel,* et al.**

On Page 19, you give me a lot more credit than is really due. Captain Marvel was created by Bill Parker in conjunction with C.C. Beck. Beck, of course, created the artwork, and just how much influence he had on the conception of the character as a whole I never did know. But certainly the two of them together in that very first story established the foundation of the character, which was altered only slightly as the years went by.

Even so, during those years many others had considerable influence. Stanley Kauffmann edited the magazines for quite a while and before him Ed Herron certainly affected the future of the Captain a great deal. In addition it was he who created Captain Marvel Jr. Writers like Joe Millard and Manley Wade Wellman also contributed greatly. Beck himself did a lot of the writing, and Marc Swayze, who was on the art staff at Fawcett, not only did a lot of the drawing, but also wrote many stories. The whole operation was in its earlier days made successful through the combined efforts of many, many people.

I never thought of Sivana as the Fu Manchu type. He was rather unique unto himself in his single-minded devotion to the conquering of the whole world, or, failing that, destroying it, and along with it Captain Marvel. The depiction of Sivana by Beck, by the way, was a caricature of a druggist he knew in Long Island, hence Sivana's costume.

Probably after your recent experience with the lawyer for Fawcett, you now realize that Fawcett can never bring these characters back to the newsstand "at will." As far as Otto's letter is concerned, I would like to clear up a few things. Ken Bald never did many layouts in Jack Binder's shop. Ken started out as main figure man and eventually replaced Pete Riss as Jack's art director. The heavy percentage of layouts were done by Bill Ward, He, on the other hand, never did much inking, and Pete Costanza never did work for Jack. Pete was an old pulp illustrator, and as the comics killed off the pulps in the late 30s, Pete got a job on the Fawcett art staff under Beck. It was he who drew the early Ibis stories. He later helped Beck on Marvel, along with Chic Stone, Dave Berg (now of *Mad*), and others. (Eddie Robbins comes to mind.)

Ray Harford and Bob Boyajian came to the Fawcett staff from Jack's shop. Harford had developed into a good main figure man, and had shown an ability to draw Captain Marvel. Marvel had become so popular that more and more stories and books were being published at great frequency. The Fawcett staff could not keep up with the work. At first they farmed out some of the work to Harry Chesler's shop. This was the shop in which Jack Binder had cut his comics eyeteeth, and where he had become art director. He eventually left to start his own shop. He was replaced by an art director named Sultan. It was Sultan who influenced George Tuska very heavily, and it is the Chesler shop work on which Tuska had some small part which you attribute to him in your magazine. Fawcett was not too well satisfied with the Chesler work, however, and they farmed it out to Binder's studio instead; Bill Ward did all the layouts, and it was on this work that Harford showed such promise that he was taken into Fawcett's own shop.

[Mike Vosburg illo]

faster
than a
speeding
bullet,
man

When the war came along, of course, most of these fellows went into the various armed forces. The books were cut down drastically, and the Fawcett shop was able to do most of it itself. Fawcett eventually disposed of the shop, with Beck taking over production of Captain Marvel on a freelance basis and having a shop of his own. Pete Costanza eventually became his partner in this, and they went on to do more work for other publishers, principally one whose magazines were distributed in Canada.

After the war Fawcett found it necessary to freelance out more of the work, and this is when Kurt Schaffenberger came onto the scene as a Marvel artist. He had started out on Ibis after he returned from the service.

As far as Captain Marvel, Jr., was concerned, he was certainly created by Mac Raboy, but Mac was an extremely slow, meticulous artist, and even with the help of his excellent background man, Ruby Zuboff, he was barely able to turn out one 13-page story a month under the expert supervision of Ed Herron in the Fawcett shop. Gene McDonald and a fellow we called "Red" (whose last name escapes me) took over some of the Marvel Jr. work. Later on, Bud Thompson came back to Fawcett after a long stint in Hollywood doing a syndicated panel on movie stars, and became the principal Marvel Jr. artist. This, of course, was after Raboy had left Fawcett to work for Ken Crossen on the Green Lama. In the halcyon days, Thompson had Joe Certa and Nick Zuraw helping him, but later he was able to do most of this work himself.

I was surprised to see Otto saying that letters were pouring in about Mr. Mind. As far as I can recall, the only time letters poured in was after Mr. Mind had been electrocuted, and for some reason or other we had requested the fans to write in at that time, although what the reason for this was, I don't remember. In any case I do recall that one little boy wrote in and protested that the trial of Mr. Mind had been unfair in that he had not been actually tried by his peers, there having been no open-minded worms on the jury.

Thanks, Wendell, for taking the time to enlighten *AE*'s readers on the artistic side of the Big Red Cheese. Now for a few comments on the writing side (as well as other matters) from the amiable Otto Binder, whose "narcissistic" reminiscences in *AE* #7 were looked on by not a few readers as being the high point of the issue:

Otto O. Binder
Former Writer: *Captain Marvel Adventures* et al.
Present Writer: *Jimmy Olsen*

Alter Ego #7 certainly "shazamed" into a super-issue! Cover: *superb*. Best likeness of the Marvel Family trio I've ever seen on a fanzine. Biljo White has outdone himself. His "Alter and Captain Ego" is a pleasing surprise, too. Clever in its subtle titling, forceful in its art, and plotted with the pro touch. To a pro like myself, your archeological digs into the origins and evolutionary patterns of early super-heroes are fascinating, indeed. I'll wager the original writer for the Human Torch will be as intrigued as I was when Dick Lupoff's fan-group (my first contact with this astonishing movement, in 1960) told *me* that Billy Batson was *not* really Captain Marvel. The proof? Billy and the Cap'n always referred to each other in the third person. Obvious though it may seem, that basic thought had never jolted me before. We didn't psychoanalyze or review our quirks of writing in those days; we just batted out scripts at a mad pace, letting the alter egos fall where they might.

"One Man's Family" gets you my "oob" (my personal

award) for the ingenious title followed by the Mightiest Marvel Review in fandom as yet, for which there ought to be a Big Red Cheese award (in the practical form of a big red cheese of good flavor).

I'm quite gratified that you liked the Sivana Family, as I always thought them my best efforts in that book. Sivana, to all of us at Fawcett, was almost "real" as compared to the other dirty dastards the Marvel Family quashed; in fact, we often privately rooted for Sivana, wishing at times he could win a round with the Marvels *licked* at the end of a book. There was talk of this for a while – and *this* would have been sensational – of giving the Sivanas their own book – namely, a comic featuring the *villains* rather than their opponent heroes. But, alas, publishers have a limited imagination and just could not accept this pretzeling of the traditional comics format. Ah, well, we have our memories...

Mort Weisinger
Editor: *Superman*, etc.

It was thoughtful of you to send me a copy of your *Alter Ego*, which impresses me as quite a superior production. (What an improvement over the first fanzine, which Julius Schwartz and I launched more than three decades ago!)

I found Otto Binder's nostalgic recap of the Marvel mags very interesting. (You may be interested to know that the Superman-Marvel court duel will be recounted by famous Louis Nizer in his forthcoming book, which is a sequel to his best-selling *My Life in Court.*)

Gardner Fox
Writer: *JLA*, etc.

My deepest thanks for putting me on your *Alter Ego* mailing list. Quite honestly, I just don't understand how you put out such a superior zine! It is professional. That is the only word I can call to mind which properly describes it. I know all the others: sensational, colossal, magnificent. I prefer the "professional," since to me this connotes perfection to the point of being salable.

Some of these days, I'll stand up to a camera and get my picture taken and send it on, if you insist. However, I am one of that school which prefers authors to be invisible, even in their writings. The story is the thing. Now, if I looked like *Joy Holiday*... or maybe I could wear a mask? Hey, *that's* an idea. I'll have to work on it.

Kurt Schaffenberger
Artist: *Lois Lane*, etc.

Many thanks for the copy of *Alter Ego* and especially for your very kind letter enclosed with it. It is nice to know that I'm not just grinding stuff out for its own sake, and that some people really do stop and look at, study, and appreciate what one is trying to do. It's very easy to get the feeling that one is working in a vacuum in this business, as one never really gets to see or meet the people who buy his product. Thanks again.

Once again it seems, rather, that *we* should thank *you* – for panel art (Jerry's term) of consistent quality in *The Marvel Family* and in other comics, past and present.

Richard Lupoff
Merry Hell
Poughkeepsie, New York

The latest *AE* was some sort of Ultimate Fanzine as far as I'm concerned; it has reached the point where it is better in physical appearance, production values, and contents than many professional publications. And, with its large circulation, I wonder if it has not actually crossed the line....

Thanks for the compliment, Dick – but, personally, I'll wait until some issue I actually make a profit first.

Phil Seuling
2881 W. 12th St.
Brooklyn, New York

Re that myths and legends article in #7: that was overdue. 'Twould be a needed service to trace the mythical bases for today's hero comics, especially if you follow the thematic approach. Following the history of sun-hero/divine king/superhuman would surely be in order. A paper on totem animals might follow. Then one on old religion vs. the new (fairies, witches, trolls, *et al.*) would keep up the pace. Tree, mountain, fertility ritual, earth mother – all would be obviously applicable to comic-strip and -book fantasy.

And then, of course, *Alter Ego* 38 and 39 could begin a look at the Arthurian Cycle, which should get you up to issue 115. By then I should come up with a few sub-themes.

And, in closing:

Randy Haynes
117 McKinley Ave.
Washington, Ohio

I received my first ish of *Alter Ego* the other day and all I can say is WOW! It's not what I expected at all.

FAMOUS BLAST WORDS
(thomas/kinney)

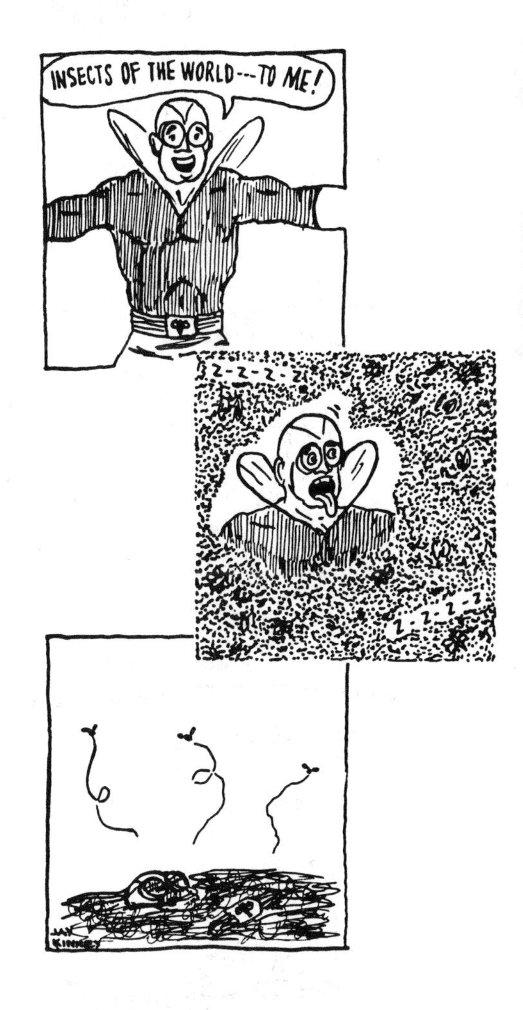

See you next ish?

About the cover of **Alter Ego** ***#9 (August 1965):*** Alter Ego*'s first (and only) wraparound cover displayed various Mexican super-heroes. Starting to the right of the* AE *mask and moving clockwise: Relámpago (Lightning), Neutrón, Santo, Blue Demon, El Hombre Invisible, Tawa (a jungle hero), Supercharro riding Criollo, the Invincible Horse, and El Piloto Fantasma.*

Alter Ego #9 – Notes & Commentary

AE #7 ("Fall 1964") and AE #8 ("Winter 1965") had very nearly lived up to the announced quarterly schedule. But AE #9's indicia billed the zine as published "three times yearly."

For, in the interim, Roy had suddenly found himself working in the comic book industry. Two events happened in such rapid succession that, today, he's a bit vague about which occurred first:

(a) Pat Masulli, executive editor of Charlton Comics, sent a form letter to myriad fanzines, challenging fans to submit scripts for either Son of Vulcan *or (pre-Ditko)* Blue Beetle. *Roy became the first fan to sell scripts to both comics; and though $4 a page wasn't going to make him rich, it wasn't a negligible sum to a guy making under $6000 a year – especially since he and the local superintendent had mutually agreed that Roy would not be teaching for a fourth year at Fox High School in Arnold, Missouri.*

(b) Around the same time, thanks to his correspondence with Julius Schwartz and Mort Weisinger, and maybe just a bit to the copies of AE *#7 & #8 which he (like Jerry and Ronn before him) had sent to every comics pro he could reach, Roy was offered a job in New York: assistant editor to Weisinger on DC's Superman titles.*

Putting a foreign-relations graduate fellowship on hold, Roy accepted the offer, but was not allowed to tell fans about it. Thus AE *#9's editorial referred only to his two scripts sold to Charlton, though with vague promises of more to come.*

At the time, Roy naively hoped to continue publishing Alter Ego, *so he simply downgraded its announced frequency to buy a little time. In June of 1965 Roy, armed with a suitcase and a portable Smith-Corona, arrived in Manhattan in the middle of a taxi strike and walked the dozen blocks from the bus terminal to DC's offices.*

How Roy worked for two weeks for Mort Weisinger (one week paid, one unpaid) and then left DC to become Stan Lee's protégé and eventual successor as Marvel's editor-in-chief was related in Bill Schelly's The Golden Age of Comic Fandom, *and is outside the scope of this book except as it impinges on the story of* Alter Ego. *But of course it did – and* how.

Meanwhile, Roy had foolishly pre-paid his St. Louis printer, who had done a good job on AE *#8. Once Roy was out of the state, the printer stalled long and shamelessly before delivering copies of* AE *#9, and did a very uneven job on them.*

Still, Roy was proud of the big fat issue – 48 pages, up from 40. Once more Biljo White ably provided much of the artwork, though Roy did a few drawings himself and even reproduced a few illustrations from comics and pulps.

Fred Patten provided the second part of "Supermen South," covering a super-hero called Relámpago (Lightning), a ghostly Piloto Fantasma, and three masked wrestlers (Santo, Neutrón, Blue Demon) who had their own comics and even films in Mexico.

Shel Kagan's "Great Guardians" covered E.E. "Doc" Smith's Lensmen, from the science fiction pulps of the 1930s, which Kagan (like Roy) believed had been at least a subconscious influence on the modern Green Lantern, if only because of editor Julius Schwartz's SF-fan background. Glen Johnson contributed a piece on All-Star Comics' *two Injustice Societies. "Re:" featured a long letter (with photos) from John Fahey on his visit to DC – the first look most fans had at any professional comics offices.*

Equally groundbreaking was "Otto in Binderland," featuring some of the mid-40s photos provided by Binder of himself and fellow Fawcett pros C.C. Beck, Kurt Schaffenberger, Wendell Crowley, et al. *We have reproduced most of these, as well as others which were squeezed out of* AE *#9 due to space limitations and are thus published herein for the first time ever.*

Otto also provided another real scoop – six daily comic-strips of "Mr. Tawny," the talking tiger of later Captain Marvel tales, by Binder and Cap's original artist, C.C. Beck.

AE *#9 likewise featured "I, Robotman," a first-person narration allegedly by the 1940s super-hero whose 60s counterpart currently co-starred in* Doom Patrol. *Actually, Roy wrote the piece, as he wrote and illustrated "A Treasury of Mortal Verses," parodies of famous poems, including an on-target "Oliver Fannish."*

Interestingly, in AE *#9 Roy also quoted extensively from a recent article on comic books in his home-county newspaper,* The Southeast Missourian, *written by one Dennis O'Neil. By this time Roy had contacted Denny, who was only a year or so older than himself; and later he would help the St. Louis-born journalist get a staff job at Marvel. Denny would go on to become a major writer and editor in the comics field, from 1965 to the present.*

With youthful optimism AE *#9 announced the "partial projected contents" for the tenth issue: part three of "Supermen South"; "The Cult of Mercury" (Flash's imitators) by Derrill Rothermich; a by-mail interview with Gardner Fox (arranged before Roy realized he'd soon meet the JSA/JLA writer in person); articles on Plastic Man by Don Thompson and on the Red Skull by L.L. Simpson; "a great new comic-strip, and other smash features!" The strip would hopefully be the Thomas-scripted, Foss-drawn "Warrior of Llarn," featured in a full-page pin-up.*

In fact, when AE *#10 would finally surface,* four years *after #9, it would contain not a single one of the above projected contents – and would be a professional publication, not really a fanzine at all....*

The Editors

OTTO in

[Otto Binder circa 1947*]

Quoted Commentary by OTTO BINDER

From the article "Captain Marvel's Mouthpiece" by Gerry de la Ree in the Bergen Evening Record, Hackensack, NJ, Feb. 7, 1953:

"[Otto] Binder gained quite a name for himself as a science fiction author between 1932 and 1940.... [He and his brother Earl] used the name Eando Binder, which was devised from the names 'Earl and Otto.' When Earl left the writing field, Otto retained the name of Eando, under which all his science fiction work appeared.... He switched to the comics field around 1941...."

"Here's my writing studio, circa 1944. During this era of greatest production, I did up to 200 scripts a year.

"Pajamas and robe represent 'working clothes.' I was so busy I didn't have time to dress and go out for days at a time – no joke. When my wife was out and I answered the door for random salesmen and callers, I'm sure they thought I was a 'kept man.' True irony! I was working like a dog!"

"This is 'The House That Captain Marvel Built,' Englewood, New Jersey."

[Right: Kurt Schaffenberger and daughter Susan, age ten months, circa 1948."*]

[*Note: These captions and photos were squeezed out of *AE* #9 due to space considerations and intended for later issues.]

BINDERLAND

"[Above] is Charles Clarence Beck, chief artist for Captain Marvel from the very start to the very end – 1940 to 1953. He is now living in Florida and doing commercial art. That's just a friend in the middle; on the right is Pete Riss, deceased some years ago, who worked in Jack's art shop while it lasted, then did his own features, including many romance comics, westerns, and such for Fawcett, Goodman, and several other old-time comics publishers."

[Above left: Otto & Ione Binder, with Jack & Olga Binder*]

"At left below is Wendell Crowley, chief editor of all Marvel comics at Fawcett from 1943 to 1953. He is now half-owner of a lumber company. At right are my brother Jack and his two sons, circa 1946."

"This is me playing the accordion (a hobby of mine), circa 1945. The interested bystander is one of my many nephews."

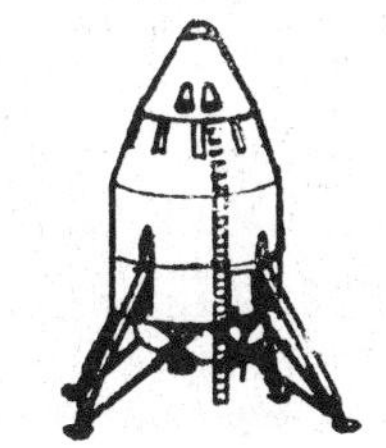

Left: "oob," Otto's personal studio-symbol

[Otto – 1948*]

[Jack Binder and Pete Riss, circa 1950*]

"Not in these photos, but a part of our social group, were Ken Bald, Carl Pfeufer, Rod Reed – well, too many to think of now. We had poker parties, baseball games, bowling contests (two teams), etc. Really a gala era!"

You know, I'll just bet it was! 

TAWNY TIGER, BURNING BRIGHT...

In Alter Ego #7, *as mentioned earlier, Roy Thomas announced over-optimistic plans to publish a sister fanzine called* Alter Ego Comics, *devoted entirely to comics material by fans.*

"Entirely"? No ... make that "mostly."

For, in a letter to Roy in 1964, Otto Binder, longtime Captain Marvel *scribe, mentioned he still had in his possession six never-published comic-strip dailies starring Tawky Tawny, the talking tiger who had been a major supporting character in Cap tales starting in the late 40s – and that those strips could be published in* AE Comics*!*

When Fawcett had folded its comic book line in 1953, Otto and artist C. C. Beck had received permission to market a "Mr. Tawny" strip to newspaper syndicates. If it had made the jump, it would have stood alongside Walt Kelly's "Pogo" as a comic strip having its origins in a defunct comic book. Presumably Fawcett would have retained some rights in the strip, though Otto never indicated as much.

The Tawny comic strip never really got off the ground. Binder and Beck produced only six dailies, far fewer than a syndicate would have needed to see before making a decision to buy – plus six dailies for each of two other strips also done in the 50s: "Frank and Ernest" ("a zany scientist on earth") and "Brian the Brain" about "a goofy (humorous) kid-genius who has fantasy adventures (with ghosts, witches, etc.)." Always eager to help fan projects, Otto eventually sent all eighteen dailies to Roy.

As for "Mr. Tawny," Otto wrote that the six strips were all "fully inked by C. C. Beck ... he answered and says for you to 'go ahead' with them. I'll get around to writing more script but let's start off with those six strips first in the issue you're shaping up."

Yes, you read it right: Otto Binder, writer of more than 18,000 comic book pages, fully intended to turn out additional "Mr. Tawny" scripts for free – perhaps with an eye toward interesting a syndicate at this late date, but still basically for free. Since C. C. Beck was pursuing a commercial art career in Florida, the plan was for future strips to be drawn by a fan – most likely Biljo White, the most Beck-influenced fan-artist of that era.

Otto also sent Roy scripts for other comic-strip notions he'd had: "Jon Jarl, Space Cop" (featuring the hero of many text stories in Captain Marvel *comics credited to Otto's pseudonym, "Eando Binder"); "Flint Kinkaid, Mars Marshal," a space western; and "Anton York, Immortal Man," adapted from a short-story series Otto had written years earlier, when he was a big name in science fiction pulp magazines.*

The originals of the "Mr. Tawny" strips are long since lost, alas – never returned by the St. Louis printer of AE *#9 after Roy relocated to New York City. Thus, we must be content with second-hand reproductions of these six dailies of Tawky Tawny from the striped tail-end of the Golden Age of Comics.*

But, the way we look at it, our cup isn't just half full ...

It runneth over.

The Editors

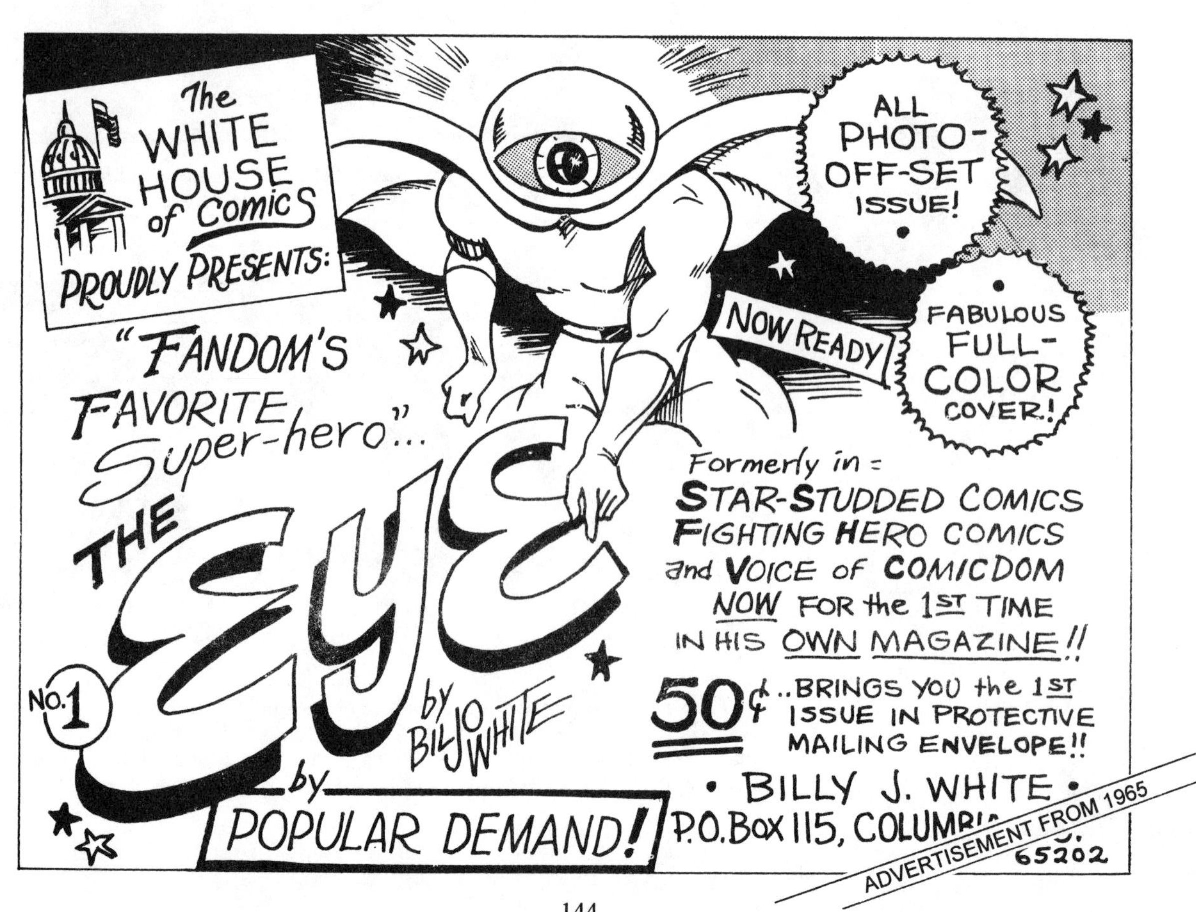

ADVERTISEMENT FROM 1965

MR. TAWNY

AN INVITATION TO A COSTUME BALL - THAT OUGHT TO BE FUN! WHAT COSTUME SHALL I WEAR? INDIAN CHIEF...?
TWO GUN TAWNY ?
NOW I CAN'T SLEEP - I'LL USE THE GOOD OLD METHOD
Z Z Z Z
THEY'RE SUPPOSED TO BE SHEEP - OH WELL, THEY'LL DO
BECK
HI, JOE - GOSH, I WISH I COULD DECIDE ON A COSTUME TO WEAR TO THE BALL
I HAVE JUST THE THING, MR. TAWNY - COME INSIDE
A PIRATE OUTFIT - TRY IT ON
GREAT, JOE
ER -- IT'S A LITTLE TIGHT...
TAKE IT OFF, QUICK - YOU'LL HAVE TO REDUCE, MR. TAWNY
RIP
RIP
BECK
I'LL HELP YOU IN MY HOME GYM - MASSAGE FIRST
E-EASY, JOE - MASSAGE, NOT MANSLAUGHTER - I MEAN TIGERSLAUGHTER
BAM
BAM
BAM
POW
YOU'RE STILL OVERWEIGHT, MR. TAWNY - LOTS MORE FAT HAS TO COME OFF BEFORE YOU CAN WEAR MY PIRATE COSTUME TO THE BALL
ONLY TEN MORE ROUNDS AND YOU CAN RELAX
YOU MEAN COLLAPSE - UGG!
BOP
BOP
BOP
BOP
BOP
I'LL REDUCE YOU IF IT KILLS ME
YOU'RE A REAL FRIEND, JOE
BLAM
SNIFF - WHAT DO I SMELL COOKING, JOE?
YOU, MR. TAWNY - HEH HEH - I'D BETTER TURN DOWN THE HEAT
INFERNO STEAM CABINET
BECK

MR. TAWNY IS REDUCING IN ORDER TO WEAR HIS FRIEND JOE'S PIRATE COSTUME TO A BALL
ONLY TEN MORE MILES, MR. TAWNY- FASTER- MAKE LIKE A GREYHOUND
PUFF PUFF PUFF
HOT DOGS
FOOD - FOOD - I'M STARVED
WHOA, BOY- MUSTN'T LET OURSELVES SLIP, YOU KNOW
HERE'S OUR LUNCH - DIG IN
MUNCH CRUNCH
ONE LETTUCE LEAF ? THAT'S ALL I GET ?
I'M NO RABBIT, I'M A TIGER ! HERE, LITTLE BUNNY - MY, AREN'T YOU FAT ?
BECK

PUFF ! I'VE ROWED SIX TIMES ACROSS THE ATLANTIC !
OKAY, MR. TAWNY- COME AND GET WEIGHED
HURRAY ! I'VE DROPPED FIFTY POUNDS !
NOW YOU CAN WEAR MY PIRATE OUTFIT TO THE COSTUME BALL
I'LL PUT IT ON
HOLY MOLEY !
GOSH - LOOKS LIKE WE REDUCED YOU TOO MUCH !
BECK

I CAN'T WEAR YOUR COSTUME, JOE - I'M TOO THIN NOW
COME ON, WE'LL RENT SOMETHING AT A SHOP
THEY'RE ALL CLOSED, MR. TAWNY- YOU'RE OUT OF LUCK
COSTUMES
I'LL JUST HAVE TO GO WITHOUT A COSTUME
Later...
DID YOU HAVE TO THINK OF THIS, TOO- WEARING A TIGER SKIN ?
UH--ER--- SORRY, SIR - IT WAS ALL I HAD !
BECK

re:

About three months prior to publication of this issue of *Alter Ego*, executive editor Pat Masulli of Charlton Comics in Derby, Connecticut, made an astounding offer to fandom: Write a script for either *Blue Beetle*, *Captain Atom*, or *Son of Vulcan* which meets Comics Code standards and which has maximum salability. At about the same time Mr. Masulli sent *Alter Ego* a missive which, because of both its controversial nature and its general interest, is reprinted below. It is hoped that readers, both professionals and fans alike, will make known their views re this challenging letter for publication in the next issue. Meanwhile, ye editor's personal thoughts on the matter are printed after the letter itself, but with no suggestion than they be considered final or incontrovertible.

Pat Masulli
Executive Editor: Charlton Comics

Thank you for sending issue #8 of *Alter Ego*. *AE* is by far the best printed fanzine that there is. Your type is the only thing which identifies it as an amateur publication. This is not meant to be a dig, for I understand the reasons for the typewriter and I am well acquainted with costs and production problems – the exact reasons why Charlton has the "stiff lettering" which you cannot abide.

My only complaint and suggestion with comic fandom is that it is too widespread and has too many members who are zealous but uninformed. This creates a problem because, being so widespread, it has no official voice, and therefore no buying power or influence. Just about all fanzines will agree that *Superman* is old hat, unsophisticated, and should be put in mothballs; yet no one, including Stan Lee, can come up with anything that sells like *Superman*. How can editors sell their publishers on the value of fandom in the face of that one glaring fact? Criticism, to be of value, must be constructive, and must take all of the facts into account. Fandom is guilty of being only taste-conscious and not sales-conscious. This does not mean that I am against this type of thing, because it still serves a purpose. However, I do believe that with the proper approach you people can exert more influence and be of more value to the comics industry.

Another example of shooting loaded dice is the case of the amateur comic art appearing in the fanzines. The artists ignore the fact that the Comics Code exists. Believe me, Roy, pro artists, including Charlton's, can draw girls as full-bosomed as the amateur artists can. We can also create evil monsters complete with talon and fang; we can also create more violence; we can also be sadistic. However, none of this could pass the Comics Code Authority, and with good reason. The comics industry went overboard some time back and we nearly lost the industry. Now that *Creepy* magazine is around, there is a good possibility that comic publishers might throw caution to the wind and succeed in wrecking the comic industry completely. This is not good business, and this is not good morally.

I did not mean to lecture, but I think that these might be some points for *Alter Ego* to consider and present to its readers.

Cordially,

Pat Masulli

1997 NOTE: Pat Masulli was also the author of another paragraph (below), printed in the "Other Side of the Mask" section of AE #9 which dealt with comics in the news media, in this case Stan Lee and Marvel Comics. Masulli gave Roy permission to print it, but not under his name, because of his connection with a rival company. *The Editors*

Stan has (intentionally or not) hit on a great formula for the times by having his heroes motivated by introspective stimuli. This is a time when all of our society has turned to looking *in* rather than *out*. With no great disaster actually upon us (the 1929 Depression, WWII), everyone – including the kid who buys these comics – has been, by habit, concentrating on himself. This has led to the rebirth of "ennui" in the neo-realistic writers and their works, and to self-searching and a good deal of discontentment. Stan's

"Wait till
Otto Binder
sees *me!* –
I'm
Captain
Supermarvel
Shazam Man....
Holy Moley!"

formula allows more chance for reader-identity because the heroes are not *super* but *tragic.* They all look *in,* not *out!* Naturally, a hero cannot cavort through twenty-plus pages beating his chest in anguish, but believable motives are lacking in the heroes of most companies.

Alter Ego wishes to thank Mr. Masulli sincerely for taking the time to express his views on some faults of comic fandom, as well as to congratulate him for being the *first* pro editor to offer fans – through *The Comic Reader,* etc. – a chance to write scripts for pro heroes. I hope that various readers – fans and pros alike – will make known their views re his comments on comic fandom.

For my own part, I have no doubt that Mr. Masulli's major premise – that fandom is primarily taste-conscious as opposed to sales-conscious – is correct; otherwise, fandom would be a dreary hobby indeed. However, the fact that the executive editor of Charlton Comics went to the *fans* for new writers is in itself something of an admission that he has perhaps overstated his case.

I doubt, too, that Mr. Masulli will claim that even Leonard Darvin's ultra-sensitive Code Authority would object to "Captain Ego," "The Eclipse," or the average story in *Star-Studded Comics.* And if *Fantasy Illustrated* and perhaps segments of "Warrior of Llarn" are not grist for Mr. Darvin's mill, they are likewise, in my opinion, worth publishing just the same and are unlikely to corrupt anybody but the Code and perhaps Dr. Wertham if he is looking in....

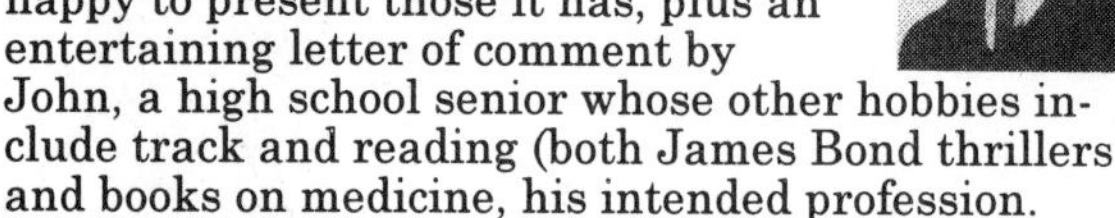

Last issue *AE* promised to feature photographs taken by John Fahey on a recent trip to the National offices in New York. Although a number of the photos were ruined by an unfortunate accident in developing, *AE* is still happy to present those it has, plus an entertaining letter of comment by John, a high school senior whose other hobbies include track and reading (both James Bond thrillers and books on medicine, his intended profession.

John Fahey
Springfield, Pennsylvania

At seven o'clock on the morning of December 29, 1964, I left my home in Springfield for a long-awaited trip to the offices of National Periodical Publications, Inc., more familiarly known as DC.

It was a beautiful day for such a trip, and everything seemed to be going my way. I hopped the 7:10 bus for Philadelphia, which is only eleven miles away, and arrived at the station only to be greeted by the sight of the 7:45 New York-bound train pulling out. Ordinarily I would have admired the efficiency of the Pennsylvania Railroad for sticking rigidly to its time schedule, but just that moment my mind was filled with less laudatory thoughts.

When I finally arrived in New York, I ran to the nearest phone booth to call DC editor Julius Schwartz. I had already arranged to visit with him for several weeks beforehand, but I wanted to pinpoint the exact time which would be most convenient for me to drop in. He told me to come at 1:30; and, as it was only 11:30, I had two free hours. I took the subway to 57th and Lexington Avenue, one block from the building in which the DC offices are located, and passed some time in the Cathedral Branch of the New York Library, across the street.

Since I had recently landed a role in our school's version of "Camelot," I was pleased to find a copy of that play on one of the shelves, and, when next I looked up, I was shocked to see it was 1:20. So I hastily returned the book and dashed across the street, narrowly avoiding a one-way trip to that Great Big Drugstore in the Sky.

Outside the elevator on the eighth floor of 575 Lexington Avenue I saw the words "National Periodical Publications, Inc." emblazoned on a large window, so I passed through the door and announced myself to the attractive secretary at the switchboard. A minute later Mr. Schwartz arrived and escorted me to his office.

We walked down a long corridor, flanked on one side by large filing cabinets bearing the names of various DC comics (and containing proofs for each issue of that particular magazine) and on the other by numbered doors.

Mr. Schwartz's office was of medium size. Opposite the door was a window overlooking the city. Along the right wall was a low cabinet, and from where I stood I could see hundreds of comics filed upright.

Julius Schwartz

The editor's desk occupied the other side of the room. it was actually two desks in one, being divided in the middle by a stack of comics two feet high, as well as numerous reference books, including dictionaries, science texts, etc. Around the desk were several modernistic pastel-colored chairs, one of which Mr. Schwartz offered to me.

I had prepared an interview, and he was most cooperative about answering my questions on such varied topics as the line-up of the next JLA-JSA story to the possibility of a revival of that greatest of ghosts, the Spectre. The interview lasted about half an hour, but, as most of the topics discussed either are now common knowledge or were "off the record," there is little use in rehashing it here.

Julie with Sid Greene

Just as I was running out of questions, Sid Greene and John Broome came in to discuss a forthcoming Green Lantern story, so, for the time being, Mr. Schwartz couldn't devote any more time to me. Walking over to the cabinet, he pulled out several bound comics volumes and showed me from his office to a very large room across the hall in which several men were busily at work.

Happy at being allowed free run of the place, I walked about to see what I could learn about the workings of a large comics company. Several artists were filling in the colored plates for printing. At another table a man was busy proof-reading for minor mistakes in some completed pages of artwork.

After watching these various operations for some time, I commenced to examine the rest of the room more closely. Along the right wall was a low cabinet filled with myriad comics, color proofs, etc. On the opposite side was another door, leading to a small room used for developing photostatic proofs.

My curiosity finally satiated, at least for the time being, I focused my attention on the books which Mr. Schwartz had previously handed me. You can imagine the feeling I had when I saw they were bound volumes of *All-Star Comics* (#1-12 and 37-57)! Gingerly I leafed through them and saw that they were all in mint condition. I tried furiously to think of a legal way to make them mine, but, unfortunately, none occurred to me.

After some time I looked up to notice Mr. Schwartz re-entering the room. As he crossed the room toward me, however, he was intercepted by one of the artists, who asked him to clear up a point: Is it *white* or *black* which is the absence of all light? (All the while I had been in the room, several of the artists had been arguing this among themselves.) Mr. Schwartz, an avid SF fan himself, settled the matter by stating that *black* is the absence of light.

Then Mr. Schwartz and I said good-bye, as I resolved to accept his invitation to return in summer. And I *will*, too!

Bob Butts
719 Pierce St.
South Bend, Indiana

There were several things in your Blackhawk article which were "conspicuous by their absence."

You made absolutely no mention of Miss Fear, Blackhawk's gal Friday. Fear was a beautiful combination of sex and sadism. She felt no compunction about killing a man who deserved to die and often used her physical charms to achieve her ends. And she usually left the Blackhawks stymied. After all, they couldn't gang up on her as if she were a common crook (though if they had I'm sure she'd have given a good account of herself!) and she'd never allow them to incarcerate her. So each story became a delightful runaround with Fear chasing the crooks and the Blackhawks chasing Fear. The Hawks not only had to catch the crooks but they had to keep them out of Fear's sights – literally. Give her a target – even a small one – and you'd have a dead man on your hands. That's one way of solving the population problem, I guess.

I own four issues with Fear in them and each is a gem. The first is *Modern* #49, where she made the scene for the first time. The other three are *Blackhawk* #14, 19, 22 – all by the great Reed Crandall. I can see where you might omit anything about Fear since she arrived on the scene so late, but omitting the following is inexcusable.

Military #16 was entitled "The Witches of Death." The story itself was typical, not too much different from the 15 which had gone before it, except that it was narrated by the three witches, Trouble, Terror, and Mystery. To those who fondly remember the Ghoulunatics of EC, this seems nothing spectacular, but this antedates them by at least ten years! Whether or not this story served as an inspiration to the EC'ers is, of course, only conjecture. It does supply food for thought, however.

Although Derrill and I wish that Fear *had* been inside the scope of our article, we saw (and see) no particular similarity between the *Military* witches and those in EC, except that both enjoyed exceptional artwork.

In closing, *AE* offers this "Famous Blast Words" cartoon by reader Marshall Lanz as an afterthought to Biljo's beautiful *AE* #8 cover.

See you next ish?

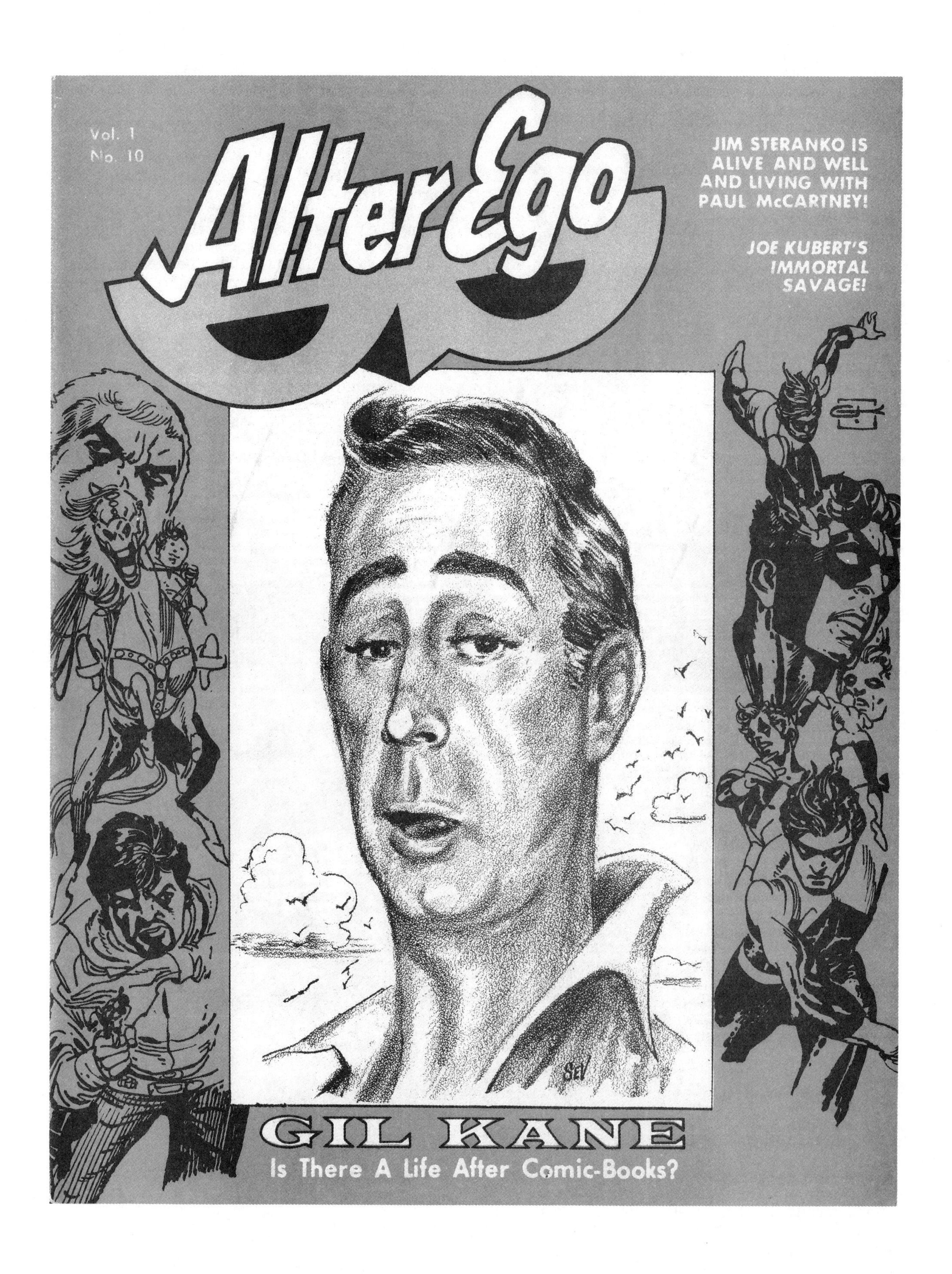

About the cover of* Alter Ego *#10 (1969): *Marie Severin's caricature of Gil Kane is considered by aficionados to be a classic. Gil provided the framing artwork, to make the cover of* AE *#10 truly memorable.*

Alter Ego #10 – Notes & Commentary

When Roy moved to New York in mid-1965, Alter Ego *#10 was already well under way.*

To spotlight the proposed Gardner Fox by-mail interview, Sam Grainger, a commercial artist from North Carolina, had drawn a dramatic cover of Fox with four of his creations: the Warrior of Llarn, Dr. Fate, and the Silver Age Hawkman and Flash.

Of course, Robert Kanigher, not Fox, had scripted the origin tale in Showcase *#4 (1956), so Grainger intended to replace that Flash with the Golden Age speedster; although, as writer/creator of the first Flash, Fox must be considered a co-creator of the second, as well.*

For four years Roy immersed himself in his new career as a writer and associate editor at Marvel. That, plus his 1968 marriage, forced continual postponements of publication of AE *#10. As Bill Schelly wrote in* The Golden Age of Comic Fandom, *by the late 60s "fans were greeting his annual assurances of publication with either bemusement or outrage." Few, however, took him up on his offer to return their money.*

Those years also saw the rise of the "pro-zines" – fanzine-like publications put out by professionals, starting with Wally Wood's Witzend *#1. Meanwhile, Roy found that, despite his hectic schedule of office work and "freelance" writing on evenings and weekends, he missed doing* AE, *especially since he was less than sanguine about the current fanzine scene, as he would describe it in* AE *#10:*

"A thundering horde of fanzines, most of them founded on the twin premises that enthusiasm equals quality and that careful tracing equals good drawing. A motley myriad of interviews with pros, but nearly all belonging to the What-Are-You-Doing-Next-Week school. Hasty sketches badgered from harried pros, and then advertised as significant contributions in order to bolster sales which didn't warrant bolstering. Pointless arguments about which current comics company is best – and why EC can never be surpassed anyway. And, worst of all, an almost total editorial irresponsibility toward such matters as punctuation, spelling, and general literacy.

"A handful of truly good zines, yes. But most of these seemed oriented almost solely toward original strips, whether by pros or gifted amateurs. And certainly none were doing precisely what I felt a comics fanzine should try to do."

Then, surprisingly, Stan Lee and Marvel production manager Sol Brodsky came to the rescue, proposing to Roy that they become his "silent partners" in publishing Alter Ego. *Roy promptly scrapped all prepared material, though the completed first part of "Warrior of Llarn" – drawn by Grainger when Ronn Foss had withdrawn – eventually saw print* in Star-Studded Comics. *Fans Mark Hanerfeld and Tom Fagan were titular assistant editors. But, as it turned out, there would be no non-pro contributors to* AE *#10, since even Mark wrote a story or two for DC about that time.*

For reasons obscure, Stan withdrew from the partnership after a few weeks, but Roy and Sol went ahead. Brodsky was invaluable in doing layouts and moving things along, even arranging for a small ad for AE *#10 to run in the Marvel comics. Some 5000 copies of the issue were printed, on a thick paper stock.*

Although AE *#10 was indeed a professional magazine, it consisted mostly of filler. But it was* good *filler:*

Roy's friend Len Brown of Topps (the gum company) arranged for AE *#10 to reprint two of the dozen-plus super-hero parodies which he, Roy, Wally Wood, and Gil Kane had done two years earlier, but which had had virtually no distribution.*

This full-color ad appeared in all Marvel Comics cover-dated Oct. and Nov. 1970.

Phil Seuling, comicon entrepreneur with whom Roy played poker most Friday nights in Brooklyn's Coney Island district, wrote about his 1969 New York Comic Art Convention, with Roy adding mildly humorous dialogue to con photos of Frank Frazetta, Hal Foster, Neal Adams, and others.

Since few fans had ever read the Comics Code adopted in 1954, it was reprinted in full, along with a photo of (and an article by) the Code's administrator, attorney Len Darvin.

To fill a last-minute hole, Roy banged out a piece titled "Jim Steranko Is Alive and Well and Living with Paul McCartney," of which all he will say today is, "Well, it seemed like a good idea at the time" – the time being the late 1960s.

Mark Hanerfeld's survey of Joe Kubert's landmark Tor *comics of the early 1950s was of more significance than most of the above, partly because Kubert drew a strong pin-up of Tor for the back cover – but even more so because Roy's favorite artist graciously allowed* AE *to print, for the first time ever, six pages' worth of an unsold "Tor" newspaper strip by himself and Carmine Infantino, done circa 1959.*

AE *#10's other highlight was a bit of serendipity.*

Longtime EC fan John Benson had previously conducted and published interviews with EC creators Harvey Kurtzman and Bernie Krigstein, and was looking for someone to print an interview he planned to do with Green Lantern and Atom artist Gil Kane. Gil and Roy had formed a mutual admiration society ever since working together on Captain Marvel *#17-21, turning Marvel's Kree hero into a science fiction* *answer to the Big Red Cheese; so Roy eagerly volunteered to print the interview.*

Having a clear vision in his head as to how he wanted the printed piece to look, John laid it out himself, mostly at Roy's East 86th Street apartment, cutting and pasting to intersperse the text with pertinent artwork from many sources to illustrate Gil's points.

Despite the fact that at the last moment Gil insisted on expunging a few of his more acidic comments, the interview created something of a stir. Like many others, Roy recognized its significance at the time, stating in the issue's editorial:

"Few can equal the range and sweep of Gil's outspoken opinions. That what he has to say will anger some, I am sure; that I personally disagree with some of his conclusions, I am certain. Still, the piece is one of the most important ones printed in the history of comics fandom – and if you don't believe me now, come back and read it again in five or ten years."

As it turned out, Roy had grossly underestimated. Would you believe – more than 25 years?

The Kane/Benson interview is still remembered by pros and fans alike. And when Gil did an even longer, two-part interview for The Comics Journal *a quarter of a century later, it was the one in* AE *#10 with which that was compared. Truly amazing, especially since the interview has never been reprinted... until now.*

For this book John Benson has laid out the interview, substituting photographs of Gil originally intended to accompany the piece, and providing new copies of many of the art examples used in AE *#10. Aside from a few minor changes in punctuation and a word here or there, the text is presented just as it originally appeared. The interview remains what it was in 1969 and has been considered ever since – one of the best comics-related interviews ever done, with one of comicdom's most articulate spokesmen. Roy then prevailed upon Hulk/Dr. Strange artist Marie Severin to draw what turned out to be a brilliant caricature of Gil for the cover. When Gil first saw it, he winced, saying: "She leaves me no illusions." In truth, Gil loved the caricature, so Marie gave it to him; it still hangs framed in the Kanes' home.*

Beneath Marvel letterer Sam Rosen's modified Alter Ego *logo, Gil drew a frame for the caricature, depicting Mar-Vell, Green Lantern, "His Name Is Savage," and several generic heroes. The frame was colored red; the picture of Gil (despite the artistic license taken on the cover of* this volume*) was left in black-and-white. This caricature-in-a-frame format for covers would be continued nearly a decade later, when AE #11 was finally published.*

Roy and Sol had big plans for future issues, including showcasing Jack Kirby's dramatic costume designs for a college production of Julius Caesar. *Among other things, upcoming issues would feature "The Artwork That Made Pros of: Steranko! Barry Smith! Sal Buscema!" (This was to be Steranko's pages of a motorcycle-riding super-hero Jim had shown Stan Lee in 1966, which landed him the "S.H.I.E.L.D." assignment – Barry (now Windsor-) Smith's "Inhumans" pages mailed from London which had led Stan to invite him to drop by if he was ever in town, little dreaming the young Brit would hop the next cattle-boat for the States – and sample pages by John Buscema's younger brother which were later used in an* Avengers *issue.)*

Once again, however, it would actually be years – this time, nearly a decade *– before the next issue of* Alter Ego *would see the light of day. By then there would be a new publisher and co-editor, and of all the projected contents only a lengthy interview with Sub-Mariner creator Bill Everett would make what would turn out to be the final cut....*

The Editors

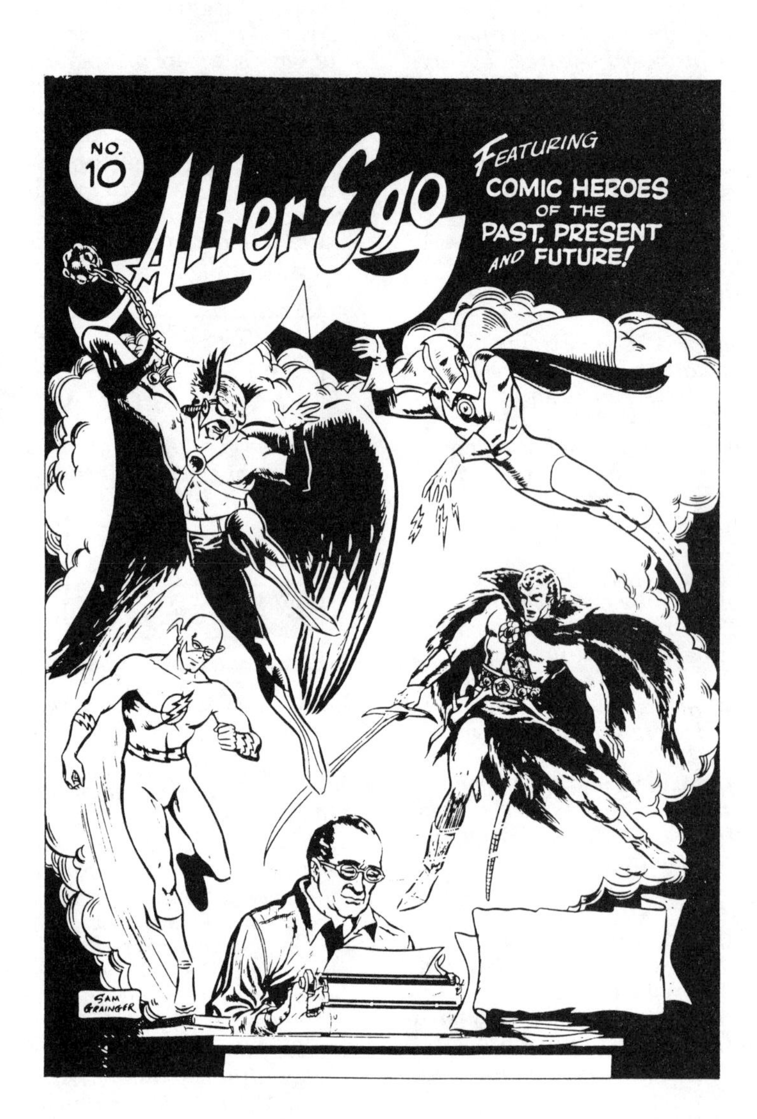

Above: The original cover intended for the 10th fannish issue of Alter Ego, *drawn by future Charlton and Marvel artist Sam Grainger.*

The issue was to have been especially dedicated to the career of AE "patron saint" Gardner F. Fox, including an interview which was completed but, unfortunately, never published – since AE was greatly delayed due to Roy Thomas' pro writing commitments.

NEW!

Humor in a Jocular Vein: From EC to *AE*

In putting together Alter Ego *#10 in 1969, Roy was surprised and delighted at the cooperation he received from what were now his fellow professionals with regard to printing previously unpublished material. All those asked (Joe Kubert, Gil Kane, Jack Kirby, Marie Severin, John Buscema) gave their enthusiastic okays, while Marvel artist John Verpoorten drew a new illo of Marvel's Forbush-Man staring at a pasted-up photostat of DC's then-mascot Johnny DC.*

Marie Severin, 1950s EC colorist par excellence *and by 1969 an artist on Dr. Strange and the Hulk, was famous in both the EC and later Marvel bullpens for her caricatures and office cartoons, some of them scathing, many of them hilarious. She graciously allowed Roy to print an atypical, gentler, hero-oriented offering – and somebody sometime should collect as many of Marie's private cartoons as can be located. They'd be doing a real public service.*

Another EC alumnus, the legendary Wally Wood, found his way into AE #10 in a more roundabout way:

In 1967, with Marvel's Not Brand Echh *and DC's* Inferior Five *looming on the horizon, Len Brown, assistant director of product development at Topps (the company that makes Bazooka Bubble Gum) and incidentally scripter of the first two Dynamo stories for Tower's* T.H.U.N.D.E.R. Agents, *asked Roy to work with him on a series of miniature eight-page, one-panel-to-a-page comics that parodied current super-heroes.*

Len and Art Spiegelman (later a Pulitzer Prize winner for his graphic novel Maus*) designed the* Mad*-style covers; Spiegelman wrote and drew ad spoofs for the back covers; while Len and Roy each wrote some of the six-page lampoons in between. Wally Wood and Gil Kane each penciled about half of the dozen or so mini-comics, with Wally inking them all.*

Alas, though all the mini-comics were printed, they didn't fare particularly well in limited test-marketing. In areas where comics were sold, they evidently did fairly well; in other areas, they didn't. So Topps shelved the project.

Len arranged informally for AE *#10 to feature two of the Wood-drawn parodies, and Roy planned to spotlight the remainder in future issues. To date, however, only the two printed in #10 have seen the light of day since that initial, very limited distribution.*

Since it seems a shame for any artwork by the late, great Wally Wood to bloom unseen, re-presenting those two in this volume is a distinct pleasure.

The Editors

Cover concept:
Len Brown & Art Spiegelman

Script: Roy Thomas
Art: Wally Wood

THE OLD, un-mod Blunder Woman

Script: Roy Thomas
Art: Wally Wood

Cover concept:
Len Brown & Art Spiegelman

– From the sketchbook of Gil Kane

A/E INTERVIEW: GIL KANE

a candid conversation with the comics' most articulate artist

The occasion which precipitated this interview was the 1965 comic book convention. The hot, stuffy atmosphere and the panels of bored artists and writers being prodded into recollecting insignificant anecdotes had done little to change my limited interest in super-hero comics, but for some reason I stayed for the last panel discussion, which featured *Creepy* publisher James Warren. For the first time the convention came to life as Gil Kane engaged Warren in a lively debate from the floor. Kane's perceptive comments about the comic industry impressed me so much that, though I had never met him before, I approached him immediately after the panel with the suggestion of doing a long in-depth interview with him.

Kane was very receptive to the idea, but although we would periodically renew each other's interest in the project, it was not until Roy Thomas suggested that the interview run in *Alter Ego* that we finally got together with a tape recorder in August of 1967.

Once, when asked for a resumé of his career, Kane stated simply that he'd "worked for every comics outfit there ever was." At the time of the interview he had been illustrating DC's *Green Lantern* and *The Atom* for some time. He had not yet announced plans for his own magazine, *His Name Is... Savage*, which is therefore not mentioned directly in the interview, although many of his general remarks obviously relate to that project.

Kane is currently [*1969*] active on a variety of projects, including material for both Marvel and DC. He recently worked on *Captain Marvel* and *Captain Atom* for those two companies, breathing considerable life into two characters who had shown scant promise until that time.

Our plan was not to do the "definitive" Kane interview, but only to touch only on certain subjects. I believe the resulting interview is more all-encompassing—and also more exciting—than either Gil or I had anticipated. Gil speaks not only as an artist but as a critic and a theorist, and to those who do not know him in the latter roles I hope the following conversation will serve as an introduction.

— John Benson

AE: *You have said several times that cartoonists do not pay enough attention to craft. What is your definition of craft?*

KANE: Most cartoonists are emotionally drawn into the field. They are attracted to it because it fills their needs and because it's a proper means of expression for them. But nearly always, they possess an insight, a single sensitivity; that's where the empathy comes in. Craft comes in when they attempt to augment this natural facility with formal techniques. Unfortunately, most artists tend to be betrayed by their facility. They get easy acceptance from editors, and as a result they never feel the need to press harder or to examine what they do. Rejection would be an excellent thing for them. The only people who manage to escape this are people who have a facility that borders on genius, like Jack Kirby. Jack is so fertile and inventive that he has taken one corner of the field and sewn it up completely as his. I don't think there's any doubt that Jack is the epitome of an artist doing super-hero work.

AE: *Isn't there a problem in talking about craft, in that craft is not art? There's a difference between the*

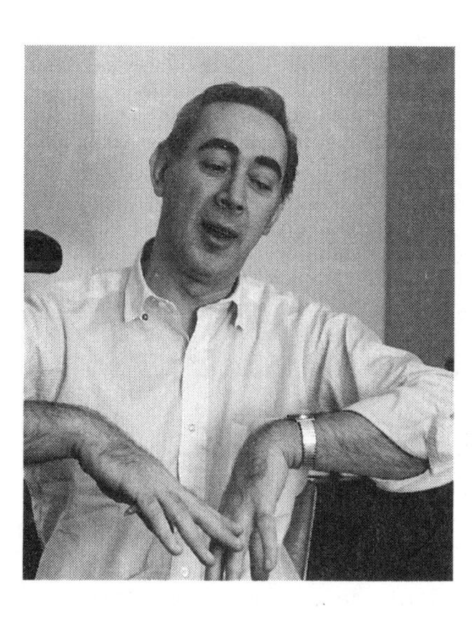

"I believe that the drawing in comics, while its appeal is primitive, is extremely sophisticated; and the stories, on the other hand, while they are written by reasonably sophisticated people, are extremely banal and primitive."

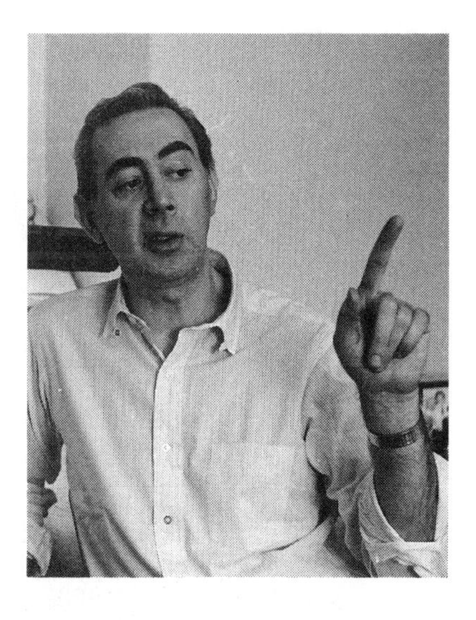

"Here were these magazines that were distributed and merchandised by the biggest outfits in the world, and Biro came in with three stinking little magazines and within a period of two years he was outselling every one of them."

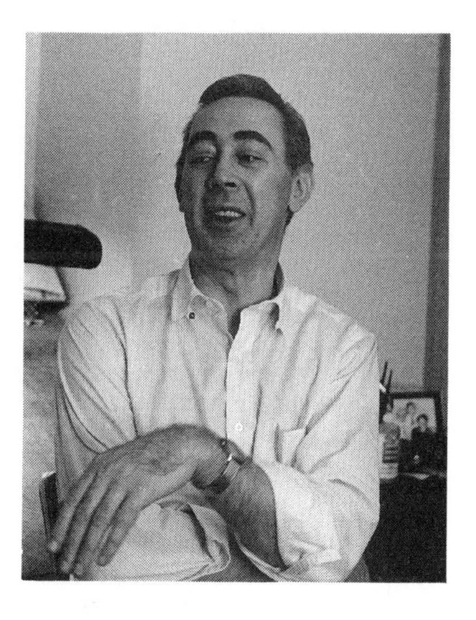

"There isn't any one of us, not even the mildest guy in the field, who comes into this field for any other reason except for the fact that the field releases all his suppressed fantasies; but then that's the truth about any creative effort."

two.

KANE: Craft is merely the springboard, it's the ability to give wings to your expression. Otherwise your expression bangs around in an inarticulate way and comes out thick and untutored; you're just throwing away range and scope. For instance, an intellectual artist would be somebody like Hal Foster,

who is not as supreme a draftsman as, say, Alex Raymond was, and who is not as supreme a designer as Noel Sickles is, yet *was* a good designer, *was* a good draftsman. He built up all these qualities through formal techniques. As a result, the things that he did do naturally—storytelling and movement—were immeasurably supported. He could try anything he wanted to. That's the beauty, for instance, of learning the figure. If you really know it, you're not stopped by anything, and you can make it do anything you want. Once you stop worrying about whether you can do it, and merely give thought to what you want to do, it's something else entirely.

AE: *So craft is what is necessary to have art?*

KANE: Not always; some primitives communicate perfectly. But on a more complex plane, I couldn't agree with you more.

AE: *Using the words in a different way: are there any real artists in the comic field, or are they mainly craftsmen?*

KANE: I think essentially they are mainly craftsmen. A lot of the things that are done are artful, but I don't think that more than a few through the years would quality as artists. I would point to Hal Foster, Will Eisner, Harvey Kurtzman... and Alex Raymond, who communicated a universal quality of barbaric lyricism and fantasy in the early days of

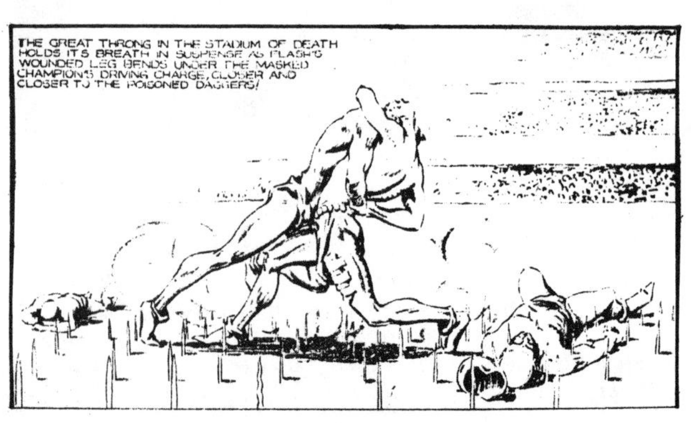

Flash Gordon that was just unbeatable. There were sequences during the tournaments of Mongo that I don't believe have ever been duplicated, catching all the wonder and glory of the savage encounter. That was beautiful stuff; poetry! If anything can be classified as an artistic achievement, I'm sure that can.

AE: *This is perhaps a digression, but do you think of yourself as a producer of children's literature? Is the comic field primarily children's literature?*

KANE: Yes. I believe that the drawing, while its appeal is primitive, is extremely sophisticated; and the stories, on the other hand, while they are written by reasonably sophisticated people, are extremely banal and primitive. The comics have endured despite the innocuous pap which the writers have contributed over the years. Comics is a medium in which I think it was intended for the artist to be the storyteller, not only through pictures but through the prose as well, because writers who aren't artists have never done anything except fill space. The only worthwhile things have been done by artists who either controlled the writing or did the writing themselves.

AE: *Then you would say that Richard Kyle's theory that the editor is the real creator of comics is a lot of baloney.*

KANE: I think it's just enormous bull. If an editor controlled the magazine, then all the art would look identical, and it doesn't. Because even when an editor insists that you hew to a particular drawing style, the fact remains that there are enough variations within the individual styles—approaches to composition and design—which are so opposed that there is absolutely no relationship except in the most superficial sense. Editors have so little knowledge of any of the formal art techniques that, outside of seeing a superficial resemblance, they can't begin to understand the differences that occur in two artists' work. A perfect example would be Lee Elias and Milton Caniff, who superficially have a similar style but who are light-years apart in every way: in mood, in their

Left: Elias. Right: Caniff.

senses of design, the way they tell a story, and the way they use their spatial relationships. I can't begin to tell you how far apart these two artists are. I myself have been forced to follow Kirby at times, and, believe me, if I managed any kind of resemblance to Kirby's work, it was only on the most superficial level, because Kirby's approach is so uniquely his own that I couldn't begin to duplicate it. In fact, I found I was rooted in my own frames of reference, and I had a great deal of difficulty even duplicating him superficially.

AE: *You would say, then, that the best way to produce art in comics would be for the artist to also be the writer.*

KANE: Yes. However, many artists don't have a

Left: Kirby. Right: Kane.

literary background and don't know what structure is in a story, though they are superb for dramatic effects. You let an artist write a story and the thing that he will do beautifully is create dramatic visual effects, but they'll be totally unrelated one to the other. Worst of all, the dramatic backbone to the whole story will be so spindly and weak that it simply won't stand up. That's where a good editor with an understanding of dramatic structure would come in—not to change the artist but merely to give him a better idea of what he is up against when he tries to organize a story.

AE: *Perhaps, then, we are talking in hypotheses. Just because most of the artists today are not dramatic wonders doesn't mean that the person to create real comic art will not be the artist who can write.*

KANE: Yes. Many artists have been misused for years, in that they are assigned by editors who can't even analyze the nature of their work properly. As a result, somebody like, say, John Severin will be assigned to do a science-fantasy story, which is ridiculous. Or, conversely, someone like Al Williamson will be given a contemporary strip. Al's entire focus is on communicating something very ethereal

and lyrical; he's less at home with a contemporary setting or with creating contemporary characters. He is diametrically opposed to the most contemporaneous artist there is today, Alex Toth. Toth has the most contemporaneous style, with a real feeling for the angularity and pattern that is reflected in everything from mechanical design through fashion and architecture. He once did Zorro... and while it was an interesting Zorro in some respects, it was terribly faulty because it didn't have any of the mood or the

lyricism... In fact, I thought that Warren Tufts, while he is not nearly as skilled technically as Alex, was much more sympathetic to Zorro.

AE: *You've said that each artist is in the field only because of a certain attraction to it. What attracted you to the form?*

KANE: If I have a natural facility (and I don't say that everyone's natural facility is developed to the same degree)... but if there is one attraction the field held for me, it was action. Figures and movement are the things that I am most concerned with and most sensitive to. Unfortunately, I am not a natural designer, I'm not even a natural storyteller, and so I've had to build up piece by piece all sorts of formal techniques to augment my natural facility. But when you become introspective about your work, it does an enormous amount of good for it, and too many artists are not introspective, analytical, or intellectual enough about the work. They depend on their feel for the material to carry them through, and it does, because what they do is good enough. But what they do is only the merest indication of what could be done with this tremendous potential that most of them have.

AE: *What about the potential of the form?*

KANE: The form is a tremendously exciting one; everyone approaches it differently, and I am not strong visually. For example, Alex Toth is a brilliant designer—if he were given free rein on a story, his approach and his point of view might differ entirely from mine. My feeling for a story hangs very heavily on telling the story *per se* in narration. I believe in a well-structured story, and I also believe in using a tremendous amount of prose to augment to pictures. I believe, unlike a good many people, that pictures alone are not sufficient, and there is no reason why text and pictures can't be combined to give comics a three-dimensional quality, rather than the quality of a silent movie.

AE: *Suppose we assume that this is so. Would you say, perhaps, that most comics have been using this combination of text and image in the wrong fashion?*

KANE: Yes, I think so. For instance, I always thought Al Feldstein was one of the best writers in the field, and also had the best feeling for story values in comics. Unfortunately, he had a very poor visual approach; he would strangle his pictures by over-

Kane. *His Name is... Savage.* [Not from *AE* #10]

writing his captions. But you can learn a tremendous lesson from that. The artists who worked for Feldstein, despite their technical shortcomings, did probably the most impressive work of their lives, and in most of the cases still have not exceeded what they did for him.

AE: *I don't know if that followed from his use of captions.*

KANE: Yes, and I'll tell you why. The captions in those stories were so complete and would create such a total mood that when they said that "the door opened slowly and light filtered in through the dark room and the figure advanced into the square of light on the floor and looked to the left and then looked to the right," it would be impossible with such an explicit caption to do anything except draw what it says. He is not allowing you any freedom in terms of what you have to put down. How you put it down is an entirely different matter. But he tells you exactly what you must put down and to a great extent he made storytellers out of artists who were not storytellers. When somebody would make a drawing of a face which would be totally expressionless, but beautifully drawn, and Feldstein had a caption that read that the character was torn with anguish, all of a sudden he would give dimension and body to a picture that was merely a meaningless display of technique.

AE: *Do you know Pudovkin's famous example of taking an expressionless face and through film montage giving this face expression by intercutting emotion-laden images, like a crying mother?*

KANE: It doesn't have expression, but the expression has a reason.

AE: *Right. So I don't see how you can use this as a defense for text, because you could just as well use pictorial montage in comics.*

KANE: No. Take a fight scene in comics, for instance; you can have two guys biffing each other with all the loud sound effects you want, but if in one caption you say "he hit the villain with enormous impact and he could feel the shock run up his arm as two teeth crumbled beneath his fist," that gives you an image that doesn't displace the picture, but augments it so that you get insight into the picture that didn't exist before.

AE: *Suppose we go back to the expressionless face in Feldstein's comic, with his text describing the character's revulsion. Wouldn't the same effect take place if you could juxtapose the man's face and the image of the horrible thing he has seen?*

KANE: Yes, to a great extent, but why does it have to stop there? You can create a mood in movies without the use of background music and all sorts of devices, but nothing says that these things won't heighten an already successful effect.

AE: *On the other hand, words can detract from an already successful film image.*

KANE: The trouble is that films create absolute reality and comics don't. When you have two people fighting in a film, they're fighting. (It makes no difference how badly, they're fighting to the extent of their abilities.) But in comics a lot depends on the artist's ability to capture action. I just want to make one more point. I think that *Little Orphan Annie,* for instance, does little more than use symbols. Harold Gray could almost use lumps for figures, but his

dialogue was so expressive in terms of characterization that he took these symbolic lumps and through dialogue gave them personalities that the drawings themselves didn't have.

AE: *I get the feeling that you are saying that text can overcome the faults of a bad artist.*

KANE: I don't think it can overcome...

AE: *It can minimize...*

KANE: I think it can, to some extent, if you are thinking about salvaging a job. But if you are thinking about a successful job, I never saw where the two are in conflict. Look how successfully Harvey Kurtzman utilized lettering for sound effects in his

war books; he developed it into a fine art. Yet there would be periods of physical conflict where the struggle did not have an enormous amount of suspense, because it was like watching a silent movie. You felt somehow removed from what was going on. There was a lack of immediacy that for me would have been filled if there were the exact same pictures, and riding overhead, without crowding the picture... It's important to understand that I am for the use of text as long as it doesn't interfere with or minimize the effect of the picture, but only augments the picture. I don't say that you have to use text for everything. I can see comic stories done in pantomime; it has been done, and sometimes quite successfully. Each story creates its own conditions. But for myself, the kind of story that I would like to do would be approached by using a great deal of narrative prose and also by utilizing a great deal of space. And I don't mean a 12-, 15-, or 20-page story; I am for lengthy, extended pieces of work where characterization can be developed, and not superficially or on a primitive level the way it is developed in comics today.

AE: *There's an Eisner story where the Spirit is marooned on an island with Sand Saref, and he's delirious, and she's swabbing his forehead, and he murmurs, "Ellen, Ellen"; the next panel shows Sand standing off alone on the beach. Without any words,*

he's said more about her feelings than words could have told.

KANE: I agree with you; there are conditions under which you can successfully make a point without text than with text. But I would have used text up to that point. I would have stopped it for that picture, and then gone back to using it.

AE: *Wouldn't it be more useful to think of it in visual terms first and then utilize text?*

KANE: Absolutely; that's exactly the way I advocate doing it. The story should be broken down visually without relying on text at all, and after the whole story is broken down visually so that it reads properly, then, just like supplying sound to a silent movie, that's where text can point up the situation. And where a beat, a silent, dramatic moment with no text or dialogue, is needed, I believe it ought to be utilized, too. I don't see why they can't work perfectly well with one another. I don't believe in being a purist and denying myself the dimensional qualities that prose and prose alone can deliver in certain instances.

AE: *Would you feel that Eisner was probably the most expert in knowing when and when not to use text?*

KANE: Will Eisner did little morality stories, which were very moving, but they had the quality of reading a children's picture book; he could be quite dramatic, but always on a kind of innocent level. He never had the complex, subtle characterizations that, say, some of Harvey Kurtzman's war stories had, and Harvey would augment a lot of his stuff with prose. I remember he had a story about Napoleon, which was told totally in captions, and was absolutely brilliant.

AE: *Many of his great war stories were ballads.*

They had stanzas and refrains, and they returned to the story's starting point.

KANE: Yes, he utilized text in a very effective way. I think the stories could have been amplified more than they were, but of course then they would have been done a little differently than Harvey intended. I favored what Feldstein was doing, but I abhorred his visual approach; everything he did could have been three times as long as it eventually came out. For instance, I thought that most of the Ray Bradbury adaptations were brilliant pieces of work. They were very fortunate in their choice of artists, and the material was ideally suited to comics. Virtually every Bradbury job was a classic of its kind. I remember one that Krigstein did which was absolutely exquisite. There were some by Al Williamson which I thought were very lovely jobs. There was a wonderful little story that Wally Wood did, "There Will Come Soft Rains," which was also beautifully done, and,

again, ideally suited to Wally and his feeling for gadgetry at the time. The choice of the material and the artists was so great that I really feel that these were a high point of comic book art.

AE: *I think you started to say that they should be longer.*

KANE: I think the Bradbury stories were perfect, but I don't see why the form has to be restricted to short stories.

AE: *You didn't feel, then, that those particular Bradbury stories were squeezed into fewer pages than they needed?*

KANE: Some of them were. I particularly remember a lovely job by Williamson called "A Sound of Thunder." Now I am very familiar with that story, and the editing cut away about one-third of the story. The text was so heavy that it would often describe four and five actions, and Williamson, in the space that

was left in the panel, would only be able to do the last one. I thought it was a poor treatment on Feldstein's part. But there were others that weren't squeezed, that were better paced. "The One Who Waits," as I remember, was well done; it wasn't squeezed and the art was very effective. But in every one of Feldstein's adaptations, I feel that he could have utilized more space; he could have used all the text if only he had extended the amount of pages involved. Feldstein's whole problem was that he would narrate and not dramatize, and I believe that every one of the multiple actions deserved a panel of its own. There wouldn't have been any trouble expanding it. It's just that all of that good comics writing and all of that good comics drawing was unfortunately squeezed and crowded together, watering down the effectiveness of the whole page. But I believe that Feldstein's stories had content and that what Feldstein was doing was an indication of where comics are going, where they must go. Comics must broaden their appeal in order to survive, because the narrow market that they had prior to 1962 was absolutely destroying them.

AE: *What was it in that period that was so limiting?*

KANE: Well, from the time that EC went out of business until the time that Stan Lee gave the superhero a new dimension, that ten-year period was probably the most banal, the blandest, the least creative period in comics.

AE: *I want to backtrack momentarily. You spoke of directions the form can take. Do you feel that comics can be introspective, or utilize material that doesn't depend on action, as effectively as other art forms?*

KANE: The simple fact is that comics have very few limitations. Their only real limitation is the difficulty in overcoming a static form and overcoming a lack of continuity in the drawing. You have to reestablish continuity every time you go on to the next panel by arranging your composition in such a way that there is a smooth, unbroken flow of movement. In fact, where the composition isn't carefully considered and the effects are terribly scattered and you find the character on all sides of the panel, it's the same problem that you have in movies, when they enter from stage right or left.

AE: *It's even more tricky in films, because if you are standing in a room you don't realize that when you move the camera across the room it's going to reverse screen direction.*

KANE: That's right, it's a very tricky device, and I also find that in action. I find it's very hard to be very convincing in a fight scene. I also think that most fight scenes in comics are too short. I don't believe in two people pummeling each other, just throwing punches right and left, but I think the way a good fight scene is done in the movies can be done exactly the same way in comics. When it's over, it should have a shattering effect; it should be a point of tremendous relief. You never even begin to approach that effect in the best things ever done in comics; they have never achieved anywhere near the vicarious feeling of watching a fight that you get in a movie.

AE: *Even in films they rarely use this kind of continuity. George Stevens is one who did.*

KANE: He does more than set up a fight. He provokes a fight and creates such emotional tension before the fight begins that when the first blow is struck, it is such a release from all the frustrations imposed on you by the director. Not only is the first blow important as a release, but it is nearly always the most dramatic blow struck. In *Shane*, the first

blow broke Ben Johnson's nose and spilled blood all over the front of his face and down his shirt, and it was such a violent release.

AE: *There is no question, then, that the comic form is as legitimate an artistic form as any other?*

KANE: Except for the fact that it has been dealing with pap. I feel that is has succeeded despite what the writers have done, and it is strong and viable as a result of the artwork; the storytelling developed by the artists has created a viable medium that has survived the onslaught of rapists for years. And it is just waiting for somebody like Kurtzman or Eisner, someone to come in and control and utilize the medium and give it direction and purpose, and not just come in there like a bunch of kids playing with sand. To create something mature within such an exciting form is hard to do; it's no snap. For instance, they don't do it in syndicated work; comics is by far the better way to tell a story.

AE: *I'm glad to hear you say that, because it's disappointing to me that the French comic enthusiasts are only interested in newspaper strips.*

KANE: Yes, and to me it's also disappointing that the things they are interested in are only vacuous displays of technological virtuosity, and they always shunt aside guys who are creative, inventive, and very original, but who are not the most superb draftsmen. They take people with very academic approaches and glorify them; and I don't think that most syndicated artists do anything more than clear, understandable diagrams that are not terribly inventive or interesting visually. The mere fact that Eisner is not being exhibited along with the ridiculously empty technical displays that they are putting on at the Louvre is just ridiculous, because Eisner was the best. The French just solicit guys with academic techniques and approaches. They also slight Foster, and what Foster did in the 1930's was the highest kind of comic art. The only parallel between Eisner and Foster is the fact that Eisner did the highest kind of comic art in the 1940's; nobody even began to approach him. In fact, it's interesting that Lou Fine, who used to *breathe* beautifully—his people were like Greek gods and he never did a drawing that wasn't the epitome of a Germanic hero—and yet when he came in to substitute for Eisner he was a poor substitute. He didn't begin to measure up to the quality Eisner had infused into *The Spirit*, even though he tried to acquire the style and technique. His goals were so different from Eisner's that within a year he abandoned Eisner's style and he became very illustrative until finally the

strip almost died, and it took Eisner to come back and buttress up the sagging thing.

AE: *Let's assume that some fluke occurs, and comics are able to jump from their trough, and that they go as far as the form allows. How far would you say they are now?*

KANE: Except for having someone like Eisner or Kurtzman come in and develop a grammar for the field, it is still waiting for someone to do something not only interesting from a visual point of view but in terms of dramatic structure. I thought that Harvey had begun to do that; his Civil War stories were very fine mood pieces, beautifully capturing the period. They were beautifully researched, the writing was absolutely marvelous, and there was a feeling for human things, a feeling for profundity. People didn't just die, but *human beings* died in human and affecting terms. There would be a stink and reek of

death and sense of futility about war that just never occurred in anything else that I have read in comics. That was very strong writing; that is what comics should be, and I believe that is only the beginning of what comics could be.

AE: *Could you recommend any of the comics coming out today to a non-enthusiast?*

KANE: I think it's mostly crap. The biggest problem with comics today is that they have to be turned out too fast.... Jack Kirby can sit down and on any day that he works he can do between three and six pages of the most complete and beautiful pencils you ever saw in your life, and he can even do more if he has to. Jack's a very special case; but that doesn't work for someone who has a style that requires greater concern for literal drawing, and it means that, working at Jack's rate, most artists can only hack. As a matter of fact, I think that Jack is probably doing the best work of his life. I think that Jack's whole approach is very satisfying. If the science-fantasy of the thirties were to make a comeback (and it seems to be—Ace is turning out volumes every month), I couldn't think of anyone better in the whole world to illustrate it than Jack.

AE: *Would you suggest the work of any other current artists?*

KANE: There are many who do some very nice work, but I would say that while it's nice, I would hardly regard it as milestones of comic art, as I regard Kirby's work.

AE: *Are you familiar with the work of Carl Barks?*

KANE: Not really. As a matter of fact, I used to swipe a lot when I first broke into the field. I had nothing to fall back on because I was so poorly trained. I had all this tremendous expression yearning for release and I didn't have the technical skill with which to articulate it. If I did something on my own, the idea would be good but the execution would be absolutely miserable. One of the reasons for that is that I started as a penciller and stayed a penciller instead of starting as an inker and then converting to penciller. As an inker you pick up all the external tricks that you need to succeed with an editor. That is, you learn to create a professional-looking finished picture; not that the composition is any good, not that the figure articulation is any good, but the rendering of the picture ultimately is strong and sure. You learn how to draw and how to spot your blacks; those are the two most pragmatic things that you have to learn when you first start. And I never learned how to draw in those days, and to this day I have trouble spotting blacks.

AE: *How does this relate to Carl Barks?*

KANE: Well, from time to time in trying to improve my figure articulation—because I felt that one of the things that I missed most was not having worked in an animation studio—I very often bought animated comic books, and some of them struck me as being superb and some were very schlock. I don't know whether it was Carl Barks, but some of them were absolutely great. I've heard quite a few people talk about him, and the people who speak very highly of him are very fine designers and animators.

AE: *You spoke of rendering as something you missed early in your career. Don't you consider composition more important than rendering?*

KANE: Oh yes, there's no getting away from it. Telling a story is the most important thing; and the most natural thing that comes out of a storytelling style is composition, because composition focuses the eye on the most important thing in the picture, and of course that's what good storytelling does. The most important single element outside of storytelling is picking up a sense of design; it's more important than drawing to me. And there are some superb draftsmen who, lacking design, lack the crowd-pleasing qualities. Raymond had design in his figures and Foster didn't; so Raymond, while he was by far the lesser artist... In fact, he often took chapter and verse from *Tarzan*; whatever Foster was doing, Raymond would ultimately be two months behind. But the point is that nevertheless he had an excellent sense of design, which Foster never had in his figure structures. This is why Foster was not the most appealing artist to the layman. His best qualities were so subtle that they eluded most laymen.

AE: *If this is true, then why would not storyboard work be rewarding?*

KANE: It is to some artists. It's satisfying for Alex Toth because Alex is the perfect designer, and he is sometimes more concerned with visual effects than with dramatic ones.

AE: *But storyboards tell a story.*

KANE: Yes, but they tell a story that nobody's interested in. I mean, who cares? We are drawn into this business because it offers a perfect release for fantasies, and storyboards don't do that. Storyboards are purely the most cold-blooded way of applying your skills, and this field does not appeal to cold-blooded people. Everyone in it is motivated by all sorts of fantasies.

AE: *Is there any topic that you'd like to bring up?*

KANE: Yes. I would like to point up the disparity between the choices of the fans and of the pro artists. Fans tend to focus on the artist who is regarded as a good working professional, but hardly with the high regard that fans have. Professionals, on the other hand, single out people that I never read about in any fan magazine.

AE: *One would be Toth.*

KANE: Toth is one. Dan Spiegle is another. Spiegle created *Hopalong Cassidy* for the newspapers and then went into and still works for Gold Key, and for years he did *Lawman*, and I think now he does *Space Family Robinson*. But his organizing of a picture is probably the finest demonstration I have

[Not from *AE* #10]

ever seen of a guy dealing in spatial relationships. And on top of that, he can create a three-dimensional scene. Most artists in comics, since they don't understand formal techniques, tend to use the crop technique. They have something large in the foreground and a contrasting small shape in the background, and they never do a scene with a complicated perspective, because that takes a tremendous amount of concentration in itself. So they tend to deal just in the photography techniques, and if they do a large drawing they merely make a larger shape, but it's basically the same panel. Most comic book cartoonists are not terribly experimental. In fact, they tend to stick to figures that they've done a million times before and hardly ever attempt interesting variations or foreshortening to any great extent. Of course, if you do a couple of hundred figures every story, in the course of a year you do several thousand figures, and your stuff has a tendency to be quite similar. But you can always tell when someone is trying, and most artists play it safe, especially those regarded by fans. Because what fans like is a quality of design that is inherent in some aspect of the person's work, and not the totality of his work.

AE: *Fans have a tendency to enjoy an inking style.*

KANE: After an inker finishes rendering a page, he erases the penciling that's underneath. Most lay people tend to regard the finished product as the renderer's and very often they are right. If you have a subtle penciller and a very strong inker, the inker can just dominate. Not that he is better because he dominates the subtle penciller; he may merely have a noisy, blatant style that overcomes a more subtle drawing. A strong inker has a personality all of his own, and should be his own penciller.... For example, there are several strip artists who have other artists do much of their penciling, while their contribution is to do a clean and professional rendering. But quite obviously that contribution is mainly one of providing set decoration.

AE: *Give another example of a highly regarded professional who is not known to fans.*

KANE: Well, I hardly ever read anything about Johnny Severin. Now I know that when people talk about him they regard him highly, but I never see Johnny listed as the best penciller, or anything else.

AE: *But we've been talking about who the great artists are all evening and you didn't mention Severin.*

KANE: When we're talking about guys who dominate the field, we're talking about Kurtzman and Eisner, and Severin isn't in that class. What Severin brought in was an understated force and power, and a kind of truth. He could tell very profound stories that you couldn't tell with a super-hero style.

AE: *How did you like Severin's western in the snow for Warren?*

KANE: Ah, beautiful. I'm not especially partial to the way he draws horses, and I don't care too much for his shrubbery concepts, but at the same time there is a realism in what Severin does that makes everything else look like the difference between Matt Dillon and Roy Rogers. He really brings a tremendous force into the material; he recreates a place and a time with a feeling of accuracy. A good example of an artist who displays brilliant technical virtuosity is Russ Heath. The story he did for *Blazing Combat* was typical. First of all, everybody looked exactly alike. They all looked like the photographs he had taken of himself on which he based all the drawings, and he was so indifferent to the need for characterization that he didn't even bother with it. What he is concerned with is drawing, and it was a brilliant job of drawing, there's no getting away from it. But in Severin's work, even when they aren't meticulously drawn, there's a sense of people sweating, of people being terribly fatigued and made rawboned by war. And that never happens to a Russ Heath character.

AE: *I take it from your earlier comments that the main reason why you are illustrating super-heroes is*

that you feel that this is the area in which you are most proficient. Is that correct?

KANE: Yes and no. It's a comfortable area for me to operate in, since it depends to a great extent on action, and it also coincides with my interest at the moment, which is learning to design anatomical structure. I'm busy solving technical problems for myself, and sometimes it's very convenient when the idiom that I am involved in happens to be sympathetic to the technical problems that I am solving. But if I had my 'druthers, I would much rather do some kind of science-fantasy or western. I would much rather do that than anything else.

AE: *You did do westerns before.*

KANE: Yes, but I feel now that I would like to do them again and this time ink them myself and really apply myself. When I've solved some of the problems I'm working on now, I think I'd like to try it then. I'm interested in trying forms that are not being utilized and developed now.

AE: *Do you have any specific ideas of what kind of forms?*

KANE: Comics today are too childlike. I don't believe that comic artists have sufficient sophistication. And even if one artist did, like Will Eisner, have the sophistication to make his stuff substantial enough to interest more than just eight-and-nine-year-old kids, it's unlikely that it would happen. Not that other artists are worse than Eisner; many artists have qualities than are far superior. The remarkable thing about Eisner was his approach to telling a story; he communicated his ideas perfectly. But there were other guys who were enormous in their own areas. For instance, Charles Biro.... Eisner worked on one side of the street, that is, the very exotic kind of cinema director, and he was an extraordinarily creative but highly stylized interpreter of a story. On the other hand, Charlie Biro told a very direct story, but he told a very substantial story. His naturalistic feeling for characterization was so good that it led to the first documentary comics.

AE: *When you talk about Biro's creativity, you're talking about* Crime Does Not Pay?

KANE: Right.... What Biro did was to create a kind of "B"- picture realism, a documentary effect. He had stories that were more erotic than anything I had seen up to that day. He was attempting to stretch the rather narrow confines of the kind of story you could tell and he was doing it. He was getting much more sophisticated content, and the payoff was that he bucked every major publisher—and at the time there were half a dozen of them, all with large lines, like National, Quality, Fawcett, Archie, Timely. The point is that here were these magazines that were distributed and merchandised by the biggest outfits in the world, and he came in with three stinking little magazines and within a period of two years he was outselling every one of them, including *Superman*. Biro was using nine panels to a page, and sometimes a story would go on for 15 pages, and he would be able to tell extremely well-developed stories full of very rich characterizations. Of course, he had a tendency to always end with a corny moral. But nevertheless he was attempting and getting more characterizations and structures into the material than anybody else was doing at that time. In fact, Kurtzman was like Eisner and Feldstein was like Biro, in that Feldstein was again using literary techniques, while Kurtzman was using visual film techniques. Those are still the two valid approaches, except that I have never been able to understand why they have to be diverse, why they can't be combined.

AE: *I would say that both Eisner and Kurtzman did use a fair amount of text. But your views on Biro come as a surprise to me, because I've heard little about him except that the violence in his books paralleled that in EC's.*

KANE: I don't think Biro was grisly, and I certainly thought he was a lot less offensive than some of the bad taste that Feldstein used. Not that Feldstein's horror was bad, but he had to foul it up by talking about somebody being ground into hamburger, and you could tell that it was a tremendous joke. But the point is, that joke would come at the end of a very well-organized and well-written story, and it would be an extremely grisly, bad taste joke, which would satisfy him and offend everyone else.

Kurtzman was like...

Eisner, and...

Feldstein was like...

Biro.

AE: *I guess that's true enough. Say something more about violence.*

KANE: I think that movies are a perfect medium for violence, and as a result they are never better than when they serve the cause of violence. I have always been partial to films like *King Kong* and *Gunga Din* and *Shane*. Of course, I appreciate the other aspects, too, but when I see a marvelously-worked-out piece of action, it has such a sense of fulfillment and release and satisfaction, and everything in the world combined. I believe that when people go to a movie, it's a voyeuristic experience, and when you're a voyeur you want to have an appetite fulfilled. I think it's quite obvious that the kind of life people lead today puts them in a position where they've got to see a certain amount of violence in order to feel a sense of satisfaction, and I think it's just a natural part of living. Maybe this is a harmless way of expressing it. I don't know. But I do love movement, and violent movement especially—although controlled movement like ballet or watching a gymnast is also very satisfying. The action and violence of comics always attracted me, and it allowed me to work out my own private fantasies. I think that's the reason most creative people are drawn into whatever area most allows them the greatest freedom of expression.

Teegarden/Nash Collection

AE: *I was thinking of asking you, "What do you think attracted me to comics?" And I think you've hit on one answer here. I'm attracted to comics because it's a medium where, in certain ways, people are left unmolested to create their own fantasies. Because it's a despised form, society doesn't look at them. Nobody does except the readers, and even the editors are prone to their individual fantasies. So comics are maybe the only place where you can see an individual's pure fantasy.*

KANE: Yes, absolutely. The only trouble with the field is that it's done on a factory basis—and it wasn't when comics first started out. While there was a factory, a need for production, there weren't any restrictions imposed on the artists and writers. So while the stuff was primitive, it was very fresh and it had tremendous charm. And now the factory regimentation has become total. Now you tend to lose personality, to all meld into a single artist, a single point of view. And we are all capable, like a hand grenade separating into a million different fragments, each going our own way. You should see the stuff comic artists do privately; it's light-years away from the stuff they do for publication.

AE: *How many professionals do any kind of extensive material on their own?*

KANE: Not extensively, but they do their own material.

AE: *But mostly individual illustrations, am I correct?*

KANE: Or they create sample syndicated strips in which, regardless of what's commercially viable, they generally tend to express themselves in the terms in which they're most comfortable. It's a real insight into their personalities, even though it complies to syndicate needs. But, of course, artists change. No one is a better example than Alex Raymond, who started out as a school athlete, full of a Spartan ideal, and totally concerned with barbaric splendors. He was affected by the magazines that were being put out at that time; Talbot Mundy was a big deal, and so were Rafael Sabatini and Harold Lamb. Writing and drawing were terribly romantic and heroic. Anyway, when *Flash Gordon* started, everyone walked around in animal skins and women wore breast plates and had exposed navels, and it was the most barbaric kind of background imaginable. But within three years they had gone a millennium, because it was turn of the century Germany; everyone was wearing Bismarck costumes; they were wearing iron helmets with plumes and points on them, and epaulets and highly polished boots. It was the same Mongo and only three years had passed, but Raymond's taste had changed completely. There was very little left that was of interest except to see a display of draftsmanship, and if you wanted that you could go beyond Raymond to superb illustrators that he could never compete with. Even that was just a passing phase; the ultimate stage was *Rip Kirby*, which showed Raymond's preference for things with snob appeal, and a need to be a part of the country club set. All his interests came out—his

interest in fashion, in golf, in projecting a very urbane image—and he left the barbarian flavor so far behind him that he could never go back. But artists are always in a state of transition. In fact, the whole trouble is that when you come into this business you have childish fantasies that you have to project, but as you grow older the responsibilities that life imposes on a growing person tend to make you pragmatic and realistic, and that tends to diminish the fantasy. And when you diminish the fantasy you destroy the poet, and when you destroy the poet the technician survives. In nine out of ten cases, the most superb and promising artists end up being the shiniest kind of technicians performing empty demonstrations of technical skills, and all the poetry is gone. It's very hard to keep the boy in the cartoonist, because if you do, it means that you are talking about an individual that never outgrows his need for fantasy. There isn't any one of us, not even the mildest guy in the field, who comes into this field for any other reason except for the fact that the field releases all his suppressed fantasies; but then that's the truth about any creative effort.

AE: *You've articulated something there that I was somewhat aware of. I think, for example, that Ditko's Dr. Strange struck a real chord in me because the fantasy concept was total, and everything worked toward the central concept of a man alone, unbeknownst to the world, fighting the evil forces of the universe.*

KANE: Ditko created a concept of mysticism and interdimensional travel which I have never seen before in comics. It was absolutely believable. And I think the most successful stuff that Archie Goodwin ran in Warren's magazines are the things Ditko did for him. Because good comics drawing has force, power, and emotion behind it; and that's what Ditko has, and that's what Eisner has, and that's what Kurtzman has, and that's what Severin has, and that's what Kirby has. There's nothing wrong with incorporating good drawing in any of that, but you can't put it first; good drawing has to grow out of the dramatic qualities of the work rather than try to get these dramatic qualities to grow out of the good drawing. You know, the most brilliant draftsmen in this field never sold a nickel's worth of books. The great sellers, the guys who had tremendous circulation, were all crude artists by comparison. But it's Biro, and it's Eisner, and it's, again, Kirby; and it's never been Louie Fine or Reed Crandall or the guys who are credited with these

especially refined drawing styles, and yet the preponderance of editorial opinion constantly sides with them. There is a large body of readers merely waiting for the kind of material that would interest them so they can go back to reading comics. It seems that comics are totally dependent on their contents now; they sell on the basis of what's inside the magazines more than ever. This parallels the big-studio concept right after the war. All of a sudden people were only going to movies that they liked, and the whole concept of merchandising a movie and not giving a crap about what was in it went down the drain. As a result they had to make deals with the people who were capable of turning out highly professional and creative products, because they were the only ones who were now making money. So the studios lost their control and became what they always were, distributors and businessmen, not creative people. When they had their creative thumb in the brew, they were turning out a commercial product (which sometimes managed to be good despite their interference, but certainly not because of it), and comics are in the same position now. The focus will be thrown on the people who create comics; and those who create it best are the people who are going to be in the new position of power.

AE: *Do you really see any activity in this direction?*

KANE: I believe that there are going to be all shapes and sizes and price ranges in comics. In a way it already started when Warren succeeded to some extent with his magazines. And *Mad* magazine is a comic book, there's no getting away from it. And I think that it's possible to do the same in dramatic continuity as well as humor. A sophisticated form is still awaiting a Kurtzman or someone to come in and articulate it, and amplify it. I also feel that the economic set-up will be different, that there will be a different return to the creator. Because right now he is a factory hand and he only draws the wages of a factory hand, and until he gets to control his product he can't expect to get a better slice of whatever is coming in.

AE: *I certainly hope you are right.*

KANE: I am sure of it, even if it takes another five years. Once the breakthrough comes, it will be like the dam breaking.

AE: *Now, is this revolution going to engage adults in the form as readers?*

KANE: I should think it will. It's the nickel-and-dime mentality of most comic book publishers. For years they've avoided putting content in the magazines, even though content obviously would help their sales. But they've done everything to discourage content: they've regimented and tyrannized the guys who have worked for them; they've imposed restrictions, and I'm not talking only about the Comics Code, but all sorts of weak-sister restrictions that have just cut the guts out of the strips. So they were selling to an ever-narrowing circle of readers. They went from a million circulation down to 250,000, and diminishing

George Metzger. "Master Tyme."

still, and here they were, selling to eight- and nine- and seven-year-old kids. They had lost the teenage market, and the fringe adults who used to read comics, and for some reason they seemed to feel that there was a virtue in that. What was the virtue in going downhill? These people merely had a great thing, a gold mine, and they only knew how to do one thing, and that was to ride with it, and milk it, and never try to exploit it or develop it, because that would take imagination. Now, the most obvious thing that a comic publisher should do is to follow the lead of *Mad* and try to appeal to someone besides the fringe level of kids with more substance and another format.

AE: *But* Mad *is on a twelve-year-old level.*

KANE: Don't misunderstand me. I think that *Mad* is a totally sophomoric magazine. But by being sophomoric, it's already heads above being juvenile. The ideal thing would be to hit such a nice intermediary plane that you could appeal to all levels. But I think in the end you will have to direct 15¢ comics to kids and more elaborate books to more demanding readers. Think of the pulp magazines and the enormous success they enjoyed in the thirties. They were written the same way that comics could be written, and they had meat to interest everybody from twelve years on up, and at one time they were a multi-million-dollar business. However, the visual approach of comics was so strong it knocked them right out of the box. So, can't you imagine a marriage of a literary form with a visual form, each one amplifying the other? I still feel that for me that's the answer. I'm not sophisticated visually anyhow. That *Fantasy Illustrated* you showed me just knocked me out with the job that guy did [Metzger's "Master Tyme"]. I never in a million years could think that way; so for me, that's no answer. For me the answer is meaty, meaty story material. In fact, the most interesting things I have seen in a fan magazine were not the home-made products, because the drawing is always brutally primitive and then it's completely put under the ground by the most miserable kind of writing. But I saw an adaptation of Adam Link from an Otto Binder story, and while the drawing was primitive, like a series of diagrams, the fact is the story was so strong, and the adaptation and breakdown was so excellent, that I thought it was superior to anything I had seen in a pro magazine in years. And I saw some stuff that a fellow named Landon Chesney did. Again,

Otto Binder/Bill Spicer/Landon Chesney: "The Life Battery"

it was an Otto Binder story, and, again, I thought it was such an excellent adaptation and that Chesney's art, as crude as it was, really served the purpose of the story. I thought it was more exciting, more sophisticated, more deft artistic material than I have seen in a pro magazine. It only supports my thesis that, when you use strong material, it buttresses and gives dimension to your drawings.

AE: *But you do feel that this explosion will interest adults in the form?*

KANE: Absolutely. In fact, as bad as the garbage adults read outside of comics is, comics are still beneath that in terms of structure. When comics wakes up to the fact that it needs more than just dramatic visual effects, that what it needs is literary structure, and when it allows the artist as much freedom as he needs, I think you're going to see a whole new era.

This interview was conducted, edited, and prepared for publication by John Benson. Gil Kane reviewed and edited the manuscript at the time of initial publication. The photographs of Kane on the first page of the interview were taken in 1969 by John Benson for the original publication of this interview.

To accompany Mark Hanerfeld's article "The Tor Gambit," Joe Kubert created this full-page illustration of his justly famous caveman, the star of some of the best comics to come out of the 1950s – and the first human action hero ever to appear in 3D comics.

About the cover of Alter Ego #11 (1978): *Another great Marie Severin caricature, surrounded by Bill Everett figures color-held in blue, against a graded green background. Counterclockwise: Hydroman, Sub-Mariner, The Fin, Venus, Amazing-Man, and Bronco Bill (and Roy, who still owns the original artwork, wishes he'd twisted Bill's arm to draw Marvel Boy on that dock instead of a cowboy).*

Illustration by Moebius

Alter Ego #11 – Notes & Commentary

A GLANCE BACK BY MIKE FRIEDRICH
Publisher of Alter Ego *#11*

I look back now on Alter Ego *#11 with a mixture of pride and regret. It's good that Roy Thomas' interview with Bill Everett helped increased fans' appreciation of an old friend's seminal work. It's also pleasing that Star*Reach was the first to bring the words of Jean (Moebius) Giraud to North America. It's regretful that I didn't really have the enthusiasm and resources necessary to continue publication, to have truly made my own editorial mark on* AE. *Thus today I think of issue #11 as a footnote to the earlier ten issues, which despite the variety of people involved, were more of a single piece.*

*Be that as it may, I'm afraid you historians out there must be informed that I have little memory of how Star*Reach's solo issue of* AE *came about. Even though at this time in the 1970s Roy and I were not working together, we did meet two or three times a year, and the subject of Roy's Bill Everett interview must have come up at some point and I must have volunteered to publish it. But when, where, and how, I can't recall.*

I have a much clearer memory of meeting Jean Giraud on November 1, 1977, in his home then outside of Paris. I took the train. He met us at the station. We recognized each other from our very brief meeting five years earlier in New York. I met his son and saw pages on the drawing board from the latest "Lt. Blueberry." It was a singular experience to discuss his highly spiritual approach to drawing and storytelling. Some of that experience translated to print; unfortunately, most did not.

There are still copies of AE *#11 floating around the back-issue bins; it's worth checking out.*

Photo of Mike Friedrich, taken by Kevin Bermingham for Alter Ego *#11.*

FROM THE EDITORS:

The indicia listed Alter Ego *#10 as "a more or less quarterly publication." But Sol Brodsky left Marvel in 1970, relinquishing his interest in* AE *to John Verpoorten, his successor as production manager. Delay followed delay on the* AE *front.*

In 1971 Roy interviewed Sub-Mariner creator Bill Everett for AE *#11's centerpiece. Both Bill and Marie Severin provided cover artwork. Bill photostatted Marie's caricature of him and put it in a black T-shirt for greater contrast. The cover was even printed in fanzine ads saying* AE *#11 was "coming soon."*

Everett had been an off-and-on apartment-mate of Roy's in 1966-67, though their friendship was an often rocky one. Publishing that interview became even more important to him after Bill passed away in 1973 at the too-young age of 56.

Below: The original art by Marie Severin of her caricature of Bill Everett, which was then statted and placed (in part) in the frame provided by Bill.

However, from 1972-74 Roy served as Marvel's very busy editor-in-chief, while in '72 and '75 he went through a pair of separations from his first wife, which would eventually culminate in divorce.

In 1976 Roy was negotiating a contract calling for him to return as Marvel's editor-in-chief, when he abruptly opted instead to move to Los Angeles. The trials and temptations of a West Coast lifestyle soon pushed thoughts of continuing Alter Ego *still further into the background. And in 1977 he met Danette Couto (now Dann Thomas).*

During the mid-70s Roy flirted briefly with an offer from Phil Seuling to take over the publication and name of Alter Ego*. But when his longtime friend decided later to go in a different direction, Roy breathed a secret sigh of relief.*

Then, enter Mike Friedrich. A fan from California's Castro Valley, in the early 70s he had written comics for Julius Schwartz, later for Roy at Marvel; but eventually Mike left to publish Star*Reach*, the first "alternative comic." By 1977-78 Mike decided he wanted to publish a "fanzine" – a pro-zine, really – and his fondness for* Alter Ego *prompted him to offer to take it over.*

Roy was slightly reluctant, partly because Mike's avowed intention was to emphasize comic books' present and future, which would have left little room for the type of historical article which had been AE*'s mainstay. But Roy liked and respected Mike, and besides he wanted to see the Everett interview published; he had long since paid Don and Maggie Thompson to edit it for him. And Mike wanted to publish that interview, because he had been a close friend of Everett's during the years just before the artist/writer's death.*

So it was decided: Mike would take over Alter Ego *with #11 and would print the Everett interview-- plus one he himself had done with Jean Giraud, the French cartoonist whose work as "Moebius" had been appearing in* Heavy Metal*. Roy fully expected that, after the eleventh issue, he would have little further connection with the magazine.*

AE *#11 was duly published in April 1978 by Mike's Star*Reach Productions, with Roy and Mike as co-editors. It contained the lengthy Everett and Moebius interviews, editorials by Roy and Mike, and a reminiscence by Roy of Bill Everett. Incidentally, Michael T. Gilbert, now of* Mr. Monster *fame, did the color cover hand separations.*

Mike announced that AE *now had no regular schedule, and that he would not take subscriptions in advance: "Don't believe it until you see it!"*

As it turned out, no one ever did. Because Mike himself would soon go off in new directions, #11 turned out to be the final issue of Alter Ego *as a fanzine... but it definitely had its moments.*

And the end was not quite yet....

Portrait of the artist as a young man – circa 1939

EVERETT ON EVERETT

AN INTERVIEW BY ROY THOMAS

[Abridged from Alter Ego *#11]*

Editing Assistance by Don & Maggie Thompson

AE: Bill, could you tell us a little about your career and your life before comics?

EVERETT: After I left school, I started in newspaper work in advertising and went from there to magazine publishing. And when I returned from Chicago after my last big advertising job, I was without any work at all. I was looking for freelance work, and I met a friend who was just starting in the comic business.

AE: What got you interested in the comics medium?

EVERETT: I wasn't actually interested in it at all; I was talked into it. Not only because this friend wanted me to do it, but because I'd always done cartoons on my own, just kidding, fooling around with them. I suppose maybe I had dreamed about being a daily comic strip artist, but never had done anything about it.

AE: Your art training was mostly on-the-job, then?

EVERETT: Right. I had two years of art school [The Vesper George School of Art, 1934-35. – Ed.] I dropped out of that, too, because I was anxious to get to work.

AE: Where did your Merchant Marine career come in here?

EVERETT: That went back to when I was back in junior high school. I went away for approximately two years. I was 15 when I went in, 17 when I came out.

AE: Were there any commercial artists, or comic strip artists, whom you particularly emulated when you were first getting started?

EVERETT: There were certain artists that I admired, both in the illustration field and in comics, but I couldn't emulate them because I never could *copy* – I couldn't do anything well enough in those days. My favorite illustrators were Dean Cornwall, Mead Schaffer – and if anything resembled comic work, it would have been Floyd Davis' illustrations. I suppose the first comic artist that I truly admired as an artist was Milton Caniff.

AE: Were there any particular writers that influenced you?

EVERETT: Jack London was one of my favorites. Any adventure. As far as humor was concerned – Thorne Smith.

AE: What was your first comic book experience? Was that with the Centaur comics group?

EVERETT: Yes. That was John Harley Publications. They were just starting with original comics, picking up from what *Famous Funnies* had done. That's where I met Carl Burgos. We both started at the same time.

AE: For them you did two strips which are remembered, including "Skyrocket Steel."

EVERETT: That was the very first one I ever did. It was a Buck Rogers type of thing. I think I may have been asked to do something concerning space characters. I created *Amazing-Man* with Lloyd Jacquet and John Harley. "Skyrocket Steel" was not really a success. But *Amazing-Man* had his own book. I think I only did about the first five issues. [A-Man, the Amazing-Man, named "John Aman," began in *Amazing-Man #5,* Sept. 5, 1939. Bill did the character in 1939-40; the comic ran through #27, Feb. 1942. – Ed.]

AE: Several people feel that this was your best early work. You worked for Timely – before it was Timely. How did that association come about?

EVERETT: Well, I left Centaur with Lloyd Jacquet and another chap whose name was Max. Lloyd had been an editor for Centaur. He had an idea that he wanted to start his own art service -- to start a small organization to supply artwork and editorial material to publishers.

AE: In other words, whole comic books packaged and then sold?

EVERETT: A package deal, right. He asked me to join him. He also asked Carl Burgos. So we were the nucleus of what was later to become known as Funnies, Incorporated. And one of the members of the organization was the sales manager, Frank Torpey, who had a friend, Martin Goodman, who was in the publishing business; and Frank talked Martin into going into publishing comics.

AE: So you did the entire comic, coming up with Sub-Mariner (in your case) and with the Human Torch (in Burgos' case) – and then the other characters. And then Mr. Goodman bought the entire package?

EVERETT: Right.

AE: Didn't you become, at some point, along here, art editor of Funnies, Incorporated?

EVERETT: Yes. The artists, including myself, at Funnies, worked on a freelance basis. But it got to the point where there was so much editorial work and so many corrections to be done that someone had to be in charge of it, and I was made (in name at least) the art director.

AE: Which means that you did the dirty work?

EVERETT: That's right. I had to assign and edit all the artwork.

AE: In Marvel Comics *#1 the two feature characters had the twin gimmicks of fire and water. Was this pairing conscious?*

EVERETT: No, it was done almost simultaneously, and I've been trying and trying to remember just how it came about. I honestly can't remember the exact instant. We were asked to develop new characters, and Carl and I were quite close friends. Between us somewhere – I don't know whether it was his idea or mine or a combination – we came up with the two elements and what we could do with them. I think, if I'm not greatly mistaken, that the Human Torch idea came first – the idea of a character turning himself into flame. And then, for an adversary, we decided, well, what better natural adversary for flame than water? So that part of it was my idea. But it was so dovetailed that it's hard to remember this many years later just exactly how it commenced.

AE: There is a text story, Bill, in an old Timely comic about you and a storm at sea and a hand that shoved you out of the storm's way when you were in the Merchant Marine. The story claims this had some connection with your later coming up with the Sub-Mariner. How much of this was fact and how much fiction?

EVERETT: We can be honest about it now. I think I wrote the story myself, and we needed a filler. It just seemed apropos at the time. It was just a little incident that happened when I was at sea, and it was dramatic, and it *did* scare me. But this is not where I actually got the idea for the Sub-Mariner. It just seemed like a good idea to *say* that it was.

AE: Did your having been in the Merchant Marine had some influence in the creation of good Prince Namor?

EVERETT: Definitely! Sure! Because I had always been interested in anything nautical, anything to do with the sea – ever since I was born, I guess.

AE: Both of these characters (Human Torch and Sub-Mariner) were obviously inspired by Superman, who had originated about a year before. And yet they were supermen each with his own gimmick. Was this because National had successfully sued a couple of other publishers over alleged copyright infringement?

EVERETT: I don't think it had anything to do with lawsuits. I don't recall ever being afraid of anything like that. It was just the idea that, when I did anything, I wanted it to be different, entirely and totally different, from anything else. It was pretty darn hard to do, because almost everything was being done at that time. This happened to be a lucky guess and it *was* something that had not been done.

We tried to outdo Superman, because Superman had come from another planet. I had to dream up some reasons for this character to have these prowesses. To be able to fly, he had to have wings. I didn't want to put wings on his back and make him look like an angel, so we put them on his feet – which was inspired by the statue of Mercury [Giovanni Bologna, 16th century. – Ed.]

AE: You and Carl Burgos were working fairly closely together off and on during the early days?

EVERETT: We worked together but we didn't work on the strips together. But we always discussed them.

AE: In a friendly way?

EVERETT: Well, not always.

AE: Was there friendly rivalry of any sort going on between you and Burgos, because of the fact that both of your characters were fairly popular?

EVERETT: No, not until we conceived the idea of bringing the two together to fight each other.

AE: What led to the Torch/Sub-Mariner battles?

EVERETT: Everything then was done with an eye for sales, because we had such tremendous competition. I can't honestly remember how it started, or whose idea it was. At the point that we first began discussing it, Mr. Goodman himself was having an awful lot to say about what the editorial content was. And whether this idea came from his office, or whether it was Lloyd's idea, or whether it was a combination of Carl's and mine, I can't honestly say. I do think that Carl and I dreamed it up. But just the fact that the two opposite elements had had their *own* stories – now what would happen if we ever got them together to fight each other?

AE: You drew the Sub-Mariner. And Burgos drew the Human Torch. How did you work out the stories in which they appeared together?

EVERETT: It was written by a team of writers, and Carl and I would work out the plots until the story was finally formed up so we could start on the drawing. We worked together on the penciling. In the actual completed work, if I recall, one would be about the Human Torch, and the Sub-Mariner would be the incidental character. So the majority of that was done by Carl. And then I would do the finished work on the Sub-Mariner.

AE: How about the longer stories – 20 or 30 pages in length?

EVERETT: We worked those out together. There were quite a number of people involved – two or three writers and pencilers, people we had doing backgrounds, for example.

AE: Was the pace pretty frantic in those days?

EVERETT: It was extremely frantic. It might not have been if we were ever on time, but we did a lot of playing as well as working, and we were usually behind on our schedules. But, yes, the deadlines were pretty tight. We didn't have nearly the artists available that we have today. We were shorthanded. I only had one or two guys I could count on to assist me, and the same with Carl.

AE: Wasn't there a story about how one of these whole books was completely done over a weekend?

EVERETT: Yes. As I recall, it was a 64-page book, and we did turn it out something like between Wednesday or Thursday and the following Monday. We may have had a synopsis, but we still had to write the entire book and draw it and have it completed and ready to deliver by – well, we'll say Tuesday. So our deadline would have been Monday. There were quite a few of us that got together and went to my apartment and did the whole thing. We just stayed there the entire weekend. Nobody left except to go out to get food or more liquor and come back and work. We had four or five writers, and we had at least six artists including Carl and myself. Oh, anything up to a dozen people, in and out constantly, working on this thing. It was a pretty wild weekend!

AE: One of the reasons that no one was able for years to reprint the first two Sub-Mariner stories is the rather strange process that you used in those issues of Marvel Mystery.

EVERETT: That was my own idea. I wanted to get a sort of third-dimensional or a painting-type effect, rather than the flat black-and-white and color. We used what is known as a Craftint Board, which is chemically treated, an illustration board, in which you use chemicals to bring out cross-hatching for tonal value. And we thought this might be a very good idea to get grays into it and to get the feeling of water – of depth under water. The first issue didn't work out well, because the printer who printed it had never done a comic before. He wanted to break into the field. He just didn't know how to handle it and slopped it up pretty badly, so it was pretty muddy. The second issue was much better. It was much cleaner.

AE: Why was it abandoned with the third issue?

EVERETT: Because it still wasn't good. You see, you had a cross-hatching effect and then put a Ben Day color over it – you put a dot on top of the cross-hatching, which gave a very muddy effect. We decided to heck with it! We'd go back to the black-and-white. It was an experiment. It just didn't please us.

AE: Tell me about the name "Sub-Mariner."

EVERETT: Okay. The "mariner" part was because I loved Coleridge's poem "The Rime of the Ancient Mariner." I just thought that this being a submarine creature, it could combine the two, the "Submarine" and the "Mariner," and by hyphenating it, it would then become the "*Sub*-Mariner." But so many kids ignored the hyphen and put it all as one word and pronounced it "Subma*reener*," because all they could think of was a submarine.

During the war, particularly when it was beginning, there had been newspaper stories and talk full of submarines and submarines and submarines. And whoever heard of a mariner? I mean, there were darn few who ever used the term. So it was logical that it would be mispronounced.

AE: But you didn't have any compunction about using that name.

EVERETT: Heavens, no! I thought anybody with any intelligence could read it as *Sub*-Mariner. If they didn't have that much intelligence, that's too bad.

AE: They could look at the pictures. About the name "Namor": why did you choose that name?

EVERETT: I can remember sitting down with a pad of paper and writing all kinds of names and writing them backwards to see which ones could make sense and which would fit the character. Why I had the word "Roman" and transposed it to "Namor" I don't honestly remember, but everyone liked it.

AE: In your strip all the men were large, bug-eyed green freaks (where they are not all blue freaks), while the women were somewhat more attractive and colored in what we used to call "flesh." What was your intention?

EVERETT: That was not my doing. My concept was that the Sub-Mariner race – whatever I called them – were closer to the fish species. They were actually mutants, I suppose you'd call them. But I tried to make them resemble fish, which is why the big eyes. But his father, Sub-Mariner's father, was an American – a human – and the mother, she looked pretty much like a fish, too. But I had to make her look a little glamorous, so I had long eyelashes and stuff like that.

AE: You didn't worry about being accused of miscegenation?

EVERETT: No, no. We didn't worry about anything in those days. This was the way I conceived him. There may be a little bit of Jules Verne and a little bit of fantasy that I'd read somewhere along the line. I used to edit some dime novels of science fiction for Teck Publications, and I bought a lot of artwork from guys – you know, comic illustrations – that were really great, and I think I was influenced by a lot of those. As far as the coloring, I had nothing to do with that. I did want all characters to be green except the Sub-Mariner.

He had the flesh tone because it was inherited from his father, and I wanted him to be more human. I think, in fact, somewhere along the line in one of the early issues, I sort of got into the genetics of it. I think I intimated somewhere that his mother was like a quadroon or something. The reason he looked so human, which he really shouldn't have, was that she had some human blood in her, anyway, before she ever met MacKenzie, the kid's father. I had to explain it somewhere along the line. I was forced into it, I think – but I'd rather have left it alone. I picked the Antarctic for his origin because, again, that was a fascination.

I used to read all of [Admiral] Byrd's exploits and expeditions. I can tell you all the geography of the Antarctic. I could rattle off every camp that was ever put up there – I mean, how deep they were and everything, because it was something I wanted to do. I muffed a beautiful opportunity – two of them. I could have gone on one Byrd expedition if I'd wanted to. I thought, well, here's the Antarctic, and who knows very much about it? Not too many people. And here's a case of educating kids to some degree, to teach them something about it.

Because everything that I wrote was factual. Because everything I drew was factual. The ice-breakers, the depth of ice, even. I didn't go into too much historically or geographically, because there wasn't any point to it. I created a mythical kingdom underneath the ice, and I thought it would just be different enough so that it would click.

Atlantis did have something to do with it. Another book I'd been fascinated with was *A Dweller on Two Planets*. It was supposedly written through a medium, like spirit writing, written by an Atlantean. You can

Carl Pfeufer art

get halfway through the book and you believe it. By the time you finish, you do believe that Atlantis existed and that this book was written by an Atlantean who had passed into the beyond and then his spirit would come back and –

AE: It was interesting, then, that you didn't call your submerged world "Atlantis."

EVERETT: No, I didn't want to, because Atlantis to me was another world and a world that existed and I still believe it does, somewhere. I don't think it's alive, but I think the remnants and relics are there somewhere. I think it was a continent that did exist at one time, so I didn't want to go that far. But the idea of the submerged continent came from Atlantis.

AE: Did you think of your work you were doing as anything that would be collected later?

EVERETT: Never! I never saved a comic book! I don't have one.

AE: You don't even save your own work?

EVERETT: No. I still don't. I guess my kids have got them, but I don't. I used to collect covers – originals – I had a whole bunch of those, and I threw them out. And they'd be worth a fortune today. Just threw them all out.

AE: You worked on the Sub-Mariner only up to about the beginning of the war, as I recall.

EVERETT: Right. I went into the service in late '41.

AE: Several other people worked on the Sub-Mariner, both as writers and, of course, as artists, in particular Carl Pfeufer.

EVERETT: Yes. I think he was the first one who took over when I went into the service.

I was gone for five years. I suppose a great number of people did Sub-Mariner. I had absolutely no interest in it at all during the five-year span. I didn't see any of them during the war, so I didn't know what had been done until I came back to it in '46 or '47.

AE: One of the more interesting characters about that time was Namora, Namor's cousin [introduced in Marvel Mystery *#82, May 1947]. How and why was she brought in?*

EVERETT: I had wanted to feature a girl counterpart of the Sub-Mariner, almost from the beginning. Rob Solomon, I think, was handling the editorial work then. It might possibly have been my own idea. The name – I think it was my own, but Stan may have had something to do with it. But the costume was mine. The costume was changed several times; changed editorially, that is, by the people at Timely. I'm sorry I'm vague on that. I always felt it was my character, but I could be wrong.

*AE: She was obviously popular. She even had a couple of issues of her own book [*Namora *1-3, Aug. '48-Dec. '48].*

EVERETT: It was a good character, but I guess it was a little bit late to bring a gal in. I had also wanted to feature Dorma more than I did. But I wasn't allowed to do it then.

AE: You did your own lettering mostly, too, through the 40s and 50s, didn't you? The very tall lettering which was quite distinctive?

EVERETT: Yeah. Lettering was a real problem in the beginning, because no one was a professional letterer as far as comics were concerned. The artist did his own or he got a friend to do it. And, again, I wanted to be different, and I didn't care much for any of the styles of what was being done at the time. Lettering of newspaper strips all looked exactly alike.

AE: How did the famous Bill Everett signature evolve?

EVERETT: Oh, Lord!

AE: It was a very distinctive signature, which people keep asking you to duplicate for them.

EVERETT: It was developed – I don't know why I started with the big "E" and the two screwy "T's" at the end of it. Everybody was looking for a distinctive signature – one which would stand out.

When I came back from the service, I developed the signature I use now (which was based, if you look at it carefully, on an artist's palette). The "E's" shape is more or less the shape of a palette, and the two "T's" are supposed to be the brushes. I doubt that it'll change again.

AE: What happened if the editor wanted to change something in the art or lettering back in the early 40s? Was this mostly done by people on staff? Or was the artist called in to make the change?

EVERETT: That's a good question, because I don't remember ever *making* any changes. The story was scripted first, then the lettering was done right from the script. The rates being low, the letterer had to turn out a hell of a lot of work. In those days, we got 50¢ a page or something like that, but this was part of the creative work. So we took our time and we could edit our own stuff as we lettered it.

AE: Did you usually write out a whole script for yourself, or did you make up the exact dialogue as you went along?

EVERETT: I made up the dialogue as I went along – usually when I lettered it. In the *beginning*, I did it any way I wanted to because I had no supervision, but later when Timely became more active in editorial work, then scripts had to be submitted to *them* for approval before they got back to the artist.

AE: Was The Fin created to be a clothed version of the Sub-Mariner?

EVERETT: It was something I dreamed up real fast. "We need a story for a book," is what Lloyd told me. "So see what you can come up with."

"How about another water character, but not like the Sub-Mariner?"

"Okay, do anything you want to!" So I came up with that. [*Daring Mystery* #7, April 1941. – Ed.]

AE: I don't believe he breathed underwater, did he?

EVERETT: No, because I gave him an aqua-lung, and he was really a frogman.

AE: How about Hydroman?

EVERETT: Hydroman – now that was something else again. That was with Famous Funnies or Eastern Color [Printing] and Steve Douglas, who wanted me to do something original for him, for his books. I guess it first appeared in *Heroic*, didn't it?

AE: Reg'lar Fellers Heroic.

EVERETT: And the thing I did best, of course, was the water bit. I couldn't think of anything that wasn't just a copy of the Sub-Mariner or The Fin. I knew a guy who was the foster brother of a kid I'd grown up with – who was not in the business at all but very much interested in what *I* was doing – and *he* came up with the idea of Hydroman. It was his idea, and I thought it was utterly *preposterous.* It was so ridiculous that I couldn't do anything with it. And he said, "Why, sure! He could change himself into water, he can run through the sewers of New York and water mains. You could turn on the tap in the kitchen and out comes Hydroman!"

"Oh, come on! That's ridiculous! How can you draw that? You can't even illustrate a thing like that!" But he sold me a bill of goods. He kept hounding me and hounding me and hounding me. Finally, I said, "All right, I'll see what I can do," and this is what I came up with. Steve liked the idea, and so they published it. I used the name "Bob Blake" for Hydroman's alter ego, because the guy that created the idea – his name was Bob, and Blake was a good name phonetically to use. It was one way I could give

Bob credit for giving me the idea for the story without having to pay him.

AE: During this period, were you trying some non-comics writing and art as a sideline?

EVERETT: I did; I tried, but I never sold anything spectacular. I could probably paper several rooms with the rejection slips.

AE: When the United States entered the war and the Sub-Mariner switched from being a general bad guy (who spent most of his time tearing up New York) to a Nazi-fighter, was this made with your full consent, or did you prefer to keep the Sub-Mariner a bad guy?

EVERETT: No, this was a natural formula. Most of us were flag-wavers, and I was one of the biggest. I wanted to do some of that red-white-and-blue stuff as much as anyone did – and this was a beautiful outlet and a change of scenery, a geographical cure, what-have-you. I was getting tired of dreaming up situations for him, and here was a built-in, ready-made situation; it was a patriotic thing, and it was the thing to do.

AE: When you came back after the war, did you have trouble finding the right kind of motivation for the Sub-Mariner?

EVERETT: Well, he had begun to change after the war, or during the war. And there are a lot of things that I didn't like. I know that I was annoyed with a lot of synopses or story ideas that I got – and I was annoyed that a lot that I submitted wasn't accepted, was changed. I was really fighting a losing battle and I guess I knew it, and so I would naturally have to agree to whatever the editors wanted. I didn't like it much; therefore I don't think I did my best work.

AE: In other words, you wanted to go back to his being an enemy of the human race, while the editors had decided to make him into a standard super-hero.

EVERETT: Yes. Petty things like cops-and-robbers, very mundane in nature. It was beneath his dignity. He had to go for something bigger than that, and he wasn't allowed to. And I didn't like this humanizing of him at all, but it was the trend. I think that was a weak period; I didn't enjoy doing it. I enjoyed *Venus* much more. But even Namora I thought was getting too humanized. They got her into all kinds of situations which could happen to anybody. She could have been anyone.

AE: You said you hadn't cared much about Sub-Mariner while you were out of comics. Did you feel any

Bill Everett
(early 1970s)

sense of loss in '49, when he was dropped?

EVERETT: I felt a slap to my pride, I guess. Everyone must feel that way. "What the heck? You mean the Sub-Mariner, it's not selling? I don't believe you. It's impossible – my character, my baby, he's not selling? This is ridiculous! This just doesn't happen!" I think my pride was hurt a little bit, but after all, if it isn't *selling*, there's nothing you can do about it. I think, also, you always have a moment of panic – what else are you going to do? Are you going to continue working? Are they going to find something else for you to do, or are you just suddenly out of a job?

AE: It has been said that some of the Sub-Mariner stories back in the '40s, some of the particularly bloody ones, were written by Mickey Spillane. As far as you know, did Spillane ever really write any comics?

EVERETT: He wrote for the comics, yeah. He usually wrote the text stories. As far as the strips are concerned, he *tried* to write them for me. He sold a few to other people; I don't think I could ever buy one. Mickey and I became very friendly enemies because I had to edit his stuff in the '40s, and of course, he was a pretty arrogant little guy. He couldn't understand why his stuff wasn't the greatest in the world. Well, it was great, but it wasn't printable. And he wasn't bitter then, not as bitter as he became later, but it was very direct and hard-fisted stuff – and you had to edit it so much. You only got a couple bucks for the text stories, five dollars at the most. Mickey sold us some; and he did sell comics elsewhere, but he couldn't sell any after the war. That's when he got mad and wrote his first novel. It took him four weeks to write *I, the Jury*. I've seen him several times since. Whenever we see each other, we're buddy-buddy, but I never followed along with his record, like some of the other guys do. He's a great storyteller, that guy. He's a wonderful storyteller.

AE: During the period when the super-hero was really *dead, in 1950-51, you worked on a couple of characters which sort of bridged the gap between the horror comic that was then popular, and the super-hero. One of these was* Marvel Boy *[Dec. 1950-June 1951] and, in particular, the* Venus *series [Aug. 1948-April 1952]. Did you do any of the writing on any of those* Venus *stories?*

EVERETT: Yes, I did. Of course, it was not my character to start with. The original stories I got, all I did was illustrate them. I guess about the time that Stan was taking over again, I began to write them, as well.

AE: You must have been glad when the Sub-Mariner came back for a while [Dec. 1953].

EVERETT: Yes, but I wasn't greatly thrilled. By that time I was doing other things.

AE: You were mainly on the horror books?

EVERETT: Yes, and I was happy with those, so it didn't matter too much whether Sub-Mariner came back or not.

AE: Did you write some of the horror stories?

EVERETT: I wrote a lot of them. They were fun.

AE: You didn't feel, as Wertham said, later on, that you were corrupting –

EVERETT: – the morals of the minors. Hell, no!

AE: You had children at that time, didn't you?

EVERETT: Yes, but they couldn't read. Later, when they got old enough to read, they didn't care anything about it. It didn't faze them, because they saw it every day; they were immune to it. I didn't feel I was doing anyone any harm because that sort of thing was available anywhere.

That little kid in Washington who wrote that rebuff in *Saturday Review*, David Wigransky [*Saturday Review*, July 24, 1948. – Ed.] – a scathing rebuff of Wertham's picnic – he made more sense than any letter or article I've ever read. This kid was 14 years old, and got all kinds of publicity. He lived in Washington and was up before committees and all that crap. But he quoted from the Bible. He said, "If Wertham is looking for bones to pick, let him read the Bible." And he picked out sodomy, incest, murders, and fratricide, patricide, matricide, and all these things that occur in the Bible. "You could read it in the best books that are published, but why are you picking on comics?"

AE: When the super-hero characters were revived from December 1953 to October 1955, the Sub-Mariner outlasted the Human Torch and Captain America by approximately a year. During this time, I understand that there was some talk of negotiation of a possible Sub-Mariner TV series.

EVERETT: I can tell you as little as I know about it. I was called into the business manager's office, one day, just out of a clear blue sky. That was '54, I'd say, '54 or '55. I was introduced to a man by the name of Frank Saverstein, whose father was a producer, and he was following in his footsteps, and producer of some pretty good stuff. He was involved, I think, with Goodson-Todman. He had an idea to produce a Sub-Mariner series. He had been a great Sub-Mariner fan. He had Herb Shriner, the Hoosier comedian, who was also a Sub-Mariner fan.

AE: This was also during the time when the Superman show had been very popular. It began in 1950.

EVERETT: Yes, they figured if you could do it with Superman, you could do it with the Sub-Mariner. It would be different, quite a different thing and difficult to film, and novel. They had Arthur Godfrey backing them, moneywise. They went so far as to buy a PT boat and get all kinds of underwater equipment, even before they got to the business negotiations. They were that sold on the idea of making the pilot.

AE: Did they have a star in mind?

EVERETT: Yes, they wanted to use Richard Egan. I couldn't quite see it, but that was beside the point. They wanted Egan and he had agreed to make the pilot.

AE: You never met him in connection with the negotiations?

EVERETT: No. I was only in on the sessions that designated responsibility. I was to be the story consultant. The scripts would be written by their company. But I was to okay them and to advise them as to what the Sub-Mariner could and couldn't do. Frank and Herb were both fans of the original Sub-Mariner, as he was before the war, but wanted to bring him into modern situations.

AE: Probably with the same anti-communist thing which you were doing in comics.

EVERETT: We didn't get as far as discussing actual story material. Main discussions were about who's going to get credit and who's going to get paid for this, how we were going to run the operation. But it fell apart somewhere along the line, in a session that I was not involved in, and nothing ever came of it. I think demands were made that shouldn't have been and acceptances were not, but that's only a personal opinion.

AE: When one considers the fantastic financial success that Superman was – Sub-Mariner might have had a good chance to be popular. When you think of "Sea Hunt" and other programs....

EVERETT: The success of "Sea Hunt" was rather phenomenal. I thought it was a great show, and it showed me that the Sub-Mariner could be filmed.

AE: And the popularity of the Jacques Cousteau TV programs under the sea shows that there is a lot of interest in the ocean bottoms.

EVERETT: Right. It's unexplored, and you can do all kinds of fantastic things with it because we still don't know what's at the bottom of it. It ain't known. So it had unlimited possibilities, and it's just a darn shame that it didn't go through. I love "Sea Hunt," and it struck me that [Lloyd] Bridges would be a perfect Sub-Mariner. I mean, even the features – just alter them very, very slightly, and he's the Sub-Mariner. Every time I see a "Sea Hunt" I get a little twinge because it could have been the Sub-Mariner. It's just one of those things that didn't come to pass.

AE: You mentioned that Herb Shriner and Frank Saverstein were long-time Sub-Mariner fans. Why don't you mention the story about Jack Lemmon now?

EVERETT: I think somebody must have mentioned something about one of Jack Lemmon's pictures. I happened to mention he used to be one of my fans. When he was about 12 years old, my cousin was a very close friend of Lemmon's mother. I was about 20 or 21 at the time. We went to their house in Weston, Massachusetts, several times. Jack was just a little fellow, quite talented. He was interested in music; he was interested in drawing. I can't recall whether it was the beginning of the Sub-Mariner or whether it was Amazing-Man that he was particularly fond of. He was quite a follower of comics then and I think for the ensuing years through his early teens. He and I, despite the age difference, got along beautifully at the time, because he was an extremely talented kid.

AE: Very interesting that years later he made this movie, "How to Murder Your Wife," in which he was a cartoonist. During the middle 50s, weren't you and John Severin and Joe Maneely pretty well the three mainstays of the entire Timely operation? It seems as though your names were on everything.

EVERETT: "The Three Musty Beards." We were supposed to be the kingpins of Marvel – or Timely Comics as we were known then.

AE: I understand you used to lose Fridays.

EVERETT: Fridays were completely lost. They were real short until noontime and they then just sort of disappeared and the whole day disintegrated from then on. Yep, that was kind of nice.

AE: So you were a good friend of Joe Maneely?

EVERETT: Yes, we were good buddies. John, Joe, and I did the key stories for the books. Our stuff happened to sell better, perhaps, than anybody else's. Although there was Russ Heath; his stuff was very good, and Gene Colan was coming on pretty strong. But they worked at home, so this separated us. When they came in, it was to pick up stories or pick up checks or put in vouchers or something, whereas we worked in the office on staff as well as freelance. We were putting out books like *Snafu*, oddball things such as *Nellie the Nurse* and junk like that. Covers were all done on staff, but the rest of it we would take home. That sort of set us aside, so we were just the Three Musketeers off in a corner. We were Peck's Bad Boys.

AE: When Timely more or less went out of the comics publishing game in around '57, did you quit the field and go into other things?

EVERETT: Some of the kids got caught short; they just couldn't believe that it would happen. But a few of us were lucky enough to see the handwriting on the wall, and we were told what was going to come. So I didn't hang around and wait for it to happen. I went out and lined up another job in another business, which was greeting cards [Norcross. – Ed.]. So when the break did come, I wasn't without work.

AE: What were some of the factors that led to the dissolution of the Timely Comics empire in the late 50s? Was it merely the merge of the distributing arm, Atlas, with American News?

EVERETT: I would say that was a big factor. We *always* had distribution problems, anyway. As I understand it, Martin had always wanted to get another, big distributor – United or American, anybody who had something to offer – but he couldn't crack 'em. They wouldn't take the product, so he formed his own and called it Atlas. And they did all right. But he did have a chance, finally, to go with American. So he sold Atlas, and that was a mistake – not a mistake, but an unfortunate happening. And then, as I understand it, American News defaulted on a contract and defaulted with Dell, also, and left us high and dry with absolutely no distributor. Goodman had to disband and he had to cut the payroll down to nothing – which he promptly did, and then, of course, gradually got straightened out.

AE: What brought you back to comics in the early 60s? Of course, you did Daredevil *#1 [April '64] and later you came back and have been with Marvel ever since.*

EVERETT: That was just a matter of circumstance, more than anything else. I was art director for Eton Paper Corporation in Massachusetts, a very good job, and I didn't like it. I was there for about four years, and we agreed to disagree, so I left. I didn't have anything to do. Not that I needed anything particularly at that time, but I would *eventually*. I had a couple of prospects elsewhere. I wasn't really working on them, just waiting for things to develop. I picked up a copy of *Playboy* magazine which had Jules Feiffer's article in it [*Playboy*, Oct. '65, "The Great Comic Book Heroes"], and saw the pictures of Sub-Mariner in it. It was the first I even thought about the comics, and of course it was a kind of shocker to see a whole article in *Playboy* about comics. They must be doing all right, you know?

AE: With a picture and several mentions of Bill Everett's Sub-Mariner.

EVERETT: So it was worth a long shot. It was a weekend, and I couldn't call Stan; I just sent him a night letter. The following Monday he called me up and said, "Come back to work," so I did. It was as simple as that.

AE: Didn't the Playboy *article appear after the first issue of* Daredevil?

EVERETT: Yes, *Daredevil* came out first, when I was still working for Eton. I must have called Stan, had some contact with him. I know he had this idea for Daredevil. And we tried to talk it over the phone, and it just wouldn't work. So I said, "All right, I'll take a day off and come down to New York." I did the one issue, but I found that I couldn't do it and handle my job, too. I had to work overtime on the job, because it was a managerial job; I didn't get paid overtime but I was on an annual salary, so my time was not my own. I was putting in 14 or 15 hours a day at the plant and then to come home and try to do comics at night was just too much. And I didn't make deadlines -- I just couldn't make them -- so I just did one issue and didn't do anymore.

AE: When you came to Marvel full-time, you immediately started to work on the Hulk. How did you feel about that character?

EVERETT: There was a lot of controversy about how the Hulk should look. You notice that the first two or three issues I did, he was a little bit different in each issue because Stan kept saying, "Well, this issue let's try to do him this way, make this change, make that change," so eventually he said, "Well, do him the way *you* want to." And I was doing it that way when I stopped doing him and started doing Doc Strange.

AE: Well, how do you feel about that *character?*

EVERETT: It was a challenge, because I tried to do Ditko-like work and that was next to impossible. Call the artwork good, bad, or indifferent; it definitely is stylized. Ditko *is* Doc Strange and vice versa. Nobody else can do it like he does. I tried to keep *my* drawing and Ditko's influence. And it was very difficult, but it was fun.

AE: If you were asked to name a handful of people that you feel had contributed most to comic books, who do you think would be some of the giants in the field?

EVERETT: Al Williamson, Wally Wood, Reed Crandall, John Severin, Joe Maneely (I don't think he was a Great, but had he lived, he would have been; he would have come on real strong). Paul Gustavson was influential. Guys in the field like Kirby and Simon, Joe Shuster, those guys; I didn't know enough about their work at the time. There are probably a lot of candidates there. Toth, for example, and guys who came into the field in the early 50s that I didn't know.

AE: You were one of the first people ever to use television in a comic book. When we reprinted one of your early Torch/Sub-Mariner fights you and Carl Burgos did, there was one of the old type of television sets in it, in which the picture was projected on a screen from below ["The Human Torch vs. the Sub-Mariner," from Marvel Mystery *#9, July 1940; reprinted in* Fantasy Masterpieces *#8, April 1967.]; and someone wrote in saying that we had* redrawn *that and taken out a radio and put in a television set!*

EVERETT: Before I had anything to do with comics, I worked for a tech publication. I was art editor for them, and we put out two radio news magazines (they were all technical, no fan stuff, no radio stars or anything like that). Strictly for hams and professionals. And we had all kinds of TV equipment, and this was 1936. We had our own laboratory. I had to edit all the pictures that were sent in by hams. They had done this in their basement -- "and here's a way you can do a TV receiver or facsimile receiver" or whatever. I was quite fascinated watching this television. Everything was test patterns or maybe an hour show a day, something like that – it was all experimental. So naturally, when the opportunity came up, I had to throw it into my story.

AE: The Sub-Mariner seems to be one of the handful – and I mean really small handful – of old-time characters that had any *depth.*

EVERETT: It was there, except I didn't know it

AE: How do you feel about that character now? Do you feel he's been changed so much that he's no longer the Sub-Mariner you created, or do you just feel there have been a few slight adjustments here and there?

EVERETT: Well, he's not the original Sub-Mariner, by any means. Something was needed at the time Stan made the change, and I think that's why the kids bought it. But from my own personal standpoint, no, it's not the Sub-Mariner: He never talked that way, he didn't act that way. He was arrogant, but in an entirely different way, in a more *human* way. He never thought of himself as God Almighty, as is the concept now.

AE: The Sub-Mariner has been accused of being a bigot, perhaps a racist. Do you feel that your *character would have had the same charges leveled at him?*

EVERETT: I don't think the Sub-Mariner could ever be accused of being a bigot, because he had no message, for one thing. His only message was that he wanted to get even with the human race, because he thought they were trying to destroy his race. I don't think he looked down on the human race. They were just his enemies, maybe on equal terms, except he was one man fighting the entire race of beings.

AE: Well, he did occasionally mention that he was going to make himself emperor of the United States. I believe that was the story where he was talking to the mayor of New York.

EVERETT: LaGuardia. I even showed him, using the caricature. I had my little hangups like everybody else (although I liked LaGuardia). It didn't make any difference if I happened to like somebody; if they were a public figure that you could pick on, you do it anyway. He might be a hero, but you could pick on him because it's current. But I didn't have any ax to grind, really – I must have, underneath, or I never would have created this anti-hero – but I wasn't conscious of it.

AE: Of course, then, you didn't call him an anti-hero, either.

EVERETT: No, I'm using that kind of term; but no, we didn't have any fancy names for him. He was a bad guy or he was a hero, that's all.

AE: Thanks, Bill.

BILL EVERETT

THE ANCIENT SUB-MARINER

1917-1973

◆ ◆ ◆

I am, I'm afraid, no expert on the life, times, and career of the late and very talented Bill Everett.

Others more diligent than I will have to record the precise dates of his birth and death. Others more artistically aware will have to analyze the strengths, the weaknesses, the influences of his artwork. And still others more meticulously painstaking will have to catalogue his work, from Skyrocket Steel through those final Sub-Mariner tales on which he was working when, most unexpectedly and far too soon, he died.

Myself, I could never reconcile Bill the man with "Bill Everett," creator of the Sub-Mariner. After all, even though I began to read Prince Namor in his first declining period (1946-49), and even though the powers-that-were had forced Bill and others to turn Namor from a sea-going hell-raiser into a mere catcher-of-smugglers, Subby was still one of the great heroes of my youth. When I played at mock heroics in a Missouri swimming pool at the age of eight or so, it was always the Sub-Mariner (pronounced by me Sub-Ma*reen*er) I portrayed, not Aquaman. Anyone who had predicted that Aquaman would have survived as a solo star after the Sub-Mariner had passed from center-stage would have been laughed out of the deep end. It still seems vaguely unjust to me... not unlike Gene Autry being unseated as king of the cowboys by Roy Rogers while Autry was off at war.

Yet, despite all the above, Bill Everett slowly, surely, became a person to me during 1965 and 1966, soon after I came to Marvel Comics. I had heard the stories by then (from Stan Lee and Sol Brodsky, both of whom truly liked the guy) of how Bill's *Daredevil* #1, drawn while he was working full-time at another job, was so late coming in that it cost the company thousands of dollars. Literally thousands. Comic book economics being what they are and were, I was surprised that Stan was still willing, even eager, to have Bill finally dump his commercial art job and take up comics again on a regular basis.

But, that's the way Bill affected people. Though he was the most human of men, he nonetheless inspired a kind of awe mixed with a genuine liking and respect. Over the next few years he'd be given staff positions, freelance status – whatever he seemed to need to give him a chance to realize his potential. When his penciling failed to sell comics in the 1960s, he became a top-notch inker... later one of Marvel's best colorists (see *Silver Surfer* #1, for example). Stan (as well as then-publisher Martin Goodman, who had bought that first Sub-Mariner story some three decades before) was always willing to take a flyer with him. So were the rest of us.

Did I mention that Bill and I were roommates off and on in the 1960s, when I was single first time around? We were – first when I lived in Greenwich Village, later on East 87th Street. Though others such as Gary Friedrich and later Mike Friedrich were probably closer to him on a personal basis in his last few years, I spent a lot of time with him during his re-introduction to comics in the late 60s. I was enthralled and entertained, hour upon hour, by stories of the early days of comics – many of which I could not get him to remember or repeat when I pulled out a tape recorder. Though he left ink-stained handprints on the wall of my first uptown apartment, it's the mark on my life and heart that I feel the most.

Bill had his problems. Alcoholism plagued him for much of his adult life, though he kept it under control until the later years, especially after the death of his beloved wife a few years before his own. The story has a happy ending of sorts, though: Bill joined Alcoholics Anonymous and became a moving force in the New York chapter during the final couple of years of his life... and I don't think he'd want to read an accounting of his life that didn't mention that. There are a goodly number of people in New York City who hardly were aware that Bill was an artist or writer, yet who grieved when he died because of what he had meant to them as a friend, a pillar of strength in their own weak moments, after he had found himself.

When he died, something went out of all of us. With the exception of the death last December of my good friend John Verpoorten, no passing from the comics scene during my thirteen years in the field has touched me – *hit* me, really – like Bill's. He died too young, in his 50s only, doubtless partly because nothing could totally undo the ravages worked on his body in earlier years.

But he left a legacy in four colors, and that's more than most folks do. I still think of him, rather more often than I do of most living people I know. It still doesn't seem real that he's gone, even after half a decade.

He used to say to me that I reminded him of himself, when he was a young firebrand. He never told me, though, if he meant that as sincere compliment or amused dig.

I prefer to take it as a compliment... because Bill Everett was quite a guy.

Roy Thomas
4-10-78

ALTER EGO: THE COMIC BOOK

In 1980 Roy's fifteen-year relationship with Marvel came to a temporary end, and for the next six years he entered a similar writing-and-editing one with DC. During this time he also co-wrote two films (including "Conan the Destroyer" with Arnold Schwarzenegger) and a few TV cartoons, including nearly half of the only season of an animated "Fantastic Four" on NBC.

When he went to freelance status in comics in 1986, several interesting possibilities swiftly raised their heads, one of the first of which was – well, First.

First Comics of Chicago was one of a handful of dynamic new companies making inroads into Marvel and DC's domination of the market, and one reason was Mike Gold, editor and co-founder. When Mike suggested he create a series for First, Roy knew just the one he wanted to do:

Alter Ego.

With the joint blessing of Jerry Bails and Mike Friedrich (coincidentally by now Roy's agent for comics work), Roy set about to turn the Alter Ego *name and mask-logo into a full-fledged fantasy concept. His thoughts went instantly to the month-long sojourn in Mexico in 1964 in which he'd amassed numerous Spanish-language comics while making mental plans to publish* AE *#7. For during this time Roy had also birthed the name and notion of a "Limbo Legion."*

This was to be a comics feature in AE*, a JSA-style group composed of 1940s heroes in the public domain. Black Terror, Airboy, Fighting Yank, and many others were ripe for the picking, and Roy warmed to the task of working (probably with Biljo White) on an ongoing Limbo Legion feature. It was, in fact, one of the series he hoped to spin off into his short-lived dream of* Alter Ego Comics.

But that dream died unrealized... only to re-surface two decades later in response to Gold's invitation. Roy and his wife Dann (his collaborator on several DC series) developed the idea of a teenage boy who donned an eye-mask and was thereby transformed into a super-hero called – what else? – Alter Ego. (This was, of course, several years before The Mask *from Dark Horse.)*

What's more, the donning of the mask would throw the boy-in-a-hero's-body into another dimension, one in which the heroes and villains of various 1940s comics actually existed – while the baddies had discovered a way to cross over to our continuum, as well. To combat them, Alter Ego would head – the Limbo Legion.

The boy was christened Rob Lindsay, after Jerry's "Robert Lindsay" nom de plume *used in various letters to Julius Schwartz's comics circa 1961. Ron Harris, a client of Mike Friedrich's Star*Reach agency who'd worked with Roy on DC's* The Young All-Stars, *signed aboard as artist (Rich Burchett would later ink two chapters), and a four-issue mini-series was born.*

Mike Gold made three wise suggestions: (a) that the names of the Limbo Legionnaires be slightly, er, altered, *so that Black Terror became Holy Terror, Airboy became Skyboy, Fighting Yank became Yankee Doodle, etc.; (b) that Roy place an ad for the AE comic into interstate commerce at once (see above, left); and (c) that, since Roy still had his old AE lists, it be announced that any subscriber to the fanzine who contacted First would receive a free copy of the first issue of the comic.*

Unfortunately, while the comic was still in the planning stage, Mike left his position at First. After that, except for the actual writing, Roy found himself frozen out of the creative process by later editors, so that Alter Ego's finished costume was not wholly to his liking, the comics' title logo retained upper-and-lower-case lettering (Roy wanted to switch to all-capitals for the comic), and the mini-series was given relatively little push by First. Whether these things made any difference or not, the four issues of Alter Ego *were only moderate sellers, though fan mail – even from those who had never heard of the original fanzine – was enthusiastic.*

But, more than a decade later, the concept of Alter Ego *the Comic Book remains nearly as dear to Roy's heart as does the memory of* Alter Ego *the Fanzine; and indeed, as this volume was in preparation, the four comics issues of* AE *were being readied for "reprinting" on the Internet by Dennis Mallonee of Heroic Publishing, and can be accessed at:*

www.heroicpub.com/alterego.

As for the future – both of the fanzine and of the comic book –

Well, who knows?

The Editors

FOUR DECADES OF Alter Ego

A Brief Historical Perspective (and Epilogue of Sorts)

by Bill Schelly

"The history of the American comic book began in the pages of Alter Ego,*" Mike Benton recently wrote. "It was the first, the best, and the most important fan magazine ever done on the costumed super-heroes." Benton, author of* The Comic Book in America *(Taylor Publishing, 1989), may be overstating the case a bit, but like many active participants in comic fandom in the 1960s, he remembers how central* AE *truly was in that halcyon decade.*

When I joined comicdom in mid-1964, Alter Ego *was already firmly established as the premiere fanzine of the day. In its pages, I first learned of the wonders of comic books beyond those I could find on my neighborhood newsstand. Alongside pioneering pieces on comics from the 1940s and foreign lands, it introduced me to the world of the men and women who created the comics.* AE *recorded the memories of many key pros who are no longer with us, from Otto Binder to Gardner F. Fox to Bill Everett. But more than anything, I loved* AE *because it was flat-out fun. I was perhaps a "typical"* Alter Ego *reader: hungry for knowledge about the comics of yore, highly amused by its many humor pieces, and deeply impressed by the talents of the artists and writers who graced its pages.*

Yes, I was a typical reader... but I arrived too late to understand just how much AE *had given to fandom. Its undeniable historical importance lay in its influence on the formation of a fandom devoted to comic art.*

Jerry Bails' Alter-Ego *provided the building blocks for the comics fanzines that were the "internet" of fandom: the general interest comics zine (*AE *itself), the ad-zine (*The Comicollector*), and the newsletter of upcoming events in pro comics (*The Comic Reader*). By October 1961, what had been one publication was now three. In the spring of 1964,* The Comicollector *merged with G. B. Love's* The Rocket's Blast, *forming the dominant advertising fanzine of the 1960s,* Rocket's Blast-Comicollector. The Comic Reader *continued unabated into the 1980s.*

No less than the redoubtable Fredric Wertham, M.D., deemed Alter Ego *one of three "fanzines credited with being trailblazers," along with* Xero *and* Comic Art, *in his book* The World of Fanzines *(Southern Illinois University Press, 1973). Even Wertham couldn't get this basic fact wrong, though the rest of the book was somewhat addle-pated.*

These early fan magazines provided a focal point for the hundreds and then thousands of comics fans who were excited about the resurgence of the costumed hero in pro comics. Dealers in back issues could now "go national" in the pages of RB-CC, *and with this communication network in place, it wasn't long before fans began talking of holding a "comic book convention." What a concept!*

Hundreds of fans became "small press publishers" in the 1960s, but somehow AE *was always considered the Cadillac of the fanzine field. Few could match its easy grandeur, its editorial sophistication, or its cornucopia of talent. As the issues rolled out, and the publishing reins were passed along, I'm sure the original editors realized they had a good thing going – but they could not have foreseen that it would cast such a long shadow.*

The demand for copies was extraordinary. There never seemed to be enough, no matter how many were printed. Thus, very early on, a series of reprints was published, beginning with one by Biljo White. White produced a facsimile edition of Alter-Ego *#1 via spirit duplicator, which differs from the original mainly in the substitution of Ronn Foss' sleek logo for the rudimentary version used on the cover initially.*

Roy Thomas announced that he would publish a collection titled The Bestest of Alter Ego Nos. 1-3 *in 1965. Unfortunately, this photo-offset reprint was scuttled, owing to his graduation to the professional ranks.*

That same year, G. B. Love conceived the idea of reprinting sold-out issues, beginning with #5. (They can be identified by the substitution of the name and address of "The S.F.C.A." on the back covers.) In this way, AE *continued to be available through the 1960s and 1970s, thus maintaining the fanzine's visibility among the next generation of slicker fan and semi-pro publications.*

Despite Roy Thomas' success at Marvel, Alter Ego *remained close to his heart. When its first "pro issue" was published in 1969,* AE *created a mini-sensation by presenting John Benson's interview with an outspoken Gil Kane. Though #11 didn't appear until 1978,* AE *nevertheless staked out a place in the late 1970s with that single Friedrich-published issue, which was marketed alongside remaining copies of #10 through the decade's end.*

The 1980s, too, had its versions of Alter Ego. *We have already seen that the name provided the inspiration for a comic book by Roy Thomas and Ron Harris. In addition, a new kind of "reprint" was made available, when Bay Area artist and fan Al Dellinges put together three individual offset magazines, re-creating* AE *#1 through 3. These publications, priced at $7 each, contained all the original text and artwork, though much of it was re-drawn by Al from the original light ditto pages. (You can inquire about the availability of Dellinges'* Alter Ego *re-issues by writing him at 211 Willow Ave., Millbrae,California, 94030.)*

Talk about persistence: Begun in the 1960s ... its final issue in the 1970s ... a comic book and reprint series bearing its name in the 1980s ... and now, in the 1990s, a book collecting the highlights from its eleven issues – published by popular demand, I might add.

From my point of view, the enduring interest in Alter Ego *can be traced to the vision of its instigators. They made the costumed hero its focus, for they knew how much fun it was to find the heroic ideal within ourselves ... by following the adventures of colorful "alter egos" across the four-color pages.*

Seattle, Washington
September 1997

Where Are They Now?

JERRY BAILS

Recently, Jerry Bails wrote, "One of the earliest covers I recall from my youth was on Flash Comics #20. That issue was dated August 1941. At almost exactly the same time, I spotted All-Star Comics #6. It marked the very first time I would witness the Justice Society of America. That comic book had the most profound long-term effect upon me. Spotting the covers of #6 and #7 were ecstatic moments for me. I can still feel a rush of endorphins just recalling the covers."

Jerry retired from his academic life of 40-some years in 1996, but continues his fan activities at an enhanced level. Currently, he produces a continuously updated edition of his Who's Who of American Comic Books in quarterly installments available on the World Wide Web. He also serves in various consulting capacities to the Grand Comic-book Database, a project to index every comic book published in America. He joins scores of other panelologists-on-line who have already indexed 50,000 individual comic books, and will soon be making this material available on the Internet. Inquiries about either of these projects can be sent by e-mail to JerryBails@aol.com. Unfortunately, Jerry and Jean are in the process of finding a new home, so his permanent home address is unknown at this time.

ROY THOMAS

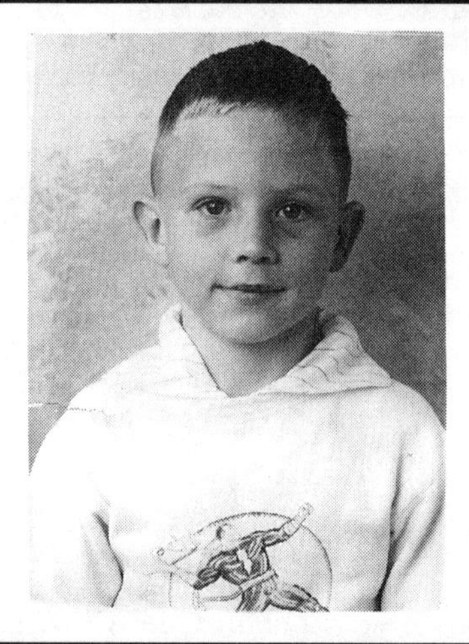

Roy (clearly, at age 6-7, already a Captain Marvel fan) was the first person to turn pro out of 1960s organized comic fandom, becoming Stan Lee's associate editor and first successor as editor-in-chief. Since 1965 he has written for Marvel, DC, Topps, and other comics companies, and has co-written two films and a few hours' worth of TV. He is best known for his 70-issue stint on The Avengers and as the original writer/editor of Marvel's Conan comics, as well as for series at Marvel and DC starring the super-heroes of World War II.

Currently, Roy writes Xena and X-Files comics for Topps, Conan mini-series for Marvel, and an occasional Superman graphic novel for DC, while serving as co-producer of several episodes of the live-action "Conan the Adventurer" TV series and pursuing interests in other media. He and his wife Dann live on a pet-infested estate in rural South Carolina – "forty acres and a pool."

RONN FOSS

Ronald Eugene Foss was eight years old in 1947, and grew up in the midwestern United States reading the comics of the post-war era. Inspired by the artwork of Al Williamson, Simon & Kirby, and especially Joe Kubert, Ronn's natural artistic flair led him to dream of an art career. After the 1960s, he became less active in comic fandom, and more involved in environmental causes and other endeavors.

Although he had work published by Marvel, and worked for a time for Russ Cochran on the EC reprint volumes, Ronn has mainly earned his living as a freelance artist, creating commissioned pieces for clients nation-wide. During the 1970s, he raised the two children he had with his ex-wife Coreen, Alexandra and Scott, who both live and work in Oregon today. Foss makes his home in the beautiful Missouri Ozarks, and from that rustic environment writes and draws the adventures of Destiny – Vampire Mermaid (created by Ronn and Dennis Druktenis). The Destiny comic strip appears in every issue of Scary Monsters magazine.

BILJO WHITE

As a youth, the budding "Capt. Biljo" spent many an idle hour putting pencil to paper, when he wasn't making the initial comic book purchases that would some day grow into "The White House of Comics." For most of his adult life, he worked as a firefighter in Columbia, Missouri, while publishing his famed fanzines such as Komix Illustrated, Batmania, The Stripper, *and* The Eye *in his spare time.*

Biljo married twice; his first wife Ruth now lives in California, as does their daughter Sunday Elizabeth. With his second wife Hazel, whom he married in 1973, the "Capt." has a daughter Toni Lynne, and a stepson Randall. The "White House of Comics" is a far cry from its former glory; now Biljo satisfies his love of the four-color medium with an extensive collection of Golden Age reprint books. Does he still draw? Yes, often – and recently completed "The Return of The Eye!" for Hamster Press' upcoming Fandom's Finest Comics *#2.*

Illo by Biljo White from AE #9

MIKE FRIEDRICH

A mid-1960s DC letterhack, Mike was one of the earliest Silver Age comics fans to make the transition to prodom, writing a Neal Adams-illustrated Spectre *story in 1967. He wrote* Justice League of America *and various comics for DC and Marvel, then published* Star*Reach, *often credited as the first "independent" or "alternative press" comic.*

*Today Mike lives in Berkeley, California, and is president of Star*Reach, a talent agency he founded to represent comic book artists and writers. He is also a member of the boards of directors both of the Friends of Lulu and of Pro/Con, and is one of the organizers of Wondercon.*

BILL SCHELLY

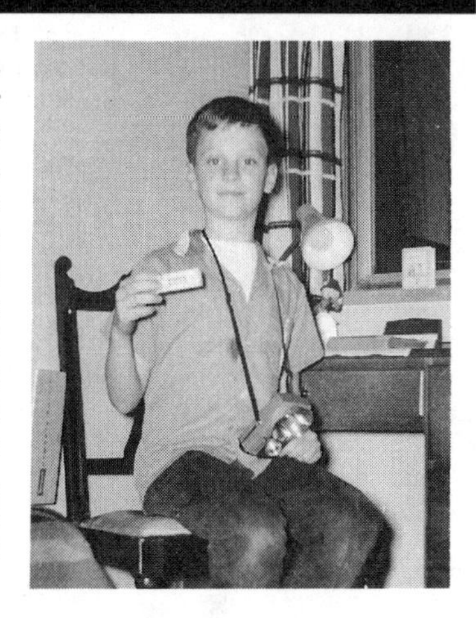

Bill was born in Walla Walla, Washington, in 1951, and grew up in Pittsburgh, Pennsylvania. The first comic book he can remember reading was the Superman Annual *#1 in 1960, and he saw his first fanzine when he was twelve years old. Within his first six months in fandom, Schelly ordered* Alter Ego *#7 from Roy Thomas, and became an avid AE reader. Inspired to publish something of his own, he produced numerous amateur magazines through 1972, the best-known being* Sense of Wonder. *His love of comicdom of the 1960s and 1970s led him to write* The Golden Age of Comic Fandom *in 1995, the first book-length history of the movement. Since then, Bill has continued to spur the resurgence of the "spirit of comicdom" by organizing a reunion of old-time fans at the 1997 Chicago Comicon, and through his company Hamster Press by publishing* Fandom's Finest Comics. *During the day, he works as a mild-mannered surety bond underwriter in Seattle, Washington, and has two children: Jaimeson (7) and Tara (5).*

INDEX

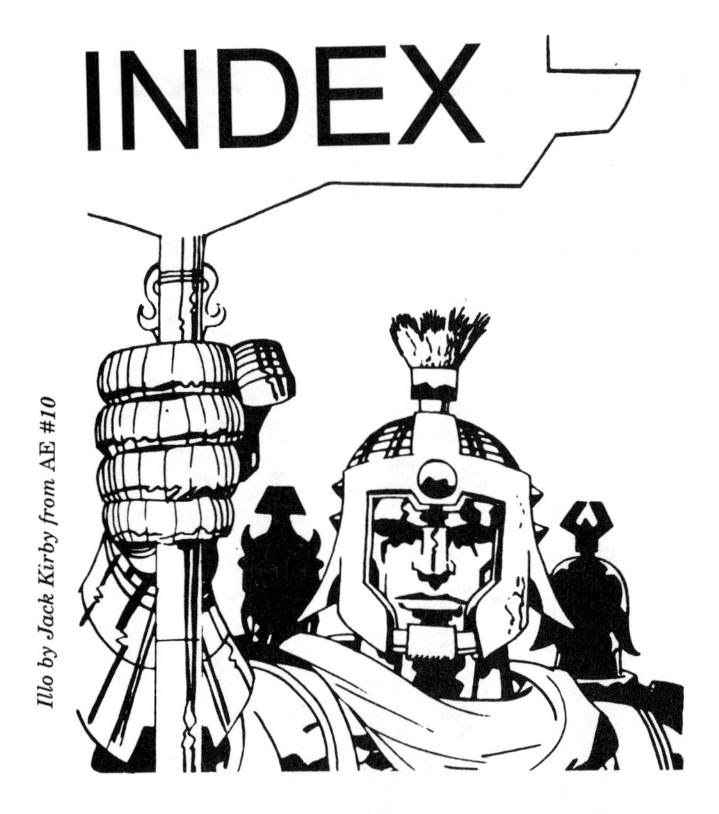
Illo by Jack Kirby from AE #10

The pros and fans in *Alter Ego*

Note: This index contains names of real (not fictional) individuals only, as they appear in the text, captions, and photographs. Publishers, comic book titles, and other subjects have been omitted due to space considerations.

From all Marvel comics dated December 1969 and January 1970

THE MYSTERY OF FANDOM

Ronn Foss illo from Alter Ego *#5*

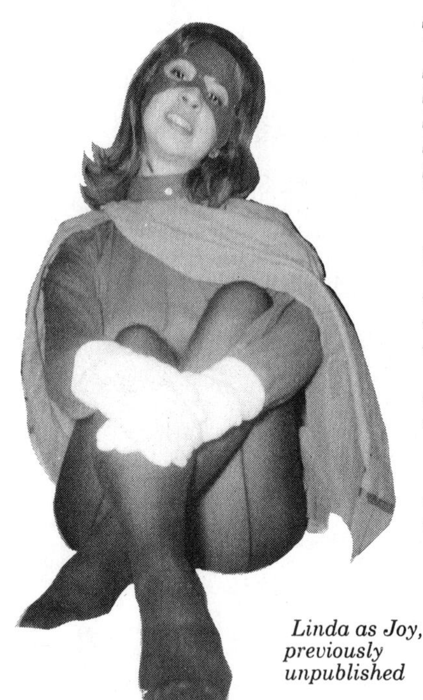

Linda as Joy, previously unpublished

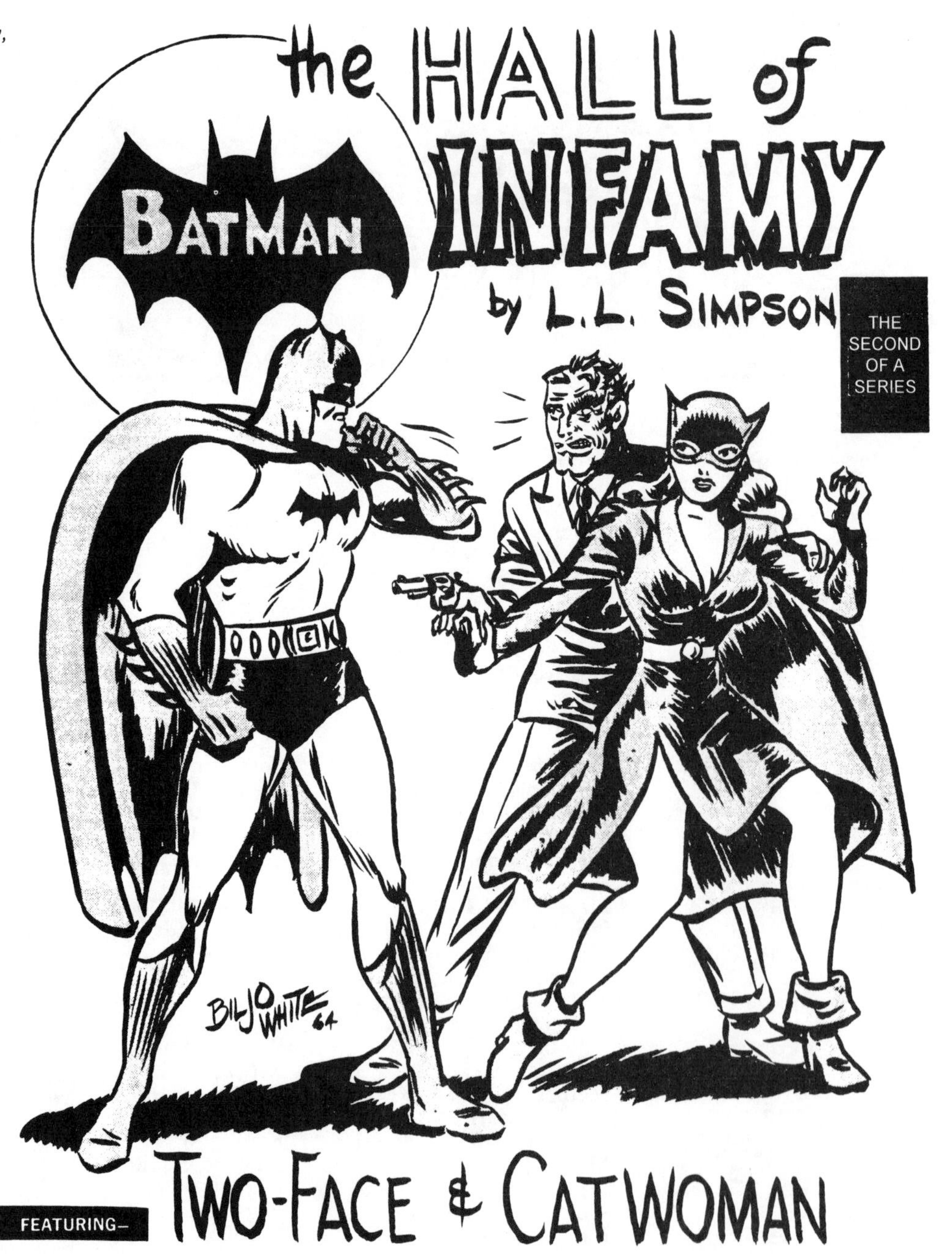

AE #6

HAMSTER PRESS PROUDLY PRESENTS ...

FANDOM'S FINEST COMICS

A TREASURY OF THE BEST ORIGINAL STRIPS FROM THE CLASSIC COMICS FANZINES (1958-1975)

With Rarities, Gems & Hidden Treasures by:

D. BRUCE BERRY
OTTO BINDER
ROGER BRAND
JOHN BYRNE
LANDON CHESNEY
DAVE COCKRUM
ROBERT CRUMB
RONN FOSS
GRASS GREEN
HARRY HABBLITZ
ALAN HANLEY
LARRY HERNDON
DAVE HERRING
LARRY IVIE
JEFFREY JONES
HOWARD KELTNER
GEORGE METZGER
JERRY ORDWAY
WENDY PINI
BUDDY SAUNDERS
BILL SPICER
JIM STARLIN
ROY THOMAS
ALAN WEISS
MARK WHEATLEY
BILJO WHITE
MARV WOLFMAN

"*Fandom's Finest* is a treasure chest full of historical firsts that shouldn't be missed. I loved it!" – Mike Allred, *Madman Comics & Red Rocket 7*

"Bill Schelly has assembled a wonderful Wayback Machine to a time when great comics inspired impassioned young writers and artists to tackle the art form on their own. I was bowled over by the sheer explosion of talent between its covers. This is a book to treasure – a splendidly-produced volume!" – Mark Evanier, *Comic Buyer's Guide*

"*Fandom's Finest* is superb and a downright steal at $17.95 for 256 pages. Incredible!" – Bill Black, *AC Comics*

Four color cover - 8 ½ x 11" trade paperback - 256 pages

20 complete comic strips by fandom's most talented writers and artists!

Compiled and fully annotated by Bill Schelly, fandom historian and author. Schelly's first book of fan history, *The Golden Age of Comic Fandom*, was nominated for a Will Eisner Comics Industry Award in 1996.

Send $17.95 plus $4.00 postage and handling to:

◆ ◆ ◆ **Hamster Press** ◆ ◆ ◆
P. O. Box 27471
Seattle, WA 98125

Back cover of Alter Ego *#11 by Moebius*